Naval Special Warfare and Marine Commando Force

NAVAL SPECIAL WARFARE AND MARINE COMMANDOS

CHALLENGES AHEAD

Capt. (Retd.) M.K.Vats

PRASHANT PUBLISHING HOUSE

DELHI-110094

Published by :

Prashant Publishing House

C-34, 28 Foota Road, Gali-3,

West Karwal Nagar, Delhi-110094

Phone : 011-22963970, Mob. : 9810396373

Naval Special Warfare and Marine Commandos

Challenges Ahead

First Pubished 2011

ISBN 978-93-80565-19-4

PRINTED IN INDIA

Published by Mr. R.K. Jha M/s Prashant Publishing House and Published at H.S. Offset House Press, Delhi.

Preface

Naval warfare is divided into three operational areas: surface warfare, air warfare and underwater warfare. The latter may be subdivided into submarine warfare and anti-submarine warfare as well as mine warfare and mine countermeasures. Each area comprises specialized platforms and strategies used to exploit tactical advantages unique and inherent to that area.

Modern submarine warfare consists primarily of diesel and nuclear submarines using weapons (like torpedoes, missiles or nuclear weapons), as well as advanced sensing equipment, to attack other submarines, ships, or land targets. Submarines may also be used for reconnaissance and landing of special forces as well as deterrence. In some navies they may be used for task force screening. The effectiveness of submarine warfare partly depends on the anti-submarine warfare carried out in response. Mankind has fought battles on the sea for more than 3,000 years. Land warfare would seem, initially, to be irrelevant and entirely removed from warfare on the open ocean, though this is not necessarily true. Land navigation, until the advent of extensive railroads was extremely dependent upon river systems and canals.

Modern naval warfare is divided into three operational areas: surface warfare, air warfare and submarine warfare. Each area comprises specialized platforms and strategies used to exploit tactical advantages unique and inherent to that area.

Modern surface warfare dates from the mid 20th century, when surface, air, and submarine warfare components were blended together as a tactical unit to achieve strategic objectives. The two most important strategic objectives are interdiction and sea control. Interdiction is the process of preventing enemy forces access to or through a location, for example: German naval objectives against Britain in World War II were primarily focused on preventing ships arriving intact with their cargos. Sea control is the dominance of force over a given area that prevents other naval forces from operating successfully, for example: the mission of the allied navies in the Atlantic during World War II was to maintain sea control and prevent Axis naval forces from operating.

In the second half of the 20th century, the importance of naval surface power was reduced as air and submarine warfare platforms demonstrated their capabilities. In the 21st century, it has been clearly demonstrated that a modern navy must be composed of all three platforms (surface, submarine, and air) to be effective in projecting naval power and maintaining sea control.

The force started off as the Indian Marine Special Force, the first batch qualifying in February 1987. It was later renamed as the *Marine Commando Force* (MCF) in 1991. The force has gradually acquired experience and a reputation for professionalism over the two decades it has been in existence. It is one of India's highest trained and best equipped forces.

The force was initially trained by the other special forces of the country, including those under the Home Ministry, the Army, Air Force, Police and paramilitary units. This was later supplemented by foreign training facilities, notably the SEALS of the U.S. Navy and further training was conducted with British Special Forces. Over the years, the force set up its own training facility, first as an adjunct of the operational company at Mumbai, later as the Naval Special Warfare Tactical Training Centre. Wide exposure to different forms of warfare have been obtained through field operations in counter insurgency and anti terrorist operations within the country, and joint exercises with more than a dozen countries across the world.

This book concludes that the only way to bring about a lasting peace and prevent more insurgencies rising up in the future is to build a state that attends equally to the interests of Naval, Marine and Warfare.

Contents

1

Naval Warfare: An Introduction

NAVAL UNITS

Naval Units operate individually in the campaign, though they are usually grouped for a mission. Most ships are represented on a 2:1 scale, with smaller vessels like submarines and destroyer escorts represented on a 3:1 scale. The only time that Naval Units interact directly with ground formations is when they are involved in a Naval Invasion. This keeps the scaling to a reasonable level, as ships are not likely to have a significant affect on a primarily land battle at this large a scale.

Naval Experience

Naval Units cannot train, but they begin the game with a set experience level based upon the naval training level of the nation in question. They may gain experience during battles, but they do not gain leaders (except for CAA units). The naval training levels are as follows:

Nations Training Level.

Germany, Japan, Britain, USA, Sweden 300.

France, Finland, Norway 200.

Italy, Netherlands, Spain, Poland, Portugal, Greece 100.

Russia, Rumania, Yugoslavia, Turkey, Belgium, Siam 0.

Ports

Ports are indicated on the map by circles, black for Minor Ports and Red for Major Ports. Each Minor Port can base up to 20 Capital Ships or 40 Escorts (or combinations with 2 Escorts = 1 Capital Ship), and Major Ports can base double that number.

Port Sides – Ports have access to all adjacent sea squares to that Port. This is because there is usually some element of coastal waters that can be used to move along if the Port is geographically located towards one side or another. Basically, to simplify just use the map as it is presented and the Port is considered that land square. The only exceptions are Ports that are along a narrow coast, for example Manila, which has land to either side as well as to the North, may only be accessed from the South.

Naval Task Force – A Naval Task Force can be called a Fleet as well, but basically any group of naval vessels that act together to perform a mission are a Task Force. For convenience they may be grouped together even when they are in port, but unlike armies a Task Force is completely flexible and can perform a mission with Naval Units being added or subtracted to any degree when the mission is launched from a Port, and sometimes it may change when the mission reaches another Port. Task Forces cannot split up or join in the middle of the sea, however, but only at friendly Ports. Any number of ships may be in a Task Force, although only 2 submarines may be attached to any Task Force as scouts.

Submarine Flotilla-Submarines were generally not fast enough to properly work with surface units, so when Submarines work together they do so in smaller groups. The Submarine Flotilla can have up to 8 Subs attached to it, but no more. This is because of the nature of submarine warfare and in fact, even the flotilla really represents a number of submarines operating over a wide area.

Raider Group – Raider groups are small groups of fast, usually long range surface ships. A Raider group can be 1 to 2 (surface) Naval Units with a speed of 3 or more. Raider groups may attack enemy shipping, and are harder to intercept or spot (-1 for each).

Disguised Merchant Raiders – The Germans used disguised merchants to good effect at the start of the war as Raiders. These operate like Raiders do, except they don't have to be fast because they rely instead on deception. They have extreme long range endurance, making them useful to send on far off missions well beyond where the heaviest convoy escorts are likely to be.

Merchant Convoy – A Merchant Convoy represents sustained economic shipping, and not a specific mission such as transporting troops or supplies. Because of the sustained nature of such shipping, a Merchant Convoy cannot be larger than 8 Transports in size.

Merchant Convoys may be provided with any Naval Unit escort or none at all as desired. The routes and numbers of merchant ships needed is dependent upon the Nation and its economy.

Naval Unit Types

The following Naval Units are available in PG II and all of them are used:

Battleship (BB) – Battleships are very hard to sink, and have long range guns. They also take up an additional hex around their location, so other ships cannot be moved adjacent to them and other BB units have to stay 3 hexes away (because they have their own "zone" or whatever it is). This is hardwired in the game.

Battle Cruiser (BC) – Faster than a BB but with less armour. There doesn't appear to be any difference between the BB and BC units in PG II, but I kept the type anyway.

Aircraft Carrier (CV) – Carriers have the same deployment zone as a BB does, and have the capacity to carry and rearm Naval Air Units (from 1 to 3). Very useful for a Naval Battle.

Cruiser (CA) – Pretty much just a smaller version of a battleship but a cruiser has no extra zone around it, reflecting its smaller size. I thought about just making classifying bigger units as CA, except that the CV is the only unit that can rearm an aircraft, so since that has the zone I might as well keep it. In addition, fixed coast guns are classed as a Cruiser. The reason for this is that they will fire back against Naval Units that attack them, assuming they are in range. Other unit types will not.

Light Cruiser (CL) – Smaller than a cruiser but a bit bigger than a destroyer, a light cruiser is otherwise no different from a cruiser as far as I can tell (in PG II terms).

Destroyer (DD) – Destroyers are vital because while their guns are weak, they are very fast and are the only Naval Units that can attack subs. Without Destroyers, other ships are dead meat when subs are around.

Submarines (SS) – Probably the most deadly unit to other naval units, a sub can't be attacked except by a DD. This means that when they attack other types of Naval Units, then tend to do a hell of a lot of damage, regardless of their Naval Attack rating. This is very oddly added into the PG II game code, but the bottom line is that almost any sub can do significant damage to a BB, for example, more than even another BB can typically do to it. They are vulnerable to air units and destroyers, and also tend to be slow. They also have a 50% chance of avoiding even a unit that can attack it (by diving). Despite these advantages, a good screen of DD units and some air can usually smash subs up quite well.

Special Naval Unit Types

These are unit types that are necessary for the game but do not fit neatly into the above standard PG II categories.

Escort Carriers (CVE) – In reality the Escort Carrier is built at a 3:1 scale, since they tend to be small, slower ships often converted to carry aircraft. However, since they don't appear until later the scale doesn't matter very much but their capabilities are built into the unit cost. A CVE carries 1 Air Unit only, and can only be used for Escort Duty (not patrol). They are great to use to guard important convoys and merchant shipping, when heavier units are needed elsewhere.

ASW Cruiser (CLD) – This is a light cruiser, usually, that has ASW capability. Since cruisers don't have that capability, they are classified for PG II as Destroyer Units. However, since they are much more expensive than DD units, care should be taken in using them in the ASW role as they are not as expendable as a DD is.

Anti-Aircraft Cruiser (CAA) – These are cruisers designed to provide air defense for a fleet by being crammed full of AA guns. Truthfully, they didn't work all that well but the PG II game doesn't properly calculate [AA] damage for higher values than 1. Therefore, I can only properly program a higher Air Defense rating for ships with more AA guns, which is important but not as effective. Therefore, I decided to have some CAA units, which are actually naval AA guns that are hard to program into a battle, but it can be done (they have to already be placed on the map, though, in order to work).

Coastal Cruiser (CC) – These are outdated heavy warships that have been relegated to coastal defense roles. They can be used for bombardment or convoy escort, but are too slow and inefficient to be used in Naval Patrols.

Destroyer Escort (DE) – These are smaller escort vessels designed to be used in a primarily ASW role. Therefore, they have very limited capacity in a fleet role and their naval attack ratings are higher than they should be against other surface ships. Therefore, the DE unit is the same as a DD except that it can only be used in a convoy escort role or to intercept Submarine Flotillas (in an ASW role). They may also be used for bombardment support, since their value as such is already quite limited.

Small Submarines (SSC) – Small subs, not necessarily midget subs but close at least, can be transported by land. These types of Sub Unit may be moved strategically from one port to another by land.

NAVAL TRANSPORT

Naval Transport in PG II is like air transport, it is supplied from the scenario and assigned as needed from ports or when a ground unit is deployed at sea. In the campaign, Naval Transports are generic for every Nation and represent any type of ship used, and in the case of some battles even river transport. In addition to moving ground units (or short ranged air units) by sea, naval transport is needed for merchant shipping (this applies to Britain, the USA and Japan only) and for Naval Invasions.

Transport Pools

Instead of being assigned to a particular port like a Naval Unit, Transport is assigned simply as a pool of units within a Sea Zone that may be drawn as needed from any friendly Port with access to that Sea Zone. Some Ports have access to more than one Sea Zone, for example Gibraltar can access both the Atlantic and the Mediterranean Transport Pools.

European Transport Pools

The European Map is divided into the Atlantic and Mediterranean Transport Pools. In addition, the Baltic and Black Sea can be appended to either the Atlantic or Mediterranean Pools if access can be established. The Baltic requires access through either the Kiel canal in Germany or Copenhagen in order to be attached to the Atlantic Pool, and access to the Black Sea is controlled by Istanbul. If these areas are not under friendly control, then the Sea is considered an Independent Transport Pool. As indicated above, Gibraltar controls access between the Atlantic and Mediterranean.

Access to the Pacific – The Atlantic Transport Pool can access the Pacific Pool via the Panama Canal, controlled by the USA, or otherwise the long route via Cape Horn.

Access to the Indian Ocean – The Mediterranean can access the Indian Ocean via the Suez Canal, and the Atlantic via South Africa.

Russian Transport Pool – The Russians only have limited access to sea areas, and most of these are small. Therefore, the Russians have a small overall Pool that they can use anywhere at all. Since it is not likely they will build much transport in any case or need much, this is not likely to be any issue.

Far East Transport Pools

The Far East has only the Pacific and Indian Ocean Transport Pools. The Indian Ocean on-Map is defined as covering the Southeast Asian Front, so in effect it also includes the small seas that make up the Dutch East Indies as well as the South China Sea.

Port Access – The Port of Foochow is only accessed by the Indian Ocean Transport Pool (it is actually the South China Sea), but Taipei has access to either the Pacific or Indian Ocean Transport Pool (Based on 6.1.2.1 Port Sides). This also means that you may only enter Taipei from the Southeast Asian Front (the scale of the Map doesn't quite show where the port is actually located). Manila is similarly restricted to the Southeast Asian Front, as is Ambon, although the latter may be invaded from the Pacific Front. Finally, Townsville is physically on the Southeast Asian Front, but its access is only to the Pacific Front and Transport Pool.

Access across the Arctic – The Arctic Ocean over Russia and Canada are only navigable during the Summer and Fall seasons.

Leningrad Canal – Russia may also send Naval Units during the Summer and Fall seasons through between Murmansk and Leningrad via Petropavlovsk.

Port Capacity – This rule has been deleted. It may be reinstated if it seems to be needed. I would like to try to play without any pre-set limits on what number of transports ports can handle. I think it may not be of any significant consequence.

Channel Crossing – Movement across a Blue Crossing Arrow by land is allowed without using any Naval Transports. Small boats and transports of that nature, rather than large ships, are used because of how narrow these waters are. An attack across such a Crossing Arrow will still involve Naval Transports for the attacking force, but these are available automatically.

Movement between Transport Pools – If Transports perform a mission that is completed in another Transport Pool, the Transports may either remain there or return to their original pool. This is indicated under the convoy sheet when their mission is given its orders. It is also possible to simply move them without a mission, creating a mission that basically has no cargo. This is most likely something that the USA may do when moving Transports from West to East, for example.

Naval Orders

Naval Units receive all of their Orders simultaneously during the Orders Phase, and then combat can take place during Operations.

Operational Range (Patrol) – The Operational Range of a Naval Unit is the distance it can travel and then return to its home base, while engaging in offensive operations like a Naval Patrol or an Invasion. Each Naval Unit has a Patrol Range = 1 for each 1,800 miles of endurance it is rated at.

1 Range = 10 Squares on-Map in Europe,

1 Range = 5 Squares on-Map in the Far East.

Sea Zones for the Atlantic, Indian and Pacific Oceans are indicated as either 1 or 2 Range for purposes of movement off Map.

A 1 Range Sea Zone is approximately 10. Latitude, and 10.+ degrees of Longitude (increased the further the distance is from the Equator). 10. of Latitude is about 690 Miles, since the circumference of the Earth is 25,000 miles and 25,000/360. = 69 miles.

Endurance – Each Naval Unit has an Endurance of 1 for each 600 miles of nautical range it is rated at. This translates into the same range system as Operational Range, but allows you to change base and provide naval escort between friendly ports.

Naval Patrol – A Naval Patrol can be undertaken from any friendly Port and out to any sea square within Operational Range. Naval Patrols allow your Naval Units to Intercept any nearby enemy Naval Missions, as well as launch Naval Air Units from the location of the Patrol.

Staging Area – If you wish to have Naval Units combine in order to launch a Patrol, they must first rendezvous at another friendly port, or staging area. The Staging Area must be either a friendly Port or Island within the Operational Range of all of the Naval Units in question. From that location, they may then choose to Patrol any square or Sea Zone within their Range. This effectively "doubles" your Patrol Range, but it requires some sort of friendly port within that range to launch from, and that may even include small islands, in addition to actual Ports, making such islands useful in the Far East.

Returning to Port – When designating Orders for a Naval Patrol, you must designate where you wish your Units to return after their Mission. This can be their home base, the staging area (if it is a Port), or any friendly Base within Patrol Range of the Patrol Square.

Patrol in a Sea Zone – To Patrol a Sea Zone requires the full range of the Sea Zone in question, and allows any task force, submarine patrol, or raider group to intercept any naval activity that passes through that Sea Zone. Note that range would be calculated by adding the squares needed to get to the Map Edge, with 5 or 10 squares = 1 Range, then adding the Range of the Zone and any Zones that must be passed through. This must be equal or less than the Patrol Range of the unit(s) in question.

Naval Transport Convoy

A Naval Transport Convoy carries units, supplies, and anything else that needs to move by sea. Usually a Naval Transport Convoy is assigned a Naval Escort to protect the transports, as well.

Embarkation – Naval Transports may embark from any friendly Port that has access to the indicated Transport Pool. Each Unit assigned may either come from a connected Army Reserve (Supplies or Units are embarked this way), or they may be ground units from a formation that has access to the Port. There can be multiple Ports of embarkation for a single convoy, but they must join together at a friendly Port and continue on from there, and usually they have escort for the various legs of their mission. The endurance of a Naval Transport is 10 as a standard for all of them, so the net range from any port of embarkation to a refuelling port cannot be greater than 10 (Naval) Range, and from there to the destination another 10. This is not likely to be an issue except when moving very long distances, usually off-map.

Debarkation – There can only be 1 port of debarkation for any transport mission. At the destination, all reserve units and supplies are added to the destination's command reserve, and ground forces continue any strategic movement their orders indicated as applicable.

Refuelling – Any friendly Territory, Island, or Port can be designated as a refuelling location, and can effectively double the overall endurance of a Naval Transport Mission. Only one refuelling is permitted per mission.

Ground Transport as Cargo – Usually if a unit already has attached Ground Transport both it and its Transport may be carried along by 1 Naval Transport. In the event that you are just moving a lot of transport, such as when Lend-Lease Transport is being shipped, each Ground unit can freely "hitch a ride" on any Transport not already carrying one, or you can put two of them in one transport at a time.

Merchant Convoys – Merchant Convoys, as well as any Tankers carrying Oil Units, are not much different from other Transport Convoys except that they can be no larger than 8 Transports each. Escort for such convoys is not limited in size. In practice, it will be difficult to cover every convoy and still have naval units free for other duties, so I don't think there is a need to impose any further constraints on escort.

Naval Escort

A Naval Escort Mission protects Transports from enemy attack. The mission can protect any single Merchant Convoy or Naval Transport Convoy. Escorting Naval Units are ordered to any Port from which the Convoy embarks, and from there they continue with the ships until their Mission is complete. The Range of Naval Escort cannot exceed Endurance Range of the Ship up to a Refuelling Port and from there to the Port of Debarkation. Naval Units that provide Escort may then return to their home port, remain in the destination port, or can re-base in any friendly port that they passed through along their route.

Reverse Escort – In some cases, especially with Merchant Convoys, the convoy route may be such that the Naval Escort is based at the destination. In this case, they can be routed to the embarkation port, then return as Escort with the Convoy (along the same route). For example, you can escort merchants that come from the Americas to Britain with ships based in Britain. This doesn't really change anything except that the mission may be intercepted on its way back, rather than on the way out, assuming you intend to target the shipping. As long as only one attack is made against the Escort and/or convoy, this does not change anything.

Partial Escort – If Escort is unable to reach the Destination Port, but can reach some friendly port to refuel along the way, it can be used to protect that portion of the route. However, if its endurance ends in the middle of the ocean, it can't be used because the endurance assumes the ability to refuel at the destination. If not, then it is possible to provide some limited escort up to 50% of endurance Range, rounded down.

Naval Invasion Orders

In a Naval Invasion, there are orders given to ground forces, naval transports, and escorting warships which all combine to form the actual invasion that takes place during Operations (assuming it has not been aborted or interrupted in the meantime).

Naval Invasion Range – The total range of a Naval Invasion is limited both in the distance to the staging area (if there is no staging area, range to staging area = 0) and in distance to the invasion square. In addition, both of these ranges affect the number of naval transports needed per unit being shipped.

The requirement is higher than that for normal movement because of the need for landing craft and other significant difficulties inherent in naval invasions. Note that the ranges are expressed like naval unit ranges, so Range 0 to 2 in the Pacific would mean a distance of 0 to 10 squares (range 1 is 5, range 2 is 10 squares) from the launch site to the staging area.. Of course, these can't exceed the operational range of the individual ships assigned as escort for the mission either.

The following table describes the ranges and transports allowed for a Naval Invasion:

Range to Staging Area Transports Range to Invasion Transports:
0 to 2 1/Unit 1 to 2 1/Unit
3 to 4 2/Unit 3 to 4 2/Unit

Ground Forces – Ground Units sent on a Naval Invasion must already be in the same Territory as the Port of Embarkation and then move to the staging area, if applicable. They may carry all of their component units, or some may be left behind and sent to the reserve if there is not enough transport available, and the same applies to any assigned supplies. Units and supply still in the reserve can't be assigned to an invasion, nor can forces that are not already in a port or formed and available.

Landing Craft – Certain Units may be assigned Landing Craft, and if so these count as 1 Transport towards the requirements above. In addition, SNLF and RMCo Units are automatically given "free" landing craft even if they have not been assigned such a unit.

Reinforcements – Note that when calculating the required Transport, a minimum of 2 Transports per Unit must be assigned, making it difficult to send a lot of forces into a battle. If you wish to invade a small island or an area with minimal or no forces defending it, the need for landing craft is minimal and it is possible to choose another option. If you make an invasion and leave some of the forces for followup waves, you can attack with all units assigned 1 less transport and they will fight the battle at half strength (5 strength). The second option is to use only 1 transport in total (assuming the normal requirement is 3 or more transports, because if it is only 2 then the former option may always be used), but these reinforcements won't appear in the battle at all, but will land once the territory has been secured.

Naval Base Change

If you choose to change base as part of any of the above missions, you may indicate such during orders and change base to any port along the route that your unit took during the Mission. If you simply wish to make a base change only, then that is a base change. There are two options when making a base change:

Operational Base Change – An operational change of base is a short movement of forces so that they may still be available for nearby operations. This is identical to a Patrol Order, except that your destination is another friendly port within patrol range. It may also include a "stage" to another port along the way. The result is that any carriers with naval air may deploy their air units during operations from the location of their new base, and any naval units in that base may intercept nearby activity or defend their port from invasion.

Strategic Base Change – A strategic base change is usually a movement across much larger distances, and is the same as a naval escort mission and uses endurance range, except that no transports are used. The ships are not active and may not be used to defend their new base and all aircraft would be considered organizing as well. If that base comes under attack, the ships will not be available either to defend or to be targeted. If a base is invaded and lost, the mission is aborted.

NAVAL INTERCEPTION

During Operations, Naval Battles will take place as a result of Interceptions against enemy Naval Missions. Naval Interceptions are announced during Ops at the same time as attacks and reactions are being made. However, they operate under their own set of rules:

Naval Routes

Every Naval Mission must assign a Route to that Mission during the Orders Phase. The Route of naval movement includes is traced on the Map (or off map through Naval Zones) step-by-step from start to finish. When tracing a route on the theatre map you may only indicate the Ports used and the Sea Squares traversed, although you may also go through straits or small islands when indicated. Coastal waters are assumed to exist in some of the land and port squares, but for game purposes all movement must be done via sea squares, again with the exception of small Islands (indicated by double blue lines around the square). Straits require control over one or both of the land sides being passed through.

Merchant Convoy Routes – Merchant Convoys are limited in size, and multiple convoys are usually required for each Nation to cover its needs. The routes established to various sources of goods are therefore indicated in a particular order of importance and the convoys need to be routed appropriately. Check each Nation for its particular requirements.

Search Range

In order to spot an enemy Naval Mission and Intercept it, ready naval or air units must be based or on Naval Patrol within search range of the Route the enemy naval mission travels. Search is a function of each naval and air unit's capabilities (this will be available on the nation's sheet for every unit). Search Range for a fleet on patrol is equal to the highest unit within the fleet. Note that you may also search diagonally using the same rules as movement, i.e. the first diagonal counts as 2, the second as 3, and so on. A Search Range of 0 is the minimum possible, and means that you only spot in the same square that is under patrol.

ASW Search – Only DD, DE, CV, CVE and Air Units have an ASW Search function (i.e. may spot a submarine flotilla), and this is always 1 less than their normal Search rating. All other Units may not spot submarine flotillas at all. While all Air Units have an ASW Search Range, only some have actual ASW capability. Only Fighters (which cannot in any case engage Submarines) and Bombers with the ASW ability are allowed to participate in a battle against a Submarine Flotilla, though other units may have spotted the activity. The one exception to this is CAP, in which case the Air Unit is part of the convoy itself, and always available to defend the convoy against any type of attack.

Carrier Task Force – If a Carrier Task Force is on Naval Patrol, its Air Units may be sent on a Naval Patrol as well, in which case they can be given a location to patrol from the Patrol square that the carrier is in. This greatly extends the ability of a Carrier Task Force to spot enemy Naval activity and intercept, often with air units alone.

Intercept Points

Basically, an intercept point is any sea square on the Map that is spotted by friendly naval forces on patrol or any naval air patrols. These represent points along the mission route that may be subject to interception.

Intercept Range – In order to make a naval intercept, an air unit must be within range of an intercept point and a Naval Unit must be on Patrol within intercept range of such a point. Unlike Search Range, Interception is only possible by individual ships and therefore the entire fleet is affected by the slowest ship.

However, it is possible to break off faster ships from any existing Naval Patrol. An Interception Range of 0 means that you have to be in the same Square as the Mission passing through. Interception Range is also adjusted by the same modifiers that affect Search Range:

Pacific Map:-1

ASW:-1

vs. Raiders:-1

Fleet Interception – Note that only 1 single fleet may intercept a single mission, no multiple intercepts are possible. Fleet interception can be split off from a single patrol, but the opposite is not possible you cannot combine two patrols against the same enemy mission. The only Naval Units eligible to intercept are those on Naval Patrol or those that are in Port (or made an operational base change to a port) and within intercept range.

Air Unit Interception – Air Units within Range of any spotted Naval Activity and otherwise Ready may be used to attack enemy naval missions, with the proviso that ASW still limits the ability of Bombers to intercept submarine flotillas.

Interception Location – The Intercept Point must be any on-Map Sea Square or off-Map Sea Zone. You may not intercept at a Port (this is represented by a land square), however. The only exception is Islands which may be passed through because of double blue lines. These are too small to take up an entire land square and are therefore considered to be both a Sea and a Land square simultaneously.

Interception in Sea Zones – Although a Sea Zone represents such a large area of the Map, it is assumed that an attempt to intercept is possible. Any Task Force or Submarine Flotilla on Patrol may intercept a convoy in a Sea Zone as well. In this case, interception range is not taken into account. However, it is harder to intercept in a Sea Zone and that is reflected in the setup of the Naval Battle. Note that

Naval Air Patrols in a Sea Zone – The only Air Units that may intercept in a Sea Zone are those that are specifically on Patrol in that Sea Zone. This is different from on-Map Interceptions because of the large area that the Sea Zone represents as well as the distance from the mainland.

Order of Interception – Interceptions are resolved in Reverse Order, so for example if Force A intercepts Force B, but then Force C intercepts Force B, you would play the C vs. B battle, following which (if they "completed" their mission by being in the target zone by the end of the battle) you could then do the B vs. A Battle, which could also be aborted if it suffered too much damage (at the attacker's discretion).

Naval Battles

Naval Battles are conducted in the Battle Phase in the Order of Interception as above, so sometimes they must be resolved in sequence as a result. However, they are all resolved during the Battle Phase. During the Breakthrough Battle Phase, special situations may arise that require Battles to be fought at this time instead (including in the Pacific Theatre).

Interception Battle – These Battles last 22 Turns, and one side may choose to Retreat on Turn 12, in the same manner as a Land Battle. The setup depends upon the theatre and the distance to the interception point. In addition, any mission is required to reach a destination zone in order to complete its mission. If it does not reach the target zone by the end of the Battle or at the time of withdrawal on Turn 12 or later, it does not complete its Mission. This may mean you choose to abort the entire mission, or you may proceed if only some units made it through.

Naval Deployment – The Naval Battle Details worksheet indicates how Naval Deployment will be determined for a Naval Battle. The PG II Ocean Map is divided into 16 squares, 4 per side, with each of the 16 squares representing a number of hexes on the map. The PG II Map Hexes chart will indicate how the hexes have been divided (as evenly as possible, but since the actual hexes may be important they are specifically delineated here). The attacker deploys within the red zone, and the defender in the blue zone.

Interception Distance – The type of interception and distance on the Map affects the deployment. This is indicated from a distance of 0 to 3 on the European and Pacific Maps separately. An attack by air units only is also a different type of deployment, and an interception in a Sea Zone will depend on the size of the Sea Zone in question.

Mission Completion – The area indicated as "Defender Destination" is the area that ships must be in order to complete their mission. This applies for every Intercepted Naval Mission that has not yet reached its destination. Even an intercepted Patrol Mission has not yet reached its destination if it is still en-route to its Patrol Square. Note that if you complete your mission, you may continue with any undamaged ships, and this includes Patrol Missions. This means that if a Naval Patrol defends itself against an Interception, it can still choose to make its own Interception as well (that doesn't count as 2 missions, as it may complete its first Mission). This is one of the few times that a fleet can be in a battle twice during the turn, but it is voluntary for the fleet since it has still only been attacked once.

Damaged Ships – If a Naval Unit sustains more than 2 points of damage in a Battle, it automatically returns to Port and cannot continue its Mission. Other Units may continue their Mission or choose to abort it and return to Port. If any Naval Units are heavily damaged following a battle, they may decide to return to a shipyard if their current base cannot repair the damage. In this case, they must choose the nearest friendly location capable of doing so and take the most direct route possible, and they may be intercepted during the Breakthrough Phase (this works like any other Interception Battle, but happens during Breakthrough instead of Operations, with Naval and Air Units that have not previously acted during *the turn)*. The other alternative is to have the ship return to port and even though it is damaged, it may make a future base change to another port with a shipyard facility. Otherwise, damaged ships may not conduct any missions until they have been completely repaired to full strength.

Evacuations – The final type of interception battle that can occur is after any land battle in which the defender has retreated by way of a Port, or in which Naval Units were displaced. This takes place during the Breakthrough Phase. Only available transports may be used to evacuate land forces, and only naval units based in that port may provide escort. Displaced naval units may form fleets and re-base to any other friendly port. After mission announcements, any interceptions may take place. This works exactly like it does during Ops. Note that in the event naval units are overrun during a Breakthrough Battle, they are all scuttled. Similarly, land units cannot evacuate by port if they are overrun in a breakthrough battle.

Merchant Ships and Tankers – Submarine Warfare is a subset of Interceptions, with convoys of merchants and/or tankers being intercepted by submarines and raiders, sometimes with limited air support as well. This is handled in the same exact way as any other interception, however the results may be calculated in a different manner. If the convoy does not "complete its mission" then oil is not delivered in the case of tankers, and if merchant ships turn back then 100 PPs of SW damage accrues for each merchant ship so doing. In addition, they can be sunk or damaged. Sinking of course accomplishes the same result as foiling the mission, except that the transport is also destroyed. Damaged ships and tankers accrue 10 PPs of SW damage for each point of damage they take, but tankers will always deliver an oil unit unless they are sunk or fail their mission.

Naval Invasion – A Naval Invasion Battle takes place whenever Naval Invasion Orders have been given, and the attack order is given during Ops. It is possible to abort a Naval Invasion by simply choosing not to attack during Ops. This does not preclude your forces from intercepting enemy naval forces nor does it preclude the same being done to your invasion fleet. Once the order is given, there are several options to consider:

Interception vs. Defense – Interception is possible prior to an Invasion taking place. If Naval Interception takes place, it may occur in any Sea Square up to and including the square adjacent to the Invasion Territory. This can take place by the usual method, with any available fleet making the interception as well as supporting air units. Note that the invasion must still be spotted, so unless an air or naval unit is based in that square, it does not automatically assume spotting occurs unless actual units do so. However, if defending naval units are based there, they will be able to make an interception. Such an interception is independent of the actual invasion battle, however. That means that you may choose not to intercept, but instead hold back air and naval units to defend against the actual landing. Naval Units may also provide defensive bombardment support, but only if they are based in the territory or have made an operational base change to that territory. Otherwise, nearby friendly naval forces could choose the intercept option instead. Both options are possible, but only 1 interception may be made against the fleet. Note that you may do both even with the same ships – i.e. intercept the fleet, then use the same ships for bombardment support. Of course, this assumes they are still afloat and capable and have not been badly damaged. Damaged ships in Port, or available after such an interception, can only participate in bombardment defense if the damage is minimal and they are at 8 or 9 strength still.

Naval Bombardment – Naval Bombardment is prohibited except in support or defense of a Naval Invasion. If there is a simultaneous land attack, the Naval Invasion force must be at least 50% of the total number of attacking units or bombardment is prohibited for both sides. Naval Bombardment may include any ship in the invasion fleet as well as any ship based in the territory under attack. However, the stacking limit for a naval invasion is no more than 8 naval units of any type, with no more than 2 submarines included as part of this force.

Reactions – Defending forces may also react to reinforce a territory under naval invasion during the ops phase, just as they would to defend any territory under attack. The same rules apply (including the fact that they will not get any entrenchment bonus for a fortified line). The attacker may do the same in regards to his air units or possible airborne units as well, or even partisans in an auxiliary role to work behind the lines (like the French Resistance did in Normandy).

Fixed Defences – Fixed Anti-Aircraft guns (some of which may have a dual function) and fixed coastal guns may be deployed. In addition, any fortified lines constructed will add +8 entrenchment for defending forces, just as they would against a land attack.

Island Invasion – Islands have a small stacking limit of 1 Division, so all ground forces are split into 5-Strength increments (or Garrisons remain as they are) and Naval and Units assigned to bombardment are also at 50% Strength (rounded up) *but are not split (so no more than 8 half-strength naval units are present per side).* This applies to both the attacker as well as the defender. Damage to those units during the Battle will occur on a 1:1 Basis. This only applies to actual Islands (with blue all around them) not to single territory islands, which have a larger stacking limit and therefore operate normally. Because of this stacking limit, the attacker is also restricted to attacking with 1 division at most, but can supplement this with special forces.

Island Defences – There are two options available for Island Defense. It is possible to have a full strength division there, or it is possible to have an island garrison, but not both. Island garrisons are normal OOB divisions at half strength (they don't count towards the force limit, either). In addition to either the division or garrison, an island can also have fixed coastal and air defense at half strength (use the normal stacking limits, but at half strength). In addition, Islands do not need fortified lines, but instead are always considered to have a fortified line. This makes taking Islands fairly difficult, but the fact that Naval Guns can usually reach the defenders quite easily on a small island can quickly degrade the entrenchment levels, so it balances out.

Air Units – Air Units are also split into 50% strength units, but although they are split the overall stacking limit of 4 fighter and 4 bomber units cannot be exceeded. Therefore, when attacking or defending against an island invasion, up to 2 full strength units of each type could be assigned, or more units, but then they would not all be employed. Damage accrues on a 1 to 1 scale, as does experience

Battle Length – Battles for Island Invasions are only 12 Turns long, because of how small the area under attack is. An Island Invasion can, however, be evacuated if at the end of the Battle there are any surviving defenders capable of making such an evacuation.

Port Attack – A Port attack is an Air attack (usually) against Naval and Strategic Targets in a Port City. A Port Attack may be made by up to 4 fighter and 4 bomber units against an enemy target during the Ops Phase, and lasts 12 Turns in the same manner as a Strategic Bombing Attack. In addition, the defender can deploy fixed air defense units as well as interceptors to defend the port.

Targets – Ports can represent target-rich environments, and that includes any factories that may also be in the target city, shipyard facilities, refineries, and of course and naval units in port or under repair or construction in the port shipyard facilities, and finally fixed coast guns can even be targeted if present. All of these targets, if available, will be present in the battle. Radar and Observation Towers are only available if there are factories, refineries or shipyards present, however (1 for each such unit).

Ships in Port – Ships in Port may be attacked if they made an Operational Base Change to that Port or have just remained in Port for the Turn. You cannot attack ships in Port if they are on any other Mission. Ships as targets of an attack can't move while in Port, and are deployed (at full strength) within a relatively small coastal area representing the port. This way they are both easily found as well as easily covered by air defences nearby. In addition, because of the fact that not all of the crew may be available, experience is reduced by 100 for any ships in Port. Damage accrues on a 1 to 1 basis from any air attacks, although if a ship sinks in a facility with a shipyard, it may be raised again and placed "under construction" in the shipyard at 2 strength (or scrapped for 1 point).

Ships under Repair – Ships in a port under repair are the same as other ships in Port but will have their strength reduced accordingly. In addition, they are reduced by 200 experience and the same rule applies if they are sunk while in a shipyard; they are placed under construction at 2 strength points.

Ships under Construction – Ships within a shipyard and under construction are placed there at their partial strength if it is from 1 to 9, with no experience. If they are destroyed, they are completely eliminated. If a ship is almost complete it is placed at 8 (strength 10) or 9 (strength 11), but in this case it has already been launched and if destroyed can be re-built from a strength of 1 (strength 10) or 2 (strength 11). Even if a ship is almost done and has been launched, however, it receives no experience. Any construction or repair that was done during orders should also be accounted for prior to setting up the ships. That means that if a ship was completed that turn, it is placed as a completed ship just like any other. The only difference being that it would not have been able to perform any mission that turn (or be placed at another port, for that matter, since that is done during logistics).

Shipyards – Shipyards are present as targets similar to factories and refineries, but 1 target is placed for each 100 capacity of the shipyard or portion thereof (i.e. a 250 capacity shipyard is 3 targets). In the case of shipyards, damage can accrue up to 2x the capacity of the shipyard, but does not do SW damage. Instead, the damage must be repaired during logistics as an infrastructure build, otherwise the shipyard is incapacitated by damage. A shipyard can be repaired immediately if PPs is available to do so, but otherwise cannot operate until all damage has been repaired. Shipyards are attacked and damage calculated against them applying the exact same rules as factories. It is also possible for any side to voluntarily "destroy" a shipyard under its control during the Logistics Phase. In this case, it may be repaired at the maximum cost of 2x the shipyard's capacity.

Pearl Harbour – Pearl Harbour is a special case for the Japanese, whose surprise attack was able to do considerable damage. The level of surprise and position of the USA fleet carriers is determined by the chart on the Naval Battles Sheet. Partial surprise allows for 1 wave of attacks at surprise, followed by an optional wave with no surprise, and full surprise allows 2 waves with surprise. Surprise reduces all ships, anti-aircraft, and air units to half strength, but damage accrues to them at 2x normal strength. In addition, all naval units that are surprised will fight at –200 experience. Finally, the "second wave" option is always available. This lets the Japanese attack twice in the turn, although any losses they suffer cannot be repaired. The second wave is optional. Note that Hawaii also has Refineries that may be attacked and SW damage can be attained by targeting these.

Vichy France – A Neutral Vichy France (not allied) can have its Algerian Fleet attacked at Oran by British Naval forces. This is a normal Port attack battle, except that British naval units are added to the battle (no more than 12 ships, but they can be independent of or in addition to air units).

Vichy French units are not prepared and therefore suffer the surprise –200 experience penalty (so for the French they would have 0 XP), but in this case they are allowed to move if enemy ships are also attacking them, but British Ships will be close enough to target them right from turn 1, and chances are they will be badly damaged by then. This is an available option as long as Vichy remains neutral, and does not cause a DoW, but it does anger Vichy and adds a +1 modifier to future diplomatic relations with Vichy.

NAVAL WARFARE-DEFINITION

Naval warfare is combat in and on seas and oceans. Mankind has fought battles on the sea for more than 3,000 years.

The many sea battles through history also provide a reliable source for shipwrecks and underwater archaeology. A major example, albeit not very commonly known, is the exploration of the wrecks of various ships in the Pacific Ocean, namely Japanese warships that sank during the Battle of Midway.

History

Naval history is the area of military history concerning war at sea. The focus is on direct combat between ships at sea rather than the use of ships to transport armies or military supplies, although frequently naval strategy hinges on the need to protect transport shipping. Naval history is of special interest not only because of the value of learning how societies of the past dealt with the double challenge of human enemies and the implacable sea, but also because ships were the first technology to enable a global civilization. In the days before radio, naval officers at remote locations were frequently called upon to singlehandedly decide the fates of their nations.

Oarsmen of the Mediterranean Sea

The first dateable recorded sea battle occurred about 1210 BC: Suppiluliumas II, king of the Hittites, defeated a fleet from Cyprus, and burned their ships at sea. Assyrian reliefs from the 700s BC show Phoenician fighting ships, with two levels of oars, fighting men on a sort of bridge or deck above the oarsmen, and some sort of ram protruding from the bow. No written mention of strategy or tactics seems to have survived. The Greeks of Homer just used their ships as transport for land armies, but in 664 BC there is a mention of a battle at sea between Corinth and its colony city Corcyra. The Persian Wars were the first to feature large-scale naval operations, not just sophisticated fleet engagements with dozens of triremes on each side, but combined land-sea operations. It seems unlikely that all this was the product of a single mind or even of a generation; most likely the period of evolution and experimentation was simply not recorded by history.

After some initial battles while subjugating the Greeks of the Ionian coast, the Persians determined to invade Greece proper. Themistocles of Athens estimated that the Greeks would be outnumbered by the Persians on land, but that Athens could protect itself by building a fleet (the famous "wooden walls"), using the profits of the silver mines at Laurium to finance them. The first Persian campaign, in 492 BC, was aborted because the fleet was lost in a storm, but the second, in 490 BC, captured islands in the Aegean Sea before landing on the mainland near Marathon. Attacks by the Greek armies repulsed these. The third Persian campaign, under Xerxes I of Persia ten years later (480 BC), followed the pattern of the first in marching the army via the Hellespont while the fleet paralleled them offshore. Near Artemisium, in the narrow channel between the mainland and Euboea, the Greek fleet held off multiple assaults by the Persians, the Persians breaking through a first line, but then being flanked by the second line of ships. But the defeat on land at Thermopylae forced a Greek withdrawal, and Athens evacuated its population to nearby Salamis Island. The ensuing Battle of Salamis was one of the decisive engagements of history. Themistocles trapped the Persians in a channel too narrow for them to bring their greater numbers to bear, and attacked them vigorously, in the end causing the loss of 200 Persian ships vs 40 Greek. At the end, Xerxes still had a fleet stronger than the Greeks, but withdrew anyway, and after losing at Plataea in the following year, returns to Asia Minor, leaving the Greeks their freedom. Nevertheless, the Athenians and Spartans attack and burn the laid-up Persian fleet at Mycale, and free many of the Ionian towns.

During the next fifty years, the Greeks command the Aegean, but not harmoniously, and after several minor wars about which we know little, in 431 BC, tensions exploded into the Peloponnesian War between Athens' Delian League and the Spartan Peloponnese. Naval strategy was critical; Athens walled itself off from the rest of Greece, leaving only the port at Piraeus open, and trusting in its navy to keep supplies flowing while the Spartan army besieged it. This strategy worked, although the close quarters likely contributed to the plague that killed many Athenians in 429.

There were a number of sea battles; at Rhium, Naupactus, Pylos, Syracuse, Cynossema, Cyzicus, Notium. But the end came for Athens in 405 at Aegospotami in the Hellespont, where the Athenians had drawn up their fleet on the beach, and were there surprised by the Spartan fleet, who landed and burned all the ships. Athens surrendered to Sparta in the following year.

Navies next played a major role in the complicated wars of the successors of Alexander the Great. *(need more?)* Rome was never much of a seafaring nation, but it had to learn, and learn fast, in the Punic Wars with Carthage, and developed the technique of grappling and boarding enemy ships with soldiers. Romans ships and fleets grew gradually as Rome found itself involved in more and more Mediterranean politics; by the time of the Roman Civil War and the Battle of Actium in 31 BC, hundreds of ships were involved, many of them quinqueremes mounting catapults and fighting towers. The Roman Empire however had little use for navies beyond periodic piracy suppression.

Dark and Middle Ages

The barbarian invasions of the 4th century and later mostly occurred by land, but there are mentions of a Vandal fleet fighting with the Romans, and a defeat of an Ostrogothic fleet at Sena Gallica in the Adriatic Sea. In the 7th century Arab fleets begin to make an appearance, raiding Sicily in 652, and defeating the Byzantines in 655. Constantinople is saved at the Battle of Syllaeum in 678 by the invention of Greek fire, an early form of flamethrower that is devastating to the ships in the besieging fleet. This was just the first of many encounters. In the 8th century the Norsemen begin to make an appearance, although their usual style is to appear quickly, plunder, and disappear, preferably undefended locations. King Alfred the Great of England built a fleet and was able to beat off the Danes.

As Arab power in the Mediterranean began to wane, the Italian trading towns of Genoa, Pisa, and Venice stepped in to seize the opportunity, setting up commercial networks and building navies to protect them. At first the navies fought with the Arabs (off Bari in 1004, at Messina in 1005), but then they found themselves contending with Normans moving into Sicily, and finally with each other. The Genoese and Venetians fought four naval wars, in 1253–1284, 1293–1299, 1350–1355, and 1378–1371. The last ended with a decisive victory for Venice, which gave them almost a century to enjoy Mediterranean trade domination before other European countries started exploring to the south and west.

In the north of Europe, the near-continuous conflict between England and France rarely entails naval activity more sophisticated than carrying knights across the English Channel, and perhaps trying to attack the transports. The Battle of Dover in 1217, between a French fleet of 80 ships under Eustace the Monk and an English fleet of 40 under Hubert de Burgh, is notable is the first recorded battle using sailing ship tactics.

Sails and empire

Technologywise, the late Middle Ages was important as the time of the development of the cogs and caravels, ships capable of surviving the tough conditions of the open ocean, with enough backup systems and crew expertise to make long voyages routine. In addition, they grew from 100 tons to 300 tons displacement, enough to carry cannons as armament and still have space left over for profitable cargo. One of the largest ships of the time, the Great Harry displaced over 1,500 tons. The voyages of discovery were fundamentally commercial rather than military in nature, although the line was sometimes blurry in that a country's ruler was not above funding exploration for personal profit, nor was it a problem to use military power to enhance that profit. Later the lines gradually separated, in that the ruler's motivation in using the navy was to protect private enterprise so that they could pay more taxes. The first naval action in defense of the new colonies was just ten years after Vasco da Gama's epochal landing in India. In March 1508, a combined Gujerati/Egyptian force surprised a Portuguese squadron at Dabul, and only two Portuguese ships escape. In the following February, the Portuguese viceroy destroys the allied fleet at Diu, thus confirming Portuguese domination of the Indian Ocean.

In 1582, the Battle of Punta Delgada in the Azores, in which a Spanish fleet defeated a French force, thus suppressing a revolt in the islands, was the first battle fought in mid-Atlantic. In 1588, Philip V of Spain sent his Spanish Armada to subdue Elizabeth I of England, but her admiral Sir Francis Drake defeated and scattered the force, beginning the rise to prominence of the Royal Navy. In the 17th century competition between English and Dutch commercial fleets came to a head in the Anglo-Dutch Wars, the first wars to be conducted entirely at sea.

The 18th century developed into a period of seemingly continuous world wars, each larger than the last. At sea the British and French were bitter rivals; the French aided the fledgling United States in the American Revolutionary War, but their strategic purpose was to capture territory in India and the West Indies.

Even the change of government due to the French Revolution seemed to intensify the rivalry rather than diminish it, and the Napoleonic Wars included a series of legendary naval battles, culminating in the Battle of Trafalgar in 1805, by which Admiral Horatio Nelson broke the power of the French and Spanish fleets, but lost his own life in so doing.

From Wood to Steel

Trafalgar ushered in the *Pax Britannica* of the 19th century, marked by general peace in the world's oceans, under the ensigns of the Royal Navy. But the period was one of intensive experimentation with new technology; steam power for ships appeared in the 1810s, improved metallurgy and machining technique produced larger and deadlier guns, and the development of explosive shells, capable of demolishing a wooden ship at a single blow, in turn required the addition of iron armour.

The famous battle of the CSS *Virginia* and USS *Monitor* in the American Civil War was the duel of ironclads that symbolized the changing times. As the century came to a close, the familiar modern battleship began to emerge; a steel-armored ship, entirely dependent on steam, and sporting a number of large shell guns mounted in turrets arranged along the centerline of the main deck. The ultimate design was reached in 1906 with the *Dreadnought* which entirely dispensed with smaller guns, her main guns being sufficient to sink any existing ship of the time.

The Russo-Japanese War and particularly the Battle of Tsushima in 1905 was the first test of the new concepts, resulting a stunning Japanese victory and the destruction of dozens of Russian ships.

World War I pitted the old Royal Navy against the new navy of Imperial Germany, culminating in the 1916 Battle of Jutland.

After the war, many nations agreed to the Washington Naval Treaty and scrapped many of their battleships and cruiser while still in the shipyards, but the growing tensions of the 1930s restarted the building programs, with even larger ships than before; *Yamato*, one of the largest battleship ever, displaced 72,000 tons, and mounted 18.1-inch guns.

Above and below the Sea

The victory of the Royal Navy at the Battle of Taranto was a pivotal point as this was the first true demonstration of naval air power and marked the end of the battleship as being the sole capital ship of naval forces. Following 7 December 1941 when the United States came into World War II, the end of the era of the battleship was confirmed, and the new importance of aircraft and their transportation, the aircraft carrier, came to the fore. During the Pacific War, battleships and cruisers spent most of their time bombarding land positions, while the carriers were the stars of the key Battle of the Coral Sea, Battle of Midway, Battle of the Philippine Sea, and the climactic Battle of Leyte Gulf, largest naval battle in history. Air power remained key to navies throughout the 20th century, moving to jets launched from ever-larger carriers, and augmented by cruisers armed with guided missiles and cruise missiles. Just as important was the development of submarines to travel underneath the sea, at first for short dives, then later to be able to spend weeks or months underwater powered by a nuclear reactor. In both World Wars, submarines (U-boats in Germany) primarily exerted their power by sinking merchant ships using torpedoes, as well as other warships. In the 1950s the Cold War inspired the development of ballistic missile submarines, each one loaded with dozens of nuclear-armed missiles and with orders to launch them from sea should the other nation attack.

Three major naval conflicts took place in the second half of the 20th century, of which two pitted fleet against fleet. One was the well known Falklands War, pitting Argentina against the United Kingdom. The other took place 11 years earlier in 1971. It was the third and last of the Indo-Pakistani Wars, in which Bangladesh gained independence from Pakistan with Indian assistance. The Falklands in particular showed the horrible vulnerability of modern ships to sea-skimming missiles like the Exocet. One hit from an Exocet sank HMS *Sheffield*, a modern anti-air warfare destroyer. Important lessons about ship design, damage control and ship construction materials were learnt from the conflict.

The third major naval war took place between Iran and Iraq from 1980 to 1988. It did not feature any large fleet battles, but it featured attacks on merchant ships as routine for the first time since 1945.

It also featured the largest surface action since WWII, when United States Navy ships went after Iranian oil rigs to punish the Iranians for their actions in the war. Iranian naval vessels intervened, and Operation Praying Mantis resulted. At the present time, large naval wars seem to be very rare affairs, with the main function of the modern navy being to exploit its control of the seaways to project power ashore. Power projection has been the primary naval feature of conflicts like the Korean War, Suez Crisis, Vietnam War, Konfrontasi, Gulf War, Kosovo War and both campaigns of the War on Terrorism in Afghanistan and Iraq.

MODERN NAVAL TACTICS

As with all other forms of battle modern naval tactics are reliant on *fire and movement*. The effective delivery of firepower results from scouting and assumption of good firing positions. Movement is a large component of modern combat; a naval fleet can travel hundreds of kilometres in a day. In naval warfare, the key is to detect the enemy while avoiding detection. Much time and effort is spent to deny the enemy the chance to detect your forces. There is also the concept of *battle space*: a zone around a naval force within which a commander is confident of detecting, tracking, engaging and destroying threats before they pose a danger. This is why a navy prefers the open sea. The presence of land and the bottom topology of an area compress the battle space, limit the opportunities to maneuver, make it easier for an enemy to predict the location of the fleet and make the detection of enemy forces more difficult. In shallow waters, the detection of submarines and mines is especially problematic. One scenario that was the focus of American naval planning during the Cold War was a conflict between two modern and well equipped fleets on the high seas, the clash of the United States and the Soviet Union. The main consideration is for Carrier Battle Groups (CVBGs). In modern naval combat there is the potential of a deadly strike being launched from up to 600 nm away. This is a huge area to scout. The double-edged answer to this is electronic warfare. Submarines are the greatest threat to offensive CVBG operations due to the stealth of modern submarines (anechoic coatings, near-silent magnetohydrodynamic drives etc.), which is the submarine's sole advantage. The move towards shallow-water operations has greatly increased this threat. The cherry-on-top is that even the *suspicion* of a submarine threat forces a fleet to commit resources to removing it as the consequences of an undetected submarine are too great.

The key threat in modern naval combat is the missile. This can be delivered from surface, subsurface or air units. With missile speeds ranging up to Mach 4 the engagement time may be only seconds. The key to successful defence is thus to destroy the launching platform *before* it fires, thus removing a number of missile threats in one go. This is not always possible so the AAW resources need to be balanced between the outer and inner air battles.

2

Naval Warfare: Historical Background

Naval warfare is combat in and on seas, oceans, or any other major bodies of water such as large lakes and wide rivers.

History

Mankind has fought battles on the sea for more than 3,000 years. Land warfare would seem, initially, to be irrelevant and entirely removed from warfare on the open ocean, though this is not necessarily true. Land navigation, until the advent of extensive railroads was extremely dependent upon river systems and canals.

The latter were crucial in the development of the modern world in the United Kingdom, the Low Countries and northern Germany, for they enabled the bulk movement of goods and raw materials without which the Industrial Revolution would not have occurred. Prior to 1750, things moved by barge or sea, or not much at all. Thus armies, with their exorbitant needs for food, ammunition and fodder, were tied to the river valleys throughout the ages.

The oceanic influences throughout pre-recorded history (Homeric Legends, e.g. Troy), and classical works like the *Odyssey* underscore the past influences. The Persian Empire — united and strong — couldn't prevail against the might of the Athenian fleet combined with that of lesser city states in several attempts to conquer the Greek city states. Phoenicia's and Egypt's power, Carthage's and even Rome's depended in no mean way upon control of the seas.

So too did the Venetian Republic dominate Italy's city states, thwart the Ottoman Empire, and dominate commerce on the Silk Road and the Mediterranean in general for centuries. For three centuries, the Northmen commonly called the Vikings raided and pillaged and went where they willed, far into central Russia and the Ukraine, and even to far off Constantinople (both via the Black Sea tributaries and through the Strait of Gibraltar). The many sea battles through history also provide a reliable source of shipwrecks for underwater archaeology. A major example, albeit not very commonly known, is the exploration of the wrecks of various warships in the Pacific Ocean.

Oars people of the Mediterranean Sea

The first dateable recorded sea battle occurred about 1210 BC: Suppiluliuma II, king of the Hittites, defeated a fleet from Cyprus, and burned their ships at sea. Assyrian reliefs from the 8th century BC show Phoenician fighting ships, with two levels of oars, fighting men on a sort of bridge or deck above the oarsmen, and some sort of ram protruding from the bow. No written mention of strategy or tactics seems to have survived.

Josephus Flavius (Antiquities IX 283-287) reports a naval battle between Tyre and the king of Assyria who was aided by the other cities in Phoenicia. The battle took place off the shores of Tyre. Although the Tyrian fleet was much smaller in size, the Tyrian defeated their enemies.

The Greeks of Homer just used their ships as transport for land armies, but in 664 BC there is a mention of a battle at sea between Corinth and its colony city Corcyra. The Persian Wars were the first to feature large-scale naval operations, not just sophisticated fleet engagements with dozens of triremes on each side, but combined land-sea operations. It seems unlikely that all this was the product of a single mind or even of a generation; most likely the period of evolution and experimentation was simply not recorded by history.

After some initial battles while subjugating the Greeks of the Ionian coast, the Persians determined to invade Greece proper. Themistocles of Athens estimated that the Greeks would be outnumbered by the Persians on land, but that Athens could protect itself by building a fleet (the famous "wooden walls"), using the profits of the silver mines at Laurium to finance them.

The first Persian campaign, in 492 BC, was aborted because the fleet was lost in a storm, but the second, in 490 BC, captured islands in the Aegean Sea before landing on the mainland near Marathon. Attacks by the Greek armies repulsed these.

The third Persian campaign, under Xerxes I of Persia ten years later (480 BC), followed the pattern of the first in marching the army via the Hellespont while the fleet paralleled them offshore. Near Artemisium, in the narrow channel between the mainland and Euboea, the Greek fleet held off multiple assaults by the Persians, the Persians breaking through a first line, but then being flanked by the second line of ships. But the defeat on land at Thermopylae forced a Greek withdrawal, and Athens evacuated its population to nearby Salamis Island. Aeschylus wrote a play about the defeat, called The Persians, which was performed at a Greek theatre contest a few years after the battle. It is the oldest known surviving play.

The ensuing Battle of Salamis was one of the decisive engagements of history. Themistocles trapped the Persians in a channel too narrow for them to bring their greater numbers to bear, and attacked them vigorously, in the end causing the loss of 200 Persian ships vs 40 Greek. At the end, Xerxes still had a fleet stronger than the Greeks, but withdrew anyway, and after losing at Plataea in the following year, returned to Asia Minor, leaving the Greeks their freedom. Nevertheless, the Athenians and Spartans attacked and burned the laid-up Persian fleet at Mycale, and freed many of the Ionian towns.

During the next fifty years, the Greeks commanded the Aegean, but not harmoniously. After several minor wars about which we know little, tensions exploded into the Peloponnesian War (431 BC) between Athens' Delian League and the Spartan Peloponnese. Naval strategy was critical; Athens walled itself off from the rest of Greece, leaving only the port at Piraeus open, and trusting in its navy to keep supplies flowing while the Spartan army besieged it. This strategy worked, although the close quarters likely contributed to the plague that killed many Athenians in 429.

There were a number of sea battles between galleys; at Rhium, Naupactus, Pylos, Syracuse, Cynossema, Cyzicus, Notium. But the end came for Athens in 405 at Aegospotami in the Hellespont, where the Athenians had drawn up their fleet on the beach, and were surprised by the Spartan fleet, who landed and burned all the ships. Athens surrendered to Sparta in the following year.

Navies next played a major role in the complicated wars of the successors of Alexander the Great.

The Roman Republic had never been much of a seafaring nation, but it had to learn, and learn fast, in the Punic Wars with Carthage, and developed the technique of grappling and boarding enemy ships with soldiers. The Roman Navy grew gradually as Rome found itself involved in more and more Mediterranean politics; by the time of the Roman Civil War and the Battle of Actium in 31 BC, hundreds of ships were involved, many of them quinqueremes mounting catapults and fighting towers. Following the Emperor Augustus transforming the Republic into the Roman Empire, Rome gained control of most of the Mediterranean. Without any significant maritime enemies, the Roman navy was reduced mostly to patrolling for pirates and transportation duties. It was only on the fringes of the Empire, in newly gained provincies or defensive missions against barbarian invasion, did the navy still engage in actual warfare.

In Ancient China

In ancient China, the first known naval battles took place during the Warring States (481 BC-221 BC), a period where regional kings battled against one another. Chinese naval warfare in this ancient period featured grapple-and-hook, as well as ramming tactics with ships called "stomach strikers" and "colliding swoopers". It was written in the subsequent Han Dynasty that the Warring States era Chinese had employed *ge chuan* ships (dagger-axe ships, or halberd ships), thought to have a simple description of a ship manned by marines carrying dagger-axe halberds as personal weapons.

The later 3rd century Three Kingdoms era Chinese writer Zhang Yan asserted in his writing that the Warring States Chinese named the boats this way because halberd blades were actually fixed and attached to the hull of the ship in order to rip into the hull of another ship while ramming, to stab enemies in the water that had fallen overboard and were swimming, or simply to clear any possible dangerous marine animals in the path of the ship.

Qin Shi Huang, the first emperor of the Qin Dynasty (221 BC-207 BC), owed much of his success in unifying China (specifically southern China) to naval power, although an official navy was not yet established. Zhou Dynasty era Chinese were known to use temporary pontoon bridges for general means of transportation, but it was during the Qin and later Han Dynasty that large permanent pontoon bridges were assembled, and used for purposes of warfare (first written account of a pontoon bridge in the West being the oversight of the Greek Mandrocles of Samos in aiding a military campaign of Persian Emperor Darius I over the Bosporus).

During the Han Dynasty (202 BC-AD 220), the Chinese discovered the use of the stern-mounted steering rudder, as well as designed a new ship type, the junk. During the late Han Dynasty into the Three Kingdoms period, significantly large naval battles like the Battle of Chibi marked the advancement of naval warfare in the East. In the latter engagement, the Chinese military strategist Zhuge Liang from the Kingdom of Shu is well known for his fire attack upon the massive naval fleet of Prime Minister Cao Cao.

In terms of seafaring abroad, arguably one of the first Chinese to sail into the Indian Ocean and to reach Sri Lanka and India by sea was the Buddhist monk Fa Xian in the early 5th century (although diplomatic ties and land trade to Persia and India was established during the earlier Han Dynasty). However, Chinese naval maritime influence would not present itself in the Indian Ocean until the medieval period.

The Europe, Middle East and North Africa

The barbarian invasions of the 4th century and later mostly occurred by land, but there are mentions of a Vandal fleet fighting with the Romans, and a defeat of an Ostrogothic fleet at Senà Gallica in the Adriatic Sea.

During the Muslim conquests of the 7th century, Arab fleets begin to make an appearance, raiding Sicily in 652, and defeating the Byzantine Navy in 655. Constantinople is saved from a prolonged Arab siege in 678 by the invention of Greek fire, an early form of flamethrower that was devastating to the ships in the besieging fleet. These were just the first of many encounters during the Byzantine-Arab Wars.

The Islamic Caliphate, or Arab Empire, became the dominant naval power in the Mediterranean Sea from the 7th to 13th centuries, during what is known as the Islamic Golden Age. One of the most significant inventions in medieval naval warfare was the torpedo, invented in Syria by the Arab inventor Hasan al-Rammah in 1275. His torpedo ran on water with a rocket system filled with explosive gunpowder materials and had three firing points. It was a very effective weapon against ships.

In the 8th century the Norse Vikings begin to make an appearance, although their usual style is to appear quickly, plunder, and disappear, preferably undefended locations. King Alfred the Great of England built a fleet and was able to stay the Viking incursions, establishing the boundaries of Danelaw in a 884 treaty.

The Norse also fought several sea battles among themselves. This was normally done by binding the ships on each side together, thus essentially fighting a land battle on the sea. However the fact that the losing side could not easily escape meant that battles tended to be hard and bloody. The Battle of Svolder is perhaps the most famous of these battles.

As Arab power in the Mediterranean began to wane, the Italian trading towns of Genoa, Pisa, and Venice stepped in to seize the opportunity, setting up commercial networks and building navies to protect them. At first the navies fought with the Arabs (off Bari in 1004, at Messina in 1005), but then they found themselves contending with Normans moving into Sicily, and finally with each other. The Genoese and Venetians fought four naval wars, in 1253–1284, 1293–1299, 1350–1355, and 1378–1381. The last ended with a decisive victory for Venice, which gave them almost a century to enjoy Mediterranean trade domination before other European countries started exploring to the south and west.

In the north of Europe, the near-continuous conflict between England and France was characterised by a number of raids on coastal towns and ports along each other coastlines and the securing of sea lanes to protect transports carrying troops from England to France. The Battle of Dover in 1217, between a French fleet of 80 ships under Eustace the Monk and an English fleet of 40 under Hubert de Burgh, is notable as the first recorded battle using sailing ship tactics. The Battle of Sluys, fought in 1340, marked the opening of the Hundred Years War; the battle saw the destruction of the French fleet in an action as decisive as Midway or Tsushima and allowed the English effective control of the sea lanes and the strategic initiative for much of the war.

The East and South Asia

The Sui Dynasty (581-618) and Tang Dynasty (618-907) of China were involved in several naval affairs over the triple-set of polities ruling medieval Korea (Three Kingdoms of Korea), along with engaging naval bombardments on the peninsula from Asuka period Yamato Kingdom (Japan). A prominent factor in the sudden decline and collapse of the Sui Dynasty was its pouring of state funds into the Goguryeo-Sui Wars, where the Chinese assembled an enormous naval fleet that in the end was unsuccessful.

The succeeding Tang Dynasty of China took on a different foreign policy, aiding the Silla Dynasty in expelling the armies and naval forces of the Japanese and conquering Silla's other Korean rivals, Baekje and Goguryeo by 668. In addition, the Chinese Tang Dynasty had maritime trading, tributary, and diplomatic ties as far as modern-day Sri Lanka, India, Islamic Iran and Arabia, as well as Somalia in East Africa.

From the Axumite Kingdom in modern-day Ethiopia, the Arab traveller Sa'd ibn Abi-Waqqas sailed from there to Tang China during the reign of Emperor Gaozong. Two decades later, he returned with a copy of the Quran, establishing the first Islamic mosque in China, the Mosque of Remembrance in Guangzhou. What followed was a rising rivalry between Arab and Chinese for dominant control of sea lanes of trade in the Indian Ocean. In his book *Cultural Flow Between China and the Outside World,* Shen Fuwei notes that maritime Chinese merchants in the 9th century were landing regularly at Sufala in East Africa to cut out Arab middle-men traders.

The Chola Dynasty of medieval India was a dominant seapower in the Indian Ocean, an avid maritime trader and diplomatic entity with Song China. Rajaraja Chola I (reigned 985 to 1014) and his son Rajendra Chola I (reigned 1014–42), who were from the Dravidian kingdom in southern India, sent out a great naval expedition that occupied parts of Myanmar, Malaya, and Sumatra. While many believe the Cholas were the first rulers noted to have a naval fleet in the Indian subcontinent, there are at least two evidences to cite use of navies. Narasimhavarman Pallava I transported his troops to Sri Lanka to help Manavarman to reclaim the throne. Shatavahanahas were known to possess a navy that was widely deployed to influence Southeast Asia. What is not known is the extent of use.

Some argue that there is no evidence to support naval warfare in a contemporary sense. Others say that ships routinely carried bands of archers to keep pirates at bay. However, since the Arabs were known to use catapults, naptha, and devices attached to ships to prevent boarding parties, one can reasonably conclude that Chola navies not only transported troops but also provided support, protection, and attack capabilities against enemy targets.

In the 12th Century

In the 12th century, China's first permanent standing navy was established by the Southern Song Dynasty, the headquarters of the Admiralty stationed at Ding-hai. This came about after the conquest of northern China by the Jurchen people in 1127, while the Chinese court fled south from Kaifeng to Hangzhou. Equipped with the magnetic compass and knowledge of Shen Kuo's famous treatise (on the concept of true north), the Chinese became proficient experts of navigation in their day. They raised their naval strength from a mere 11 squadrons of 3,000 marines to 20 squadrons of 52,000 marines in a century's time.

Employing paddle wheel crafts and trebuchet's throwing gunpowder bombs from the decks of their ships, the Chinese became a formidable foe to the Jin Dynasty during the 12th-13th centuries. With a powerful navy, China dominated maritime trade throughout South East Asia as well. Until 1279, the Chinese were able to use their naval power to defend against the Jin to the north, until the Mongols finally conquered all of China. After the Song Dynasty, the Mongol-led Yuan Dynasty of China was a powerful maritime force in the Indian Ocean.

The Yuan Emperor Kublai Khan attempted to invade Japan twice with enormous fleets (of both Mongols and Chinese), in 1274 and again in 1281, both attempts being unsuccessful. Building upon the technological achievements of the earlier Chinese Song Dynasty, the Mongols also employed early cannons upon the decks of their ships.

While the Chinese Song Dynasty built its naval strength, the Japanese also had considerable naval prowess. The strength of Japanese naval forces could be seen in the Genpei War, in the large-scale Battle of Dan-no-ura on April 25, 1185. The forces of Minamoto no Yoshitsune were 850 ships strong, while Taira no Munemori had 500 ships under his command.

In the mid-14th century, the rebel leader Zhu Yuanzhang (1328–1398) seized power in the south amongst many other rebel groups. His early success was owed to the aid of capable officials such as Liu Ji and Jiao Yu, and their gunpowder weapons. Yet the decisive battle that cemented his success and his founding of the Ming Dynasty (1368–1644) was the Battle of Lake Poyang, considered one of the largest naval battles in history.

In the 15th century, the Chinese Ming Dynasty Admiral Zheng He was assigned to assemble a massive fleet for several tributary missions abroad, sailing throughout the waters of the South East Pacific and the Indian Ocean. During his maritime missions, on several occasions Zheng's fleet came into conflict with pirates. Zheng's fleet also became involved in a conflict in Sri Lanka, where the King of Ceylon traveled back to Ming China afterwards to make a formal apology to the Emperor.

In the late 16th century, Toyotomi Hideyoshi of Momoyama-era Japan gathered an enormous fleet to assault the Joseon Dynasty of Korea when the Korean King Seonjo refused to allow Japanese armies to invade Ming Dynasty China via the Korean Peninsula as a staging ground. During the Japanese invasions of Korea (1592-1598), the Japanese employed clever close-range tactics on land with arquebus rifles, but also relied upon close-range firing of muskets in grapple-and-board style naval engagements.

The Japanese were successful in first capturing the Korean port at Busan, the capital at Hanseong (In modern-day Seoul) fell to their forces, and then proceeded to move far north into the Korean peninsula. Military aid sent by Chinese Wanli Emperor of Ming assisted the Koreans somewhat, but the farther firing range of Korean cannons, along with the brilliant naval strategies of the Korean Admiral Yi Sun-sin, were the main detrimental factors in ultimate Japanese defeats.

Admiral Yi is credited Turtle ship (Geobukseon). Turtle Ships were used mostly to spearhead attacks. They were best used in tight areas and around islands rather than the open sea. Admiral Yi effectively cut off the possible Japanese supply line that would have run through the Yellow Sea to China, as well as severely weakened the Japanese strength and fighting morale in several heated engagements (where many regard the most critical Japanese defeat to be the Battle of Hansan Island).

The Ming Dynasty Imperial Navy defeated a Portuguese navy led by Martim Affonso in 1522. The Chinese destroyed one vessel by targeting its gunpowder magazine, and captured another Portuguese ship.

A Ming army and Navy led by Koxinga defeated a western power, the Dutch East India Company at the Siege of Fort Zeelandia, the first time China had engaged against a western power and won. The Chinese used cannons and ships to bombard the Dutch into surrendering.

The Sails and Empires in late Middle Ages

The late Middle Ages was important as the time of the development of the cogs, caravels and carracks ships capable of surviving the tough conditions of the open ocean, with enough backup systems and crew expertise to make long voyages routine. In addition, they grew from 100 tons to 300 tons displacement, enough to carry cannons as armament and still have space left over for profitable cargo. One of the largest ships of the time, the Great Harry displaced over 1,500 tons.

The voyages of discovery were fundamentally commercial rather than military in nature, although the line was sometimes blurry in that a country's ruler was not above funding exploration for personal profit, nor was it a problem to use military power to enhance that profit. Later the lines gradually separated, in that the ruler's motivation in using the navy was to protect private enterprise so that they could pay more taxes.

Like the Egyptian Shia-Fatimids and Mamluks, the Sunni-Islamic Ottoman Empire centered in modern-day Turkey dominated the eastern Mediterranean Sea. The Ottomans built a powerful navy, rivaling the Italian city-state of Venice during the Ottoman-Venetian Wars (1499-1503).

Although they were sorely defeated in the Battle of Lepanto (1571) by the Holy League, the Ottomans quickly rebuilt their naval strength, and afterwards successfully defended the island of Cyprus so that it would stay in Ottoman hands. However, with the concurrent Age of Discovery, Europe had far surpassed the Ottoman Empire, and successfully bypassed their reliance on land-trade by discovering maritime routes around Africa and towards the Americas.

The first naval action in defense of the new colonies was just ten years after Vasco da Gama's epochal landing in India. In March 1508, a combined Gujarati/Egyptian force surprised a Portuguese squadron at Chaul, and only two Portuguese ships escaped. The following February, the Portuguese viceroy destroyed the allied fleet at Battle of Diu, thus confirming Portuguese domination of the Indian Ocean.

In 1582, the Battle of Ponta Delgada in the Azores, in which a Spanish fleet defeated a combined Portuguese, French, and English force, thus ending the Portuguese succession crisis, was the first battle fought in mid-Atlantic.

In 1588, Philip II of Spain sent his Spanish Armada to subdue Elizabeth I of England, but Admiral Sir Charles Howard forced its retreat, beginning the rise to prominence of the Royal Navy. However it was unable to follow up with a decisive blow against the Spanish navy, which remained the most important for another half century. After the war's end in 1604 the English fleet went through a time of relative neglect and decline.

In the 16th century, the Barbary states of North Africa rose to power and they collectively became a dominant naval power in the Mediterranean Sea due to the Barbary pirates. The coastal villages and towns of Italy, Spain and Mediterranean islands were frequently attacked by them and long stretches of the Italian and Spanish coasts were almost completely abandoned by their inhabitants; after 1600 Barbary pirates occasionally entered the Atlantic and struck as far north as Iceland.

According to Robert Davis between 1 million and 1.25 million Europeans were captured by Barbary pirates and sold as slaves in North Africa and the Ottoman Empire between the 16th and 19th centuries. These slaves were captured mainly from seaside villages in Italy, Spain and Portugal, and from farther places like France, England, the Netherlands, Ireland and even Iceland and North America. The Barbary pirates were also able to successfully defeat and capture many European ships, which was largely due to advances in sailing technology by the Barbary states. The earliest naval trawler, xebec and windward ships were employed by the Barbary pirates from the 16th century.

From the middle of the 17th century competition between the expanding English and Dutch commercial fleets came to a head in the Anglo-Dutch Wars, the first wars to be conducted entirely at sea. Most memorable of these battles was the raid on the Medway, in which the Dutch admiral Michiel de Ruyter sailed up the river Thames, and destroyed most of the British fleet. This remains to date the greatest naval defeat of England and her consecutive countries, and established Dutch supremacy at sea for over half a century. The English and Dutch wars were also known for very few ships being sunk, as it was very difficult to hit ships below the water level; the water surface deflected cannon balls, and the few holes produced could be patched quickly. Naval forces were severely weakened by casualties to the men and damage to the sails more than by loss of ships.

The 18th century developed into a period of seemingly continuous world wars, each larger than the last. At sea, the British and French were bitter rivals; the French aided the fledgling United States in the American Revolutionary War, but their strategic purpose was to capture territory in India and the West Indies—which they did not achieve. In the Baltic Sea, the final attempt to revive the Swedish Empire led to Gustav III's Russian War, with its grande finale at the Second Battle of Svensksund. The battle was unrivalled in size until the 20th century, was a decisive Swedish tactical victory but its strategical result was poor (due to poor army performance and previous lack of initiative from the Swedes) and the war ended without any territorial changes.

Even the change of government due to the French Revolution seemed to intensify rather than diminish the rivalry, and the Napoleonic Wars included a series of legendary naval battles, culminating in the Battle of Trafalgar in 1805, by which Admiral Horatio Nelson broke the power of the French and Spanish fleets, but lost his own life in so doing.

From Wood and Wind to Steel and Steam in 19th Century

Trafalgar ushered in the *Pax Britannica* of the 19th century, marked by general peace in the world's oceans, under the ensigns of the Royal Navy. But the period was one of intensive experimentation with new technology; steam power for ships appeared in the 1810s, improved metallurgy and machining technique produced larger and deadlier guns, and the development of explosive shells, capable of demolishing a wooden ship at a single blow, in turn required the addition of iron armour.

Although naval power during the Song, Yuan, and Ming dynasties established China as a major world seapower in the East, the Qing Dynasty lacked an official standing navy. They were more interested in pouring funds into military ventures closer to home (China proper), such as Mongolia, Tibet, and Central Asia (modern Xinjiang). However, there were some considerable naval conflicts during the Qing Dynasty before the Opium Wars (such as the Battle of Penghu, or the conflict against Koxinga).

The insignificant naval effort that the Manchus/Chinese pitted against the more advanced British steam-powered ships during the first of the Opium Wars in the 1840s was sorely defeated. This left China open to virtual foreign domination (from European powers and then Japan) via spheres of influence over regions of China for economic gain. Although the Qing Dynasty attempted to modernize the Chinese navy, China's Beiyang Fleet was dealt a severe blow by the Imperial Japanese Navy in the First Sino-Japanese War (1894–1895).

The famous battle of the CSS *Virginia* and USS *Monitor* in the American Civil War was the duel of ironclads that symbolized the changing times. The first fleet action between ironclad ships was fought in 1866 at the Battle of Lissa between the navies of Austria and Italy. Because the decisive moment of the battle occurred when the Austrian flagship the *Erzherzog Ferdinand Max* successfully sank the Italian flagship *Re d'Italia* by ramming, in subsequent decade every navy in the world largely focused on ramming as the main tactic. The last known use of ram in naval battle was in 1879 when the Peruvian ship Huáscar rammed the Chilean ship Esmeralda. The last known gunboat that was equipped with a ram was lunched in 1908-The German ship Emden.

As the century came to a close, the familiar modern battleship began to emerge; a steel-armored ship, entirely dependent on steam, and sporting a number of large shell guns mounted in turrets arranged along the centerline of the main deck. The ultimate design was reached in 1906 with the *HMS Dreadnought (1906)* which entirely dispensed with smaller guns, her main guns being sufficient to sink any existing ship of the time.

The Russo-Japanese War and particularly the Battle of Tsushima in 1905 was the first test of the new concepts, resulting a stunning Japanese victory and the destruction of most Russian ships.

With the advent of the steamship, it became possible to create massive gun platforms and to provide them with heavy armour protection. The Dreadnought battleships and their successors were the first capital ships that combined technology and firepower with a mobile platform. However, in the first half of the

20th century, the utility of air power in support of the fleet began to emerge;

World War I pitted the old Royal Navy against the new navy of Imperial Germany, culminating in the 1916 Battle of Jutland. The future was heralded when the seaplane carrier HMS *Engadine* and her Short 184 sea planes joined the battle. Meanwhile, in the Black Sea, Russian seaplanes flying from a fleet of converted carriers interdicted Turkish maritime supply routes, Allied air patrols began to counter German U-Boat activity in Britain's coastal waters, and a British Short 184 seaplane carried out the first successful torpedo attack on a ship.

In 1918 the Royal Navy converted an Italian liner to create the first aircraft carrier, HMS *Argus*, and shortly after the war the first purpose-built carrier, HMS Hermes was launched. Many nations agreed to the Washington Naval Treaty and scrapped many of their battleships and cruisers while still in the shipyards, but the growing tensions of the 1930s restarted the building programs, with even larger ships than before; *Yamato*, the largest battleship ever, displaced 72,000 tons and mounted 18.1-inch (460 mm) guns.

Above and Below the Surface in Royal Navy

The victory of the Royal Navy at the Battle of Taranto was a pivotal point as this was the first true demonstration of naval air power. Following 7 December 1941 when the United States came into World War II, the sinking of HMS Prince of Wales and HMS Repulse marked the end of the era of the battleship, and the new importance of aircraft and their transportation, the aircraft carrier, came to the fore.

During the Pacific War, battleships and cruisers spent most of their time bombarding shore positions, while the carriers were the stars of the key Battle of the Coral Sea, Battle of Midway, Battle of the Philippine Sea, and the climactic Battle of Leyte Gulf. Air power remained key to navies throughout the 20th century, moving to jets launched from ever-larger carriers, and augmented by cruisers armed with guided missiles and cruise missiles.

Roughly parallel to the development of naval aviation was the development of submarines to travel underneath the sea, at first for short dives, then later to be able to spend weeks or months underwater powered by a nuclear reactor. In both World Wars, submarines (U-boats in Germany) primarily exerted their power by using torpedoes to sink merchant ships, as well as other warships. In the 1950s the Cold War inspired the development of ballistic missile submarines, each one loaded with dozens of nuclear-armed missiles and with orders to launch them from sea should the other nation attack.

Against the backdrop of these developments, World War II had seen the United States become by far the largest Naval power in the world. Throughout the rest of the 20th century The United States Navy would maintain a tonnage greater than that of the next 17 largest navies combined.

The only major naval conflict that took place after World War II was the well known Falklands War in 1982, pitting Argentina against the United Kingdom. The Royal Navy fleet were dispatched over 7000 miles from the British mainland to the South Atlantic and based their task force on the sea. Their fleet consisted of approximately 100 ships however they were heavily outnumbered in airpower with only 36 Harriers from their two aircraft carriers, compared with the 200, at least aircraft of the Argentine Air Force. Most of the land-based aircraft of the Royal Air Force were not available as there was no airfield for such a base, however the Vulcan bomber did provide bombing runs on the Argentine-held airfield in Stanley. This reliance on aircraft at sea showed the importance of the unique ability of the aircraft carrier. The Falklands showed the vulnerability of modern ships to sea-skimming missiles like the Exocet. One hit from an Exocet sank HMS *Sheffield,* a modern anti-air warfare destroyer. Important lessons about ship design, damage control and ship construction materials were learnt from the conflict.

The Falklands War was a unique conflict and at the present time, large naval wars seem to be seldom seen affairs as modern day warfare seemingly evolves further from warships, which have existed for centuries, to reliance on new technologies such as military aircraft and land warfare. The main function of the modern navy being to exploit its control of the seaways to project power ashore. Power projection has been the primary naval feature of conflicts like the Korean War, Suez Crisis, Vietnam War, Konfrontasi, Gulf War, Kosovo War, the War on Terrorism in Afghanistan and the Iraq War.

HISTORY OF INDIAN NAVAL WARFARE

The old notion that the Hindus were essentially a landlocked people, lacking in a spirit of adventure and the heart to brave the seas, is now dispelled. The researches of a generation of scholars have proved that from very early times the people of India were distinguished by nautical skill and enterprise, that they went on trading voyages to distant shores across the seas, and even established settlements and colonies in numerous lands and islands.

In ancient India, owing to the geographical influence, nautical shill and enterprise seems to have been best developed in three widely separated region of the country. These were Bengal, the valley and delta of the Indus, and the extreme south of the Deccan peninsula, called *Tamilagam*.

Boat-making and ship-building industries were found in India since ancient times. In the Vedic period, sea was frequently used for trade purposes. The Rig Veda mentions "merchants who crowd the great waters with ships". The Ramayana speaks of merchants who crossed the sea and bought gifts for the king of Ayodhya. Manu legislates for safe carriage and freights by river and sea. In some of the earliest Buddhist literature we read of voyages 'out of sight' of land, some lasting six months or so.

In *Kautalya Arthasastra* the admiralty figures as a separate department of the War Office; and this is a striking testimony to the importance attached to it from very early times. In the Rig Veda Samhita boats and ships are frequently mentioned. The classical example often quoted by every writer on the subject is the naval expedition of Bhujya who was sent by his father with the ship which had a hundred oars (aritra). Being ship-wrecked he was rescued by the twin Asvins in their boat.

"There was also extensive intercourse of India with foreign countries, including the Mediterranean lands and the African continent, naturally led to piracy on the waters. There then arose the need for the protection of sea-borne trade, and we are told that "at the outset the merchant vessels of India carried a small body of trained archers armed with bows and arrows to repulse the attacks of the pirates, but later they employed guns, cannon and other more deadly weapons of warfare with a few wonderful and delusive contrivances." In the *Shanti Parvan* (59, 41) of the Mahabharata it is said that the navy is one of the *angas* (part) of the complete army. Examples of ships being used for military purposes are not lacking. When Vidura scented danger to Kunti's five sons, he made them escape to the forest with their mother, crossing the Ganges in a boat equipped with weapons having the power of withstanding wind and wave.

In the Dig Vijaya portion of the Sabha parva, it is said that Sahadeva crossed the sea and brought many islands under his sway after defeating the Mlecchas and other mixed tribes inhabiting them. If this be an historical fact the inference is irresistible that he could not have effected his conquest without the use of boats and vessels. We read in the Ramayana that Durmukha, a Raksasa, who had been fired by the impulse of anger at the deeds of Hanuman, offered his services to Ravana even to fight on the sea.

This is testimony enough of the use of a fleet for war purposes. There are other references here and there to ships in the Ramayana. When Hanuman was crossing the ocean to Lanka, he is compared to a ship tossed by winds on the high seas. Sugriva speaks of Sumatra, Java and even the Red Sea, when sending forth his monkey hosts in quest of Sita.

The Amarakosa, mentions a number of nautical terms which stand for ship, anchorage (naubandhana), the helm of the ship (naukarana), the helmsman (naukaranadhara). That there were ships-building yards in different parts could be inferred from a significant term navatakseni occurring in a copper plate grant of Dharmaditya dated 531. A.D.

About 517 B.C. according to Herodotus, Darius launched a maritime expedition under Skylax of Caryanda to the Indus Delta, and during Alexander's time, again, we read of the people of the Punjab fitting out a fleet. We have the testimony of Arrian to show that the Xathroi (Kshatri), one of the Punjab tribes, supplied Alexander during his return voyage with thirty oared galleys and transport vessels which were built by them. (source: India and Its Invasion by Alexander p. 156)

In the Manusamhita (Vii. 192), it is laid down that boats should be employed for military purposes when the theatre of hostilities abounded in water. Kamandaka (XVI, 50) alludes to naval warfare when he says:

"By regular practice one becomes an adept in fighting from chariot, horses, elephants and boats, and a past-master in archery."

Manavadharmasastra refers to sea fights and attests to the use of boats for naval warfare. The sailor is called naukakarmajiva. Thus in Vedic, Epic and the Dharmasastra literature we find that naval warfare is mentioned as a distinct entity, attesting a continuous naval tradition from the earliest times. Yukti-kalpataru specifies one class of ships called agramandira (because they had their cabins towards the prows), as eminently adapted for naval warfare (rane kale ghanatyaye). Passing on to other literary evidence, we find in the Raghuvamsa frequent reference to boats and ships. Raghu in the course of his digvijaya conquered Bengal which was protected by a fleet (nausadhanotyatan). In anther place it is mentioned that Raghu marched on Persia through the land route, and not by the sea route, thereby showing that the latter was the more common route.

Historian Dr. Vincent A. Smith says that 'the creation of the Admiralty department was an innovation due to the genius of Chandragupta. "The Admiralty as a department of the State may have been a creation of Chandragupta but there is evidence to show that the use of ships and boats was known to the people of the Rig Veda."

In the following passage we have reference to a vessel with a hundred oats. 'This exploit you achieved, Asvins in the ocean, where there is nothing to give support, nothing to rest upon, nothing to cling to, that you brought Bhujya, sailing in a hundred oared ship, to his father's house.'

Further on in the Veda, this same vessel is described as a *plava* which was storm-proof and which presented a pleasing appearance and had wings on its sides. Another reference informs us that Tugra dispatched a fleet of four vessels (Catasro navah) among which was the one referred to above. We may infer from these passages that the Asvins were a great commercial people having their home in a far-off island, and that their ruler Tugra maintained a fleet in the interests of his State. There are also other references in the Rig Veda to show that the ancient Indians were acquainted with the art of navigation. For instance, Varuna is credited with a knowledge of the ocean routes along which vessels sailed.

The Baudhayana Dharmasastra speaks of Samudrasamyanam and interprets it as *nava dvipantaragamanam*, i.e. sailing to other lands by ships. This very term occurs in the navadhyaksa section of the Kautaliya Arthasastra.

The Puranas have several references to the use of ships and boats. The *Markandeya Purana* speaks of vessels tossing about on the sea. The Varahapurana refers to the people who sailed far into the ocean in search of pearls and oysters. The ships floated daily on the shoreless, deep and fearful waters of the ocean. We are on firmer ground when we see in the Andhra period their coins marked with ships. The ship building activities were great on the east coast, and the Coromandel coast in particular. From this period to about 15th century A.D. there was a regular intercourse with the islands of the Archipelago most of which were colonized and also with ancient America right across the Pacific as testified to us by the archaeological finds and inscriptions in those parts. The Pali books of Sri Lanka like the Mahavamsa refers to ocean going vessels carrying 700 passengers. Such frequent intercourse and colonization through the ages could not have been effected without a powerful fleet.

But it is in a later work, the Yuktikalpataru of Bhoja, that we have three classes of ships-the Sarvamandira, the Madhyamandira, and Agramandira. The first was called Sarvamandira because it had apartments all around. In the Sarvamandira were carried treasures, animals, and ladies of the court. This was the vessel ordinarily used by kings in times of peace. The Madhyamandira was so called because the living quarters were situated in the middle. It was a sporting vessel and generally used in the rainy season. The vessel of the third kind, the Agramandira, took its name from the circumstance that the living room was located in front or at the top of the vessel. The Agramandira was used for distant and perilous voyages and also sea-fights.

There are also in the Yuktikalpataru other references to vessels. There are 27 types of ships mentioned here, the largest having the measurement 276 ft X 36 ft X 27 ft weighing roughly 2,300 tons. The following passage points to the use of ships in warfare. The line: naukadyam vipadam jneyam makes it clear that naval expeditions were common. Under the heading of yanam or march mention is made of expeditions by land, water and air.

Kautilya remarks: "Pirate ships (himsrika), boats from an enemy's country when they cross its territorial limits, as well as vessels violating the customs and rules enforced in port towns, should be pursued and destroyed." It is obvious that the task set forth above could only be performed by armed vessels belonging to the state. From this we may conclude that in ancient India ships were employed in warfare at least as early as the Rig Vedic times. It is an incontrovertible fact that there was a naval department in Mauryan times. We have the testimony of Megasthenes that the navy was under a special officer called the Superintendent of Navigation. This official was in turn controlled by the Admiralty department. The officer whom Megasthenes refers to as Superintendent of Navigation is called Navadhyaksa as already seen, in the Arthasastra. The Greek accounts bear testimony to the fact that navigation had attained a very high development at the times of Alexander's invasion, for we are told that the invader was able to secure a fleet from the Punjab at short notice. The Arthasastra lays down some healthy regulations relating to navigation. Vessels which gave trouble or were bound for the enemy's country, or transgressed the regulations of port towns were to be destroyed. A considerable ship building activity is evident on the west coast of India also as noted in the Sangam works of the Tamils. South India carried on political and commercial activities as far as the Mediterranean in the early centuries of the Christian era and before. The great Ceran Senguttavan had a fleet under him.

Turning to the history of South India, we have evidence to show that the country had trade and culture contacts with foreign countries like Rome in the west and Malay Archipelago and South east Asia in the east. Yavana ships laden with articles of merchandise visited the west coast frequently. There was active foreign trade between Tamil Indian and the outer world at least from the time of Soloman, i.e. about 1000 B.C. Roman historians refer to the commercial intercourse that existed between Rome and South India. In the first century before Christ we hear of a Pandyan embassy to Augustus Caesar. The Sangam classics point to the profession of pearl-diving and sea-fisheries on a large scale. We hear of shipwrecks of the early Tamils saved now and then by Manimekhalai, the goddess of the sea.

As in the case of Dwaraka, initial findings at and off Poompuhar, at the mouth of the Cauvery, show that there may well be a historical basis to this legend: apart from several structures excavated near the shore, such as brick walls, water reservoirs, even a wharf (all dated 200-300 B.C.), a few years ago a structure tantalizingly described as a "U-shaped stone structure" was found five kilometers offshore, at a depth of twenty-three meters; it is about forty meters long and twenty wide, and fishermen traditionally believed that a submerged temple existed at that exact spot. If the structure is confirmed to be man-made (and not a natural formation), its great depth would certainly push back the antiquity of Puhar.

Only more systematic explorations along Tamil Nadu's coast, especially at Poompuhar, Mahabalipuram, and around Kanyakumari (where fishermen have long reported submerged structures too) can throw more light on the lost cities, and on the traditions of Kumari Kandam, which some have sought to identify with the mythical Lemuria). We have the account of a Cera King conquering the Kadamba in the midst of sea waters. The Cera King Senguttuvan had a fleet with which he defeated the Yavanas who were punished with their hands being tied behind their backs and the pouring of oil on their heads. The Cholas also maintained a strong fleet with which they not only invaded and subjugated Lanka but also undertook overseas expeditions. Among the conquests of Rajaraja, Lanka was one, and his invasion of that island finds expression in the Tiruvalangadu plates, where it is described as follows: "Rama built, with the aid of the monkeys, a causeway over the sea and then slew with great difficulty the king of Lanka by means of sharp-edged arrows. But Rama was excelled by this (king) whose powerful army crossed the ocean in ships and burnt the king of Lanka."

Rajaraja also sent an expedition against the Twelve Thousand Islands, obviously a reference to the Laccadives and Maldives. Friendly embassies were also sent by the Chola king to China. From the evidence of the Mahvamsa as well as from a few inscriptions we are able to gather some information regarding the diplomatic relations that existed between India and Sri Lanka. We have the story of Vijaya and his followers occupying the island about 543 B.C. Vijaya was a prince of North India who was banished from the kingdom by his father. Passing through the southern Magadha country he sailed to Sri Lanka, according to the Rajavali, in a fleet carrying more than 700 soliders, defeated the Yaksas inhabiting it, and settled there permanently. This story is illustrated in the Ajanta frescoes. Numerous ships carried the troops of Rajendra to Sri Vijaya and its dependencies which he conquered. Among the places conquered were Pannai (Pani or Panei on the east coast of Sumatra), Malaiyur (at the southern end of the Malay

Peninsula), Mappappalam (a place in the Talaing country of Lower Burma), Mudammalingam (a place facing the gulf of Siam), Nakkavaram (the Nicobar islands. Besides, active trade was carried on between South India and China during this period.

At the end of the 10th century the Chinese emperor sent a mission to the Chola king with credentials under the imperial seal and provisions of gold and piece-goods to induce the foreign traders of the South Sea and those who went to foreign lands beyond the sea for trade to come to China. The facts clearly show that the Cholas maintained supremacy over the sea and kept a strong and powerful navy which was useful not only for carrying on extensive commerce with foreign countries but also for conducting military expeditions. During the days of the Kakatiyas of Warangal, Motupalle (Guntur District) was the chief port, on the east coast. Ganapatideva, the Kakatiya ruler, extirpated piracy on the sea and made the sea safe for commerce with foreign countries like China and Zanzibar. This policy was pursued by Rudramba, his daughter.

Vijayanagar kingdom also claimed supremacy over the sea. Since the days of Harihara I the rulers of Vijayanagar took the title of the Lord of the Eastern, Western and Southern oceans; and there were 300 ports in the empire. The activities of the Vijayanagar fleet on the west coast are also referred to by the Portuguese in 1506. The Vijayanagar kings sent friendly embassies to foreign courts. 'Bukka I sent an embassy through his chief explainer to the court of Taitsu, the King Emperor of China, with tributes and large presents, among which was a stone which was valuable in neutralizing poison.

ACCOUNTS OF FOREIGN TRAVELERS TO INDIA

Coming to later times we have the account of Hiuen Tsang who notices a fleet of 3,000 sail belonging to the King os Assam. There is inscriptional evidence of the possession of a fleet under the Kakatiyas and the Cholas in South India. Marco Polo testifies to the huge size and efficient construction of Indian vessels while Yule in his Cathey refers to Rajput ships en route to China. Marco Polo, a famous Venetian traveller who visited India in 13th Century also visited Thane Port. The first chapter of his book which deals with India is almost devoted to shipbuilding industry in India. Friar Odoric of Pordenone, an Italian Monk who visited India in

14th Century, in his account of his voyage across the Indian Ocean, a mention is made of ships which can carry 700 people.

"Ships of size that carried Fahien from India to China (through stormy China water) were certainly capable of proceeding all the way to Mexico and Peru by crossing the Pacific. One thousand years before the birth of Columbus Indian ships were far superior to any made in Europe upto the 18th century." Ludovico di Varthema (1503 A. D) saw vessels of 1,000 tons burden built at Masulipatnam. According to Dr. Vincent, India built great sized vessels from the time of Agathareids (171 B.C.) to the 16th century. And no wonder the Portuguese, when they first landed at the west coast, were carried away by the excellent Indian vessels. Later still, the Vijayanagar Empire, which had as many as 300 ports, had a powerful fleet. The naval commander was styled Naviyadaprabhu.

India has a coastline of about 6300 km. Extensive new archaeological, epigraphical, sculptural and literary material has been added to our knowledge since the early decades of this century. Dr. Radha Kumud Mookerji's Book Indian Shipping-A History of the Sea-Borne Trade and Marine Activity of The Indians From The Earliest Times published in 1912 Orient, is the most comprehensive study of Indian Navigation up to that period.

We now know that many ports on both Eastern and Western Coast had navigational and trade links with almost all Continents of the world. There are many natural and technological reasons for this. Apart from Mathematics and Astronomy, India had excellent manufacturing skills in textile, metal works and paints. India had abundant supply of Timber. Indian-built ships were superior as they were built of Teak which resists the effect of salt water and weather for a very long time. "The art of Navigation was born in river Sindhu 6000 years ago. The very word navigation is derived from Sanskrit word Nav (or Nav-ship) Gatih."

Lieut. Col. A.Walker's paper: "Considerations of the affairs of India" written in 1811 had excellent remarks on Bombay-built ships. He notes, "situated as she is between the forests of Malabar and Gujarat, she receives supplies of timber with every wind that blows." Further he says, "it is calculated that every ship in the Navy of Great Britain is renewed every twelve years. It is well known that teakwood built ships last fifty years and upwards. Many ships Bombay-built after running fourteen or fifteen years have been brought into the Navy and were considered as stronger as ever. The Sir Edward Hughes performed, I believe, eight voyages as an Indiaman before she was purchased for the Navy. No Europe-built Indiaman is capable of going more than six voyages with safety."He has also further noted that Bombay-built ships are at least one-fourth cheaper than those built in the docks of England. Francois Balazar Solvyns, a Belgian/Flemish maritime painter, wrote a book titled *Les Hindous* in 1811.

His remarks are, "In ancient times, the Indians excelled in the art of constructing vessels, and the present Hindus can in this respect still offer models to Europe-so much so that the English, attentive to everything which relates to naval architecture, have borrowed from the Hindus many improvement which they have adopted with success to their own shipping.... The Indian vessels unite elegance and utility and are models of patience and fine workmanship."

Surprisingly, many earlier western traders and travelers have expressed the same views. Madapollum was a flourishing shipping centre. Thomas Bowrey, an English traveller who visited India during 1669-79, observes, "many English merchants and others have their ships and vessels yearly built (at Madapollum). Here is the best and well grown timber in sufficient plenty, the best iron upon the coast, any sort of ironwork is ingeniously performed by the natives, as spikes, bolts, anchors, and the like. Very expert master-builders there are several here, they build very well, and launch with as much discretion as I have seen in any part of the world. They have an excellent way of making shrouds, stays, or any other rigging for ships".

A Venetian traveller of 16th Century Cesare de Federici, while commenting on the East Coast of India has noted that there is an abundance of material for ship building in this area and many Sultans of Constantinople found it cheaper to have their vessels built in India than at Alexandria. Nicolo Conti who visited India in 15th century was impressed by the quality Indians had achieved in ship building. He observes: "The nations of India build some ships larger than ours, capable of containing 2,000 butts, and with five sails and as many masts. The lower part is constructed with triple planks, in order to withstand the force of the tempests to which they are much exposed. But some ships are so built in compartments that should one part be shattered, the other portion remaining entire may accomplish the voyage."

J. Ovington, Chaplain to the British King, the seventeenth-century English traveller, who visited Surat, wrote a book *A Voyage to Surat in the Year 1689*. He was impressed by the skill of the Indians in ship-building and found that they even outshone Europeans. The timber used by the Indians was so strong that it would not 'crack' even by the force of a bullet so he urged the English to use that timber 'to help them in war'. Indian Teak stood firmer than the English Oak, remarked Ovington.

Thomas Herbert, a traveller who visited Surat in 1627, has given an interesting account of the arrival, loading and unloading of ships through small boats at Swally marine (Sohaly), a few kilometres away from Surat. He remarked that between September and March every year, the port of Sohaly presented a very busy and noisy scene for there came many ships from foreign lands. The merchants (baniyas) erected their straw huts in large numbers all along the sea coast, making the whole place thus look like a country fair. The merchants sold various commodities like calicoes, ivory, agates, etc.

Many small boys engaged by the merchants were seen running about doing odd jobs. The English found that the small boats used and constructed by the natives could be of immense use. This was a definite gain for both nations. Boats and rafts were used as a means of conveyance for loading and unloading ships. There were about 4200 big and 4400 small boats. There were large-sized boats that could carry even elephants. The boats used by kings and nobles were designed to look artistic.

Abul Fazl writes about the "wonderfully fashioned boats with delightful quarters and decks and gardens" Among the primitive Indian boats, the *cattarmaran* comes first. It consisted of three logs and three spreaders and cross lashings. The centre log was the largest, and pointed towards one end. Mainly fishermen used the cattarmaran for fishing. A little more skilfully made is the musoola boat, which has no iron fastening. It was mostly used in the Coromandel coast. Dr John Fryer says, "It is possible that the name musoola may be connected with Masulipatarn where boats seem to have been in use".

Another boat made in an indigenous manner was known as dingy. It was hollowed out from a single trunk. Lower down the Ganga, the name was applied to boats half-decked, half wagon-roofed and built of planks.

Purqoo was another type of boat described by Thomas Bowery. It plied between the Hooghly and Balasore. These boats were made very strong to carry 'sufficient load'. They were also used for loading ships. They could remain in water for a long time without getting damaged. As compared to the purqoo, boora was a 'lighter boat' which rowed with 29 or 30 oars. These boats were also used for carrying saltpeter and other commodities.

Sir John Malcolm (1769-1833) was a Scottish soldier, statesman, and historian entered the service of the East India Company wrote about Indian vessels that they: "Indian vessels are so admirably adapted to the purpose for which they are required that, notwithstanding their superior science, Europeans were unable, during an intercourse with India for two centuries, to suggest or to bring into successful practice one improvement."

In the middle of the 18th century, John Grose noted that at Surat the Indian ship-building industry was very well established, indeed, "They built incomparably the best ships in the world for duration", and of all sizes with a capacity of over a thousand tons. Their design appeared to him to be a "a bit clumsy" but their durability soundly impressed him. They lasted "for a century".

Lord Grenville mentions, in this connection, a ship built in Surat which continued to navigate up the Red Sea from 1702 when it was first mentioned in Dutch letters as "the old ships" up to the year 1700." Grenville also noted that ships of war and merchandise "not exceeding 500 tons" were being built" with facility, convenience and cheapness" at the ports of Coringa and Narsapore.

Dr. H. Scott sent samples of dammer to London, as this vegetable substance was used by the Indians to line the bottom of their ships; he thought it would be a good substitute, "in this country for the materials which are brought from the northern nations for our navy...There can be no doubt that you would find dammer in this way an excellent substitute for pitch and tar and for many purposes much superior to them." Alain Danielou (1907-1994) son of French aristocracy, author of numerous books on philosophy, religion, history and arts of India has written:

"India's naval dockyards, which belonged to the state, were famous throughout history. The sailors were paid by the state, and the admiral of the fleet hired the ships and crew to tradesmen for transporting goods and passengers. When the British annexed the country much later on, they utilized the Indian dockyards-which were much better organized then those in the West-to build most of the ships for the British navy, for as long as ships were made of wood." "...an Indian naval pilot, named Kanha, was hired by Vasco da Gama to take him to India.

Contrary to European portrayals that Indians knew only coastal navigation, deep-sea shipping had existed in India. Indian ships had been sailing to islands such as the Andamans, Lakshdweep and Maldives, around 2,000 years ago. Kautiliya's shastras describe the times that are good and bad for seafaring. In the medieval period, Arab sailors purchased their boats in India. The Portuguese also continued to get their boats from India, and not from Europe. Shipbuilding and exporting was a major Indian industry, until the British banned it. There is extensive archival material on the Indian Ocean trade in Greek, Roman, and Southeast Asian sources."

India became the first power to defeat a European power in a naval battle-The Battle of Colachel in 1742 CE. A dramatic and virtually unknown past, in an area of bucolic calm surrounded by spectacular hills: that is Colachel, a name that should be better known to us. For this is where, in 1741, an extraordinary event took place — the Battle of Colachel. For the first, and perhaps the only time in Indian history, an Indian kingdom defeated a European naval force.

The ruler of Travancore, Marthanda Varma, routed an invading Dutch fleet; the Dutch commander, Delannoy, joined the Travancore army and served for decades; the Dutch never recovered from this debacle and were never again a colonial threat to India.

The *Battle of Colachel* in 1742 CE, where Marthanda Varma of Travancore crushed a Dutch expeditionary fleet near Kanyakumari. The defeat was so total that the Dutch captain, Delannoy, joined the Travancore forces and served loyally for 35 years—and his tomb is still in a coastal fort there. So it wasn't the Japanese in the Yellow Sea in 1905 under Admiral Tojo who were the first Asian power to defeat a European power in a naval battle—it was little Travancore. The Portuguese and the Dutch were trying to gain political power in India at that time. Marthanda Varma defeated the Dutch in 1741. He was an able ruler. He established peace in his country-Travancore. It was a remarkable achievement for a small princely state.

DIPLOMACY AND WAR

Not withstanding the elaborate rule of war laid down in the epics and the law-books, insisting in the main that to wage war was the duty and privilege of every true Ksatriya, in several cases the horrors of war made the belligerent think of the consequences and avoid outbreak of hostilities by a well calculated policy which we now term diplomacy. Negotiation, persuasion and conciliation were cardinal points of the ancient Indian diplomatic system, and were effective instruments in averting many a war, which would otherwise have realized in much bloodshed and economic distress.

The political term for diplomacy is naya, and the opinion of Kautalya, the eminent politician of the 4th century B.C., a king who understands the true implications of diplomacy conquers the whole earth.

The history of diplomacy in ancient India commences with the Rig Veda Samhita, and the date of its composition may be taken as far back as the Chalcolithic period. In the battles the help of Agni is invoked to overcome enemies. He is to be the deceiver of foes. In pursuing his mission to a successful end, the use of spies is mentioned. This bears eloquent testimony to the system of espionage prevalent so early as the time of the Rig Veda Samhita. In the battle of the Ten Kings described in the seventh mandala, we find diplomacy of rulers getting supplemented by its association with priestly diplomacy, which exercised a healthy influence on the constitutional evolution.

International Relations-The picture presented in the epics and the Arthasastra literature seems to be confined to the four corners of Bharatkhanda. The intercourse as envisaged in the literature, shows relations to be more commerical than political in character. Strabo quotes Megasthenes and says that Indians were not engaged in wars with foreigners outside India nor was their country invaded by foreign power except by Hercules and Dionsysius and lately by the Macedonians. There were friendly relations of Chandragupta with Seleukos Nikator, of Bindusara with Antiochus, of Asoka and Samadragupta with Lanka, of Pulaskesi with Persians, of Harsha with Nepal and China, of the Cholas with Sri Vijaya. "It was always regarded as a legitimate object of the ambition of every king to aim at the position of Cakravartin or Sarvabhuuma (paramount sovereign or of supreme monarch)." This ambition was legitimate and had no narrow outlook about it. It was a fruit to be sought after by every one of the monarchs comprising the mandala. If the king is not actuated by this idea, he falls short of an ideal king according to the Hindu Rajadharma.

Diplomatic Agents-Ambassadors

Bhisma mentions seven qualifications as essential in an ambassador: he should come from a noble line, belong to a high family, be skilful, eloquent of speech, true in delivering the mission, and of excellent memory.

Espionage in War

Spies filled an important role in both the civil and military affairs of ancient India. The institution of spies had a greater utility, as the king could take action on the report of the spies. Spies were engaged to look after the home officials, including those of the royal household as well as to report on the doings in the enemy kingdoms. The Rig Veda Samhita, often speaks of spies (spasah) of Varuna. Only men of wisdom and purity were sent on this errand, thus suggesting that they should be persons above corruption and temptation of any sort. In the epics and post-epic literature in general, spies have been described as the 'eyes of the king'.

In the Udyoga-parva (33, 34) of Mahabharata, it is stated that "cows see by smell, priests by knowledge, kings by spies, and others through eyes." Spies roamed about in foreign states under various disguises to collect reliable information. In the Ramayana, a king mentions the wise adage that "the enemy, whose secrets have been known through espionage, can be conquered without much effort."

The Arthashastra, which predates Christ by centuries, dwells at length on the importance of espionage and the creation of an effective spy network. Such details may indicate the high development of the science of diplomacy in ancient India. It was the famous Indian strategist of the fourth-century B.C, Kautilya in the Arthasastra, who gave the world the dictum: "The enemy of my enemy is my friend." "The same style of Indian thought" says Heinrich Zimmer in his book, Philosophies of India, p. 139, admiringly of Kautilya, "that invented the game of chess grasped with profound insight the rules of this larger game of power."

Attitude to War

The Sangam age of the Tamils was the heroic age of the Tamil Indians. If the men of the Tamil land were heroes, then their women were heroines. A certain mother was asked where her son was, and she replied, that she was sure that the tiger that had lain in her womb would be found in the field of battle. War was the pabulum on which our ancient warriors were great in name and fame. A certain lady who gave birth to only one son and who sent him to the field of battle when there was the country's call for it. Okkurmasattiyar, a poetess, praises a certain lady dresses the hair of her only son and gives him the armour to get ready for action in the field of battle. This may be contrasted with another where a heroic mother heard the disquieting news that her son lost his courage in action and had fled in fear.

If it were true, she expressed that she would cut off her breasts that had fed him with milk. With this determination she entered the battle-field with sword in her hand and went on searching for her fallen son. When she saw her son's body cut in twain, she felt much more happy than when she gave birth to him. Flags-The origin and use of flags can be traced to the earliest Indian literature, the Rig Veda Samhita. The term *deaja* occurs twice in the Veda. Besides, dhvaja, we meet with a good number of expressions for a banner in Vedic literature. These are Akra, Krtadhvaja, Ketu, Brhatketu, Sahasraketu. It appears that the Vedic host aimed their arrows at the banners of the enemy.

The idea was that once the banner was captured, or struck, a claim was made for success in the battle over the enemy. Ketu was a small flag as contrasted with Brhatketu or the big flag. Sahasraketu may be a thousand flag, or as the knight who brought under control a thousand flags of enemies. We are told that banners and drums were counted among the insignia of ancient Vedic kings. In the Mahabharata war, every leader had his own insignia to distinguish one division from the other. Arjuna had the Kapidhvaja or the flag with the figure of Hanuman, Bhisma, Taladhvaja, cognizance of a palmyra tree etc..

3

Indian Maritime and Heritage: Its History

Indian maritime history begins during the 3rd millennium BCE when inhabitants of the Indus Valley initiated maritime trading contact with Mesopotamia. The Roman historian Strabo mentions an increase in Roman trade with India following the Roman annexation of Egypt. By the time of Augustus up to 120 ships were setting sail every year from Myos Hormos to India. As trade between India and the Greco-Roman world increased spices became the main import from India to the Western world, by passing silk and other commodities. Indians were present in Alexandria while Christian and Jew settlers from Rome continued to live in India long after the fall of the Roman empire, which resulted in Rome's loss of the Red Sea ports, previously used to secure trade with India by the Greco-Roman world since the Ptolemaic dynasty. The Indian commercial connection with South East Asia proved vital to the merchants of Arabia and Persia during the 7th–8th century. On orders of Manuel I of Portugal, four vessels under the command of navigator Vasco da Gama rounded the Cape of Good Hope, continuing to the eastern coast of Africa to Malindi to sail across the Indian Ocean to Calicut. The wealth of the Indies was now open for the Europeans to explore. The Portuguese Empire was one of the early European empires to grow from spice trade.

THE NATIONAL MARITIME DAY

April 5 1964 marks the National Maritime Day of India. On this day in 1919 navigation history was created when SS Loyalty, the first ship of The Scindia Steam Navigation Company Ltd., journeyed to the United Kingdom, A crucial step for India siping history when sea routes were controlled by the British. The National Maritime Day was first celebrated on 5th April, 1964.

Prehistory

The region around the Indus river began to show visible increase in both the length and the frequency of maritime voyages by 3000 BCE. Optimum conditions for viable long-distance voyages existed in this region by 2900 BCE. Mesopotamian inscriptions indicate that Indian traders from the Indus valley—carrying copper, hardwoods, ivory, pearls, carnelian, and gold—were active in Mesopotamia during the reign of Sargon of Akkad (ca. 2300 BCE). Gosch & Stearns write on the Indus Valley's pre-modern maritime travel:

Archaeological research at sites in Mesopotamia, Bahrain, and Oman has led to the recovery of artifacts traceable to the Indus Valley civilization, confirming the information on the inscriptions. Among the most important of these objects are stamp seals carved in soapstone, stone weights, and colorful carnelian beads....Most of the trade between Mesopotamia and the Indus Valley was indirect. Shippers from both regions converged in Persian Gulf ports, especially on the island of Bahrain (known as Dilmun to the Sumerians). Numerous small Indus-style artifacts have been recovered at locations on Bahrain and further down the coast of the Arabian Peninsula in Oman. Stamp seals produced in Bahrain have been found at sites in Mesopotamia and the Indus Valley, strengthening the likelihood that the island may have acted as a redistribution point for goods coming from Mesopotamia and the Indus area....There are hints from the digs at Ur, a major Sumerian city-state on the Euphrates, that some Indus Valley merchants and artisans (bead makers) may have established communities in Mesopotamia.

The world's first dock at Lothal (2400 BCE) was located away from the main current to avoid deposition of silt. Modern oceanographers have observed that the Harappans must have possessed great knowledge relating to tides in order to build such a dock on the ever-shifting course of the Sabarmati, as well as exemplary hydrography and maritime engineering. This was the earliest known dock found in the world, equipped to berth and service ships. It is speculated that Lothal engineers studied tidal movements, and their effects on brick-built structures, since the walls are of kiln-burnt bricks. This knowledge also enabled them to select Lothal's location in the first place, as the Gulf of Khambhat has the highest tidal amplitude and ships can be sluiced through flow tides in the river estuary. The engineers built a trapezoidal structure, with north-south arms of average 21.8 metres (71.5 ft), and east-west arms of 37 metres (121 ft).

Early Kingdoms

Indian cartography locates the Pole star, and other constellations of use in navigational charts. These charts may have been in use by the beginning of the Common Era for purposes of navigation. Detailed maps of considerable length describing the locations of settlements, sea shores, rivers, and mountains were also made. The Periplus Maris Erythraei mentions a time when sea trade between India and Egypt did not involve direct sailings. The cargo under these situations was shipped to Aden: Eudaimon Arabia was called fortunate, being once a city, when, because ships neither came from India to Egypt nor did those from Egypt dare to go further but only came as far as this place, it received the cargoes from both, just as Alexandria receives goods brought from outside and from Egypt.

The first clear mention of a navy occurs in the mythological epic Mahabharata. Historically, however, the first attested attempt to organize a navy in India, as described by Megasthenes (ca. 350 BCE—290 BCE), is attributed to Candragupta Maurya (reign 322 BC—298 BCE). The Mauryan empire (322–185 BCE) navy continued till the times of emperor Ashoka (reign 273—32 BCE), who used it to send massive diplomatic missions to Greece, Syria, Egypt, Cyrene, Macedonia and Epirus. Following nomadic interference in Siberia—one of the sources for India's bullion—India diverted its attention to the Malay peninsula, which became its new source for gold and was soon exposed to the world via a series of maritime trade routes. The period under the Mauryan empire also witnessed various other regions of the world engage increasingly in the Indian Ocean martitime voyages.

According to the historian Strabo (II.5.12.) the Roman trade with India trade initiated by Eudoxus of Cyzicus in 130 BCE kept increasing. Indian ships sailed to Egypt as the thriving maritime routes of Southern Asia were not under the control of a single power. In India, the ports of Barbaricum (modern Karachi),

Barygaza, Muziris, Korkai, Kaveripattinam and Arikamedu on the southern tip of India were the main centers of this trade. The Periplus Maris Erythraei describes Greco-Roman merchants selling in Barbaricum "thin clothing, figured linens, topaz, coral, storax, frankincense, vessels of glass, silver and gold plate, and a little wine" in exchange for "costus, bdellium, lycium, nard, turquoise, lapis lazuli, Seric skins, cotton cloth, silk yarn, and indigo". In Barygaza, they would buy wheat, rice, sesame oil, cotton and cloth.

The Ethiopian kingdom of Aksum was involved in the Indian Ocean trade network and was influenced by Roman culture and Indian architecture. Traces of Indian influences are visible in Roman works of silver and ivory, or in Egyptian cotton and silk fabrics used for sale in Europe. The Indian presence in Alexandria may have influenced the culture but little is known about the manner of this influence. Clement of Alexandria mentions the Buddha in his writings and other Indian religions find mentions in other texts of the period. The Indians were present in Alexandria and the Christian and Jew settlers from Rome continued to live in India long after the fall of the Roman empire, which resulted in Rome's loss of the Red Sea ports, previously used to secure trade with India by the Greco-Roman world since the time of the Ptolemaic dynasty.

Early Common Era—High Middle Ages

Textiles of India were in demand in Egypt, East Africa, and the Mediterranean between the 1st-2nd centuries CE. These regions became overseas markets for Indian exports. In Java and Borneo, the introduction of Indian culture created a demand for aromatics. These trading outposts later served the Chinese and Arab markets as well. The Periplus Maris Erythraei names several Indian ports from where large ships sailed towards east to Khruse. Moluccan products shipped across the ports of Arabia to the Near East passed through the ports of India and Sri Lanka. After reaching either the Indian or the Sri Lankan ports were sometimes shipped to East Africa, where they would be used for many purposes, including burial rites.

The Chola dynasty (200—1279) was at the peak of its influence and power during the medieval period. Emperors Rajaraja Chola I (985—1014) and Rajendra Chola I (1012—1044) extended the

Chola kingdom beyond the traditional limits. At its peak, the Chola Empire stretched from the island of Sri Lanka in the south to the Godavari basin in the north. The kingdoms along the east coast of India up to the river Ganges acknowledged Chola suzerainty. Chola navies invaded and conquered Srivijaya (7th–13th century) in the Malay archipelago.

The Indian commercial connection with South East Asia proved vital to the merchants of Arabia and Persia between 7-8 century CE. The Abbasids used Alexandria, Damietta, Aden and Siraf as entry ports to India and China. Merchants arriving from India in the port city of Aden paid tribute in form of musk, camphor, ambergris and sandalwood to Ibn Ziyad, the sultan of Yemen. The kingdoms of Vijaynagar and Kalinga established foothold over Malaya, Sumatra and Western Java.

The Cholas excelled in foreign trade and maritime activity, extending their influence overseas to China and Southeast Asia. Towards the end of the 9th century, southern India had developed extensive maritime and commercial activity. The Cholas, being in possession of parts of both the west and the east coasts of peninsular India, were at the forefront of these ventures. The Tang dynasty (618 – 907) of China, the Srivijaya empire in the Malayan archipelago under the Sailendras, and the Abbasid Kalifat at Bagdad were the main trading partners.

During the reign of Pandya Parantaka Nedumjadaiyan (765 – 790), the Chera dynasty were a close ally of the Pallavas. Pallavamalla Nadivarman defeated the Pandya Varaguna with the help of a Chera king.

Cultural contacts between the Pallava court and the Chera country were common. Indian spice exports find mention in the works of Ibn Khurdadhbeh (850), al-Ghafiqi (1150), Ishak bin Imaran (907) and Al Kalkashandi (fourteenth century). Chinese traveller Hsuan Tsang mentions the town of Puri where "merchants depart for distant countries."

Hindu and Buddhist religious establishments of Southeast Asia came to be associated with economic activity and commerce as patrons entrusted large funds wnich would later be used to benefit local economy by estate management, craftsmanship and promotion of trading activities. Buddhism, in particular, traveled alongside the maritime trade, promoting coinage, art and literacy.

Late Middle Ages—Modern Period

Christians missionaries traveling with trade, such as, Saint Francis Xavier, were instrumental in the spread of Christianity in the East. Christianity competed with Islam to become the dominant religion of the Moluccas. However, the natives of the Spice Islands accommodated aspects of both the religions easily. The European traveller Marco Polo (1292) described Indian vessels:"...built of fir timber, having a sheath of boards laid over the planking in every part, caulked with oakum and fastened with iron nails. The bottoms were smeared with a preparation of quicklime and hemp, pounded together and mixed with oil from a certain tree which is a better material than pith." Descriptions between the 14th-15th century indicate that the Indian vessels could carry over 100 seamen and were equipped with bulkhead (partition). Ma Huan (1413-51) reached Cochin and noted that Indian coins, known as fanam, were issued in Cochin and weighed a total of one fen and one li according to the Chinese standards. They were of fine quality and could be exchanged in China for 15 silver coins of four-li weight each.

On the orders of Manuel I of Portugal, four vessels under the command of navigator Vasco da Gama rounded the Cape of Good Hope In 1497, continuing to the eastern coast of Africa to Malindi to sail across the Indian Ocean to Calicut. The first Dutch expedition left from Amsterdam (April 1595) for South East Asia. Another Dutch convoy sailed in 1598 and returned one year later with 600, 000 pounds of spices and other Indian products. The United East India Company forged alliance with the principal producers of cloves and nutmeg.

Shivaji Bhonsle (reign 1664—1680) maintained a navy under the charge of general Kanhoji Angre (served 1698—1729). The initial advances of the Portuguese were checked by this navy, which also effectively relieved the traffic and commerce in India's west coast of Portuguese threat. The Maratha navy also checked the English East India Company, until the navy itself underwent a decline due to the policies of general Nanasaheb (reign 1740-1761).

The British East India Company shipped substantial quantities of spices during the early 17th century. Rajesh Kadian (2006) examines the history of the British navy in as the British Raj was established in India: In 1830 ships of the British East India Company were designated as the Indian navy. However, in 1863, it was disbanded when Britain's Royal Navy took control of the Indian Ocean. About thirty years later, the few small Indian naval units were called the Royal Indian Marine (RIM). In the wake of World War I, Britain, exhausted in manpower and resources, opted for expansion of the RIM. Consequently, on 2 October 1934, the RIM was reincarnated as the Royal Indian Navy (RIN).

The Indian rulers weakened with the advent of the European powers. Shipbuilders, however, continued to build ships capable of carrying 800 to 1000 tons. The shipbuilders at the Bombay Dockyard built ships like the HMS Hindostan (1795) and HMS Ceylon (1808), inducted into the Royal Navy. The historical ships made by Indian shipbuilders included HMS Asia (1824) (commanded by Edward Codrington during the Battle of Navarino in 1827), the frigate HMS Cornwallis (1813) (onboard which the Treaty of Nanking was signed in 1842), and the HMS Minden (on which The Star Spangled Banner was composed by Francis Scott Key). David Arnold examines the role of Indian shipbuilders during the British Raj:

> Shipbuilding was a well-established craft at numerous points along the Indian coastline long before the arrival of the Europeans and was a significant factor in the high level of Indian maritime activity in the Indian Ocean region....As with cotton textiles, European trade was initially a stimulus to Indian shipbuilding: vessels built in ports like Masulipatam and Surat from Indian hardwoods by local craftsmen were cheaper and tougher than their European counterparts.
>
> Between the seventeenth and early nineteenth centuries Indian shipyards produced a series of vessels incorporating these hybrid features. A large proportion of them were built in Bombay, where the Company had established a small shipyard. In 1736 Parsi carpenters were brought in from Surat to work there and, when their European supervisor died, one of the carpenters, Lowji Nuserwanji Wadia, was appointed Master Builder in his place. Wadia oversaw the construction of thirty-five ships, twenty-one of them for the Company. Following his death in 1774, his sons took charge of the shipyard and between them built a further thirty ships over the next sixteen years. The Britannia, a ship of 749 tons launched in 1778, so impressed the Court of Directors

when it reached Britain that several new ships were commissioned from Bombay, some of which later passed into the hands of the Royal Navy. In all, between 1736 and 1821, 159 ships of over 100 tons were built at Bombay, including 15 of over 1,000 tons. Ships constructed at Bombay in its heyday were said to be 'vastly superior to anything built anywhere else in the world'.

CONTEMPORARY ERA (1947–PRESENT)

Military

In 1947, the Republic of India's navy consisted of 33 ships, and 538 officers to secure a coastline of more than 4,660 miles (7,500 km) and 1,280 islands. The Indian navy conducted annual Joint Exercises with other Commonwealth navies throughout the 1950s. The navy saw action during various of the country's wars, including Indian integration of Junagadh, the liberation of Goa, the 1965 war, and the 1971 war. Following difficulty in obtaining spare parts from the Soviet Union, India also embarked upon a massive indigenous naval designing and production programme aimed at manufacturing destroyers, frigates, corvettes, and submarines.

India's Coast Guard Act was passed in August 1978. The Indian Coast Guard participated in counter terrorism operations such as Operation Cactus. During contemporary times the Indian navy was commissioned in several United Nations peacekeeping missions. The navy also repatriated Indian nationals from Kuwait during the first Gulf War. Rajesh Kadian (2006) holds that: "During the Kargil War (1999), the aggressive posture adopted by the navy played a role in convincing Islamabad and Washington that a larger conflict loomed unless Pakistan withdrew from the heights.".

As a result of the growing strategic ties with the western world the Indian navy has conducted joint exercises with its western counterparts, including the United States Navy, and has obtained latest naval equipment from its western allies. Better relations with the United States of America and Israel have led to joint patrolling of the Straits of Malacca.

INDIA'S MARITIME IN INDIAN OCEAN

The Indian Ocean, is named after peninsular India which juts into its centre and occupies a unique position. These vast waters wash the shores of the entire East Coast of Africa, the South. Coast of Arabia, the Southern shores of Iran and Baluchistan, the Malaysian Peninsula and Indonesia's Sumatra. The ingress and egress of the ocean are through the eastern and western waterways at the Straits of Malacca and Bab-el-Mandeb. The former lead to the Indonesian Archipelago, the South China Sea, the Far East and the vast expanse of the Pacific Ocean while the latter control the entrance to the Red Sea. Commanding the gateway to the landlocked Persian Gulf in the northwest is Hormuz formerly known as Ormuz. For ages, Aden, at the Southern tip of Arabia, was the home and main base of the Arab corsairs. Two off-shoots of this Ocean are the Arabian Sea and the Bay of Bengal which wash the 5600-kilometre-long shores of the Indian peninsula, Pakistan, Bangladesh, Burma and the island of Sri Lanka which is separated from India by the Palk Strait.

Because of its unique features, the Indian Ocean has always been regarded as an area of great geopolitical significance and India has been regarded as its centre of gravity. Sardar K.M. Panikkar, has said: In spite of the vastness of its surface and the oceanic character of its current and winds, the Indian Ocean has some of the features of a land-locked sea. The Arctic and the Antarctic, circling the Poles have but little connection with inhabited land. The Pacific and the Atlantic lie from the north to the south like gigantic highways. They have no land roof, no vast land area jutting out into their expanse. The Indian Ocean is walled off on three sides by land, with the southern side of Asia forming a roof over it. The continent of Africa constitutes the western wall and Burma, Malaya and the insular continuations protect the eastern side. But the vital feature which differentiates the Indian Ocean from the Pacific or the Atlantic is not the two sides but the subcontinent of India which juts out far into the sea for a thousand miles to its tapering end at Kanya Kumari. It is the geographical position of India that changes the character of the Indian Ocean.

The islands in the Indian Ocean area are neither as numerous nor as evenly spread out as those in the Pacific. The major islands in the region *Mxe* Sri Lanka and Malagasy while the minor ones are Socotra near the Arab Coast. Zanzibar and Seychelles off the African Coast, Mauritius and Reunionon the Tropic of Capricorn, Lakshadweep and the Maldives near the West Coast of India, the Bahrain group near the Persian Gulf, the Andamans and the Nicobars in the Bay of Bengal and the Diego Garcia group in the

Chagos Archipelago. Considerable geopolitical significance is also attached to the bays, gulfs and bights of the Ocean. The Persian Gulf which is virtually a land-locked sea with its choke point at Hormuz, the Arabian Sea which separates the Indian and Arabian peninsulas, the Gulf of Aden entry to which is controlled by the island of Socotra, the Red Sea whose gate-post is at Bab-el-Mandeb, the Bay of Bengal separating the Indian and Malaysian peninsulas and the Gulf of Malacca with Singapore commanding entry into it, have all played a significant role in the maritime history of the region.

Because of the unique feature of the monsoons and the development of the nucleus of civilisation around this Ocean, oceanic activity and traditions developed in this region before any other place. Centuries before the development of seafaring activities in the Aegean Sea, the littoral states of peninsular India had already built up their oceanic traditions. The strategic, naval and geopolitical importance of land-locked countries establishing links with the seas by acquiring sovereignty over waterways or even land corridors has been appreciated by politico-military thinkers for centuries. For instance, the potential of their presence in the Indian Ocean or even in its seas, bays and straits prompted some super powers of today to make attempts to gain access to this ocean over land even in the last century. The British appreciation of the balance of power in and around Asia after World War II and its future plans made during the forties also catered to these contingencies.

What is most striking and little known is the fact that Maharaja Ranjit Singh, the great ruler of the Punjab, had also realised the importance of establishing a link with the sea after his victory over the Pathans and Afghans during the third decade of the last century. To quote a historian, "If the Punjabi empire was to expand any further, it could only be across the Sindh desert to the sea or across the Sutlej to India." (The portion of India then held by the British.) The British were clever enough to persuade the Maharaja to sign a commercial treaty in December 1832 and abandon his plans to extend his empire to the sea. These facts and today's rivalry between the super powers over their presence in the Indian Ocean confirm the wisdom of the observation made by Khaireddin Barbarosa, the Egyptian Admiral centuries ago, "He who rules on the sea will shortly rule on the land also."

Another fact that emerges from a careful analysis of the sequence of events in India's maritime past is that during the last five millennia, those who came over land from other parts of the world, mainly using the mountain passes in the northwest, did rule some parts of the Indian subcontinent for a while but were eventually absorbed in the mainstream of Indian culture and traditions and, over the centuries, became an integral part of the Indian milieu. Some of these were the Aryans, Pathans, Mughals, Afghans, Sakas and even the Huns. But those who came by sea during the last two millennia, the Portuguese, Dutch, French, British, Germans, Danes, Flemish, Armenians and the Jews, did not lose their identity and came to stay for hundreds of years, some of them holding sway over larger areas and for longer periods. India's maritime history can be broadly divided into five distinct periods— the Hindu period extending from the hoary past to the middle of the 15th century A.D., the Portuguese period from the closing years of the 15th century to the end of the 16th century; two British periods— from 1612 to 1830 and from 1830 to 1947; and the Indian period which commenced on August 15, 1947. The British period is divided into two parts because in 1830, the East India Company's Navy in India underwent two major changes; it was constituted as a combatant service and given the name Indian Navy and the first ship of the Service to sail under steam, the 411-ton *Hugh Lindsay,* covered the distance from Bombay to Suez in 21 days thus ushering in the conversion from sail to steam.

The Vedas, Buddhist Jatakas, Sanskrit, Pali and Persian literature, Indian folklore and mythology and even the Old Testament bear testimony to the fact that as far back as the days of Mohen-jo-Daro, Lothal and Harappa (3,000 to 2,000 B.C.), i.e., the Indus Valley Civilisation, there was considerable maritime activity between India and the countries in Africa, Southern Europe, Western Asia and the Far East. Seals and potsherd portraying anchors and tools and kitchen implements made of coral and mussel-shell have been found at these places and Java, Sumatra, Indo-China, Sri Lanka and Egypt. A recently unearthed huge drydock at Lothal in Gujarat further confirms the existence of India's seaborne trade with these countries, especially Sumer, Egypt, Crete and countries in Central Asia and Persia at that time. Late Professor Buhler, the well-known German orientalist, expressed the view that "there are passages in ancient Indian works which prove the early existence of navigation of the Indian Ocean and the somewhat later occurrences of trading voyages undertaken by Hindu merchants to the shores of the Persian Gulf and its rivers."

This fact is further borne out by available works in the languages of the littoral states of the region; such as Sindhi, Gujarati, Marathi, Konkani, Kannada, Malayalam, Tamil, Telugu, Oriya and Bengali; the writings of foreign travellers and historians—Chinese, Arabic and Persian—which contain observations on Indian subjects; the evidence available from archaeology— epigraphic, monumental and numismatic; and Indian and foreign art and foreign literature—English, Greek, Portuguese, French, Dutch, Persian, Chinese, Japanese, Arabic, Malay, Thai, Burmese and Sinhalese.

Some of the little-known facts about the extent of commercial and cultural influence of India and sea-borne trade using ships built in India during the Hindu period (pre-Christian era to the middle of the 15th Century A.D.) are:

- The Matsya Yantra (the fish machine), an iron fish floating on oil to the north serving as a primitive compass used by Indian seafarers for several millennia (as per Hindu mythology, Matsya was the first incarnation of Lord Vishnu).
- The names of some of the places in Southern and southeast Asia such as Socotra which is a derivative of Sukhadhara (container or island of happiness); Sri Lanka which originally was Swarna Alankar (gold ornament), Nicobar which was derived from Nak-Dweep (the island of the naked) and Calicut which originally was Kallikote (in Kannada a stone-fort);
- Reference to Indians as Klings in Thailand and Telangs in some parts of Burma because of the conquests of these countries by the Kalingas and Andhras several millennia ago;
- The similarity between the Thai and Oriya scripts due to the long Kalinga rule over Thailand;
- The scriptures in a Buddhist temple in Japan which are recited by the monks every morning even today being in the 6th Century A.D. Bengali script; and

— The transfer by sea of the weary, tired and demoralised army of Alexander the Great from the mouth of the Indus to the shores of the Persian Gulf in 323 B.C. in about 800 Indian-built sailing vessels.

During this period, while the Arabian Sea and the Indian Ocean were used mainly for purposes of maritime trade, the Bay of Bengal provided a highway for the countries on the Eastern seaboard to embark on proselytising, cultural and colonising missions to Sri Lanka and countries as far as the East Indies and Japan.

During the Hindu period, considerable maritime activity took place in the waters around India. As described by Megasthenes, the royal shipyards of the Mauryas built seagoing ships of various classes. The War Office of Emperor Chandragupta had, as one of its six boards, a Nav Parishad (Board of Admiralty) which controlled national shipping. During the days of Emperor Ashoka in the 3rd century B.C., his sister, Princess Sanghamitra sailed from Tamralipta in Bengal to Sri Lanka on her historic mission of spreading Buddhism there.

Ashoka also had a strong seagoing fleet and regular commercial intercourse with Syria, Egypt, Cyrene, Macedonia and Epirus/ Between 200 B.C. and A.D. 250, the Andhras carried out maritime trade with Western Asia, Greece, Rome, Egypt, China and some other Eastern countries and had even set up embassies in some of these countries. Roman coins discovered in India, especially in the South, establish the existence of trade between these countries even before the Christian era. Persecution at the hands of the Romans forced some Jews to flee Rome and take refuge in Malabar in A.D. 68. Larger sailing vessels built by the Cholas, Pandyas and the Keralas of South India and the Kalingas of Orissa were used for trade, passenger traffic and nava l warfare. These ships were considered excellent for navigation across the oceans as their lower parts were reinforced with triple planks in order to enable them to withstand the force of tempests. Some of the leading communities in organising sea-bferne commerce were the Manigramrftan Chetties, Namdasis, Valangais and Elangais of South India. It is a fact of history that during the first decade of the seventh century, a ruler of Gujarat who was faced with defeat at the hands of his enemy, sent his son with thousands of followers comprising cultivators, artisans, warriors, physicians and writers in over 100 vessels to Java where they laid the foundation of a new civilisation whose contribution to the world is the temple and sculptures of Borobudur. The Cholas (A.D. 985-1054) maintained a strong naval fleet on the Coro-mandel Coast. The Chola emperors Rajaraja I and Rajendra I had strong armadas which were used to capture Sri Lanka and in A.D. 1007 the Cholas launched an expedition against the Sri Vijayas, who at that time ruled the Malayan Peninsula, Java, Sumatra and some neighbouring islands and the sea areas contingous to them, and defeated them to establish Chola power in the Malayan Peninsula.

Evidence from various sources confirms the existence of trade in various commodities between India and Europe for at least three millennia. India maintained trade relations with the Phoenicians, Jews, Assyrians, Greeks, Egyptians and Romans during the earlier centuries and with the Turks, Venetians, Portuguese, Dutch and English during the later part of the period. While India imported few items such as tin, lead, glass, amber, steel for arms, coral and medicinal drugs from Europe and West Asia, Arabia supplied frankincense to India for use in her temples. The items exported to Europe, North Africa and West Asia included wool from the fleeces of sheep bred on the northwestern mountain ranges, armour, onyx, chalcedony, lapis lazuli, jasper, resinous gum, furs, asafoetida, musk, balm, myrrh, embroidered woollen fabrics, coloured carpets, silk (considered most valuable and exchanged by weight with gold), various types of cotton cloth ranging from coarse canvas and calicoes to muslins of the finest texture, peacocks, apes, oils, brassware, ivory, ebony, pearls, sugar cane extracts, salt, indigo, drugs, dyes, rice, sandalwood, timber for building ships, aromatics, pepper, cinna mon and edible spices which were, during the later years, mainly traded for precious metals, especially gold.

Interrelation is further confirmed by the fact that the word for peacock is "tuki" in Hebrew and "tokei" in Tamil and by the adoption of Tamil words by the Greeks and vice-versa. There was considerable sea-borne commercial intercourse between Greece and South India during the Hindu period affirmed by the fact that the words for rice, ginger, cinnamon and foreign merchants in Greek and Tamil respectively are ryza and arisi, zingibar and inchivar, karpion and karava and Iaones and Yavana. In April A.D. 800, as described in the 199th Chapter of the Japanese document

Ruijukokushi, an Inglian was cast up on the shores of Japan and some seeds of the cotton-plant, so far unknown to that country, were found on his ship and sown in the provinces of Kii, Awaji, Sanuki, Jyo, Tosa and Kyushu. Thus cotton was introduced into Japan.

There is evidence of Herodotus (450 B.C.) who wrote about the (cotton) worn by the Indian contingent of Xerxes Army which had been woven from "the wool which certain mild trees in India bear instead of fruit that in beauty and quality excels that of sheep." Thus, it was India that introduced the use of cotton to Europe, West Asia and the Far East.

One of the most sensational discoveries that helped maintain trade between India and the West was that of the regularity of the seasonal winds of the southwest monsoon by a Greek named Hippalus in A.D. 45. His discovery helped him in finding a direct route to Malabar which was far shorter than the older coast-hugging route. Toward the end of the summer months, "ships used to depart from the mouth of the Arabian Gulf or Kane on the coast of Arabia Felix and sail straight in 40 days to Muziris (modern Kodungallur) on the West Coast of India. They began their homeward voyage in December by sailing with the North-East Wind, enter the Arabian Gulf, meet with a South or South-West Wind and thus complete the voyage by using the trade winds throughout the period." The discovery of the directions and regularity of the monsoon air current was a major contributing factor towards the continuance of maritime trade between India and the Western countries over the centuries.

That oceanic navigation was well advanced during the earlier centuries of the Christian era is further borne out by the writings of the celebrated Chinese monk, Fa Hien who came to India overland to study Buddhism at Bodhgaya, Sarnath and Varanasi in A.D. 413. On his way back to his home land he sailed from Tamralipta in Bengal and 14 days later reached Sri Lanka where he embarked for Java and called at the Nicobars before passing through the Straits of Malacca to reach the pacific.

Hindu supremacy over the Eastern waters reached its zenith during the period of 5th to 12th centuries when the Sri Vijaya Empire ruled the entire sea area between India's eastern seaboard and the. Far East. The Sri Vijayas' cultural and colonising expedition took them to such far-flung areas as Sumatra, Burma, the Malayan Peninsula, Java, Thailand and Indo-China. Besides spreading Hindu culture, they maintained regular political and commercial intercourse with the Cholas, Pandyas and Keralas. As a result of jealousy between the Cholas, the Tamil Kings, and the Sri Vijayas, however, a series of sea battles were fought between their navies toward the end of the 10th century A.D. resulting in the weakening of these empires and opening the way for Arab supremacy in the region. About the same time, the rulers of Gujarat and Calicut also maintained large fleets of sailing vessels for commercial purposes which sailed with cargoes of silk carpets, precious stones, pearls, ivory, spices and other valuable goods to Europe and West Asia. With the weakening of the Indian rulers, their sea-borne trade routes passed into the hands of the Arabs who became great intermediaries of maritime commercial intercourse between the two regions.

During this period the Arabs acted as a link between the East and Europe and used to pass the Indian merchandise to the Venetians who supplied the Indian goods to the European markets where they were in great demand. The Venetians soon became immensely prosperous which aroused the jea-lousy and cupidity of the seafarers of the Iberian nations, i.e., Spain, Portugal and other Mediterranean countries, and the quest for a direct passage to India began.

For several millennia ships had been traversing the Indian Ocean carrying valuable merchandise and cultural emissaries between India and the West. Cities that directly engaged in the maritime trade or stood on the ancient trade routes continued to grow in importance and prosperity. Some of these centres of commerce were ancient Chaldea, Babylon, Nineveh, Ophir, Tad-more and the ports in the Mediterranean, Persian Gulf and the Red Sea. The Phoenicians had for some years arrogated to themselves a major share in the Mediterranean trade but were later driven out of it by the Assyrians, Greeks and Romans but the Arabs continued to hold away over the Red Sea, Persian Gulf, Indian Ocean and the Arabian Sea.

Egypt, during the days of the Ptolemies, developed Alexandria into the most important port in the world. One of the Ptolemies, Ptolemy Philadel-phus was planning to construct a canal between the Red Sea and the Nile, a hundred cubits wide and thirty cubits in depth, in order to transport Indian goods to Alexandria wholly by water but, for reasons not known, this project was never undertaken and hence a new port called Berenike was developed on the Western shore of the Red Sea. Ships from India carried merchandise, sailing from Tatta at the head of the lower delta of the Indus or other ports on the West Coast to the coast of Persia and after following the Arabian shore to Berenike. From Berenike, the goods were carried overland to the city of Koptos, which was very close to the Nile, where they were loaded into ships which navigated along a canal to Alexandria. Carthe-gian merchants carried Indian goods to all Mediterranean ports. During the period of Egyptian supremacy, the northern countries of Europe received Indian goods which were carried overland from India to Oxus from where they went to the regions bordering the Caspian Sea and the Black Sea.

After its conquest of Carthage, Egypt and Syria, the Roman Empire monopolised trade with India for many years and Alexandria continued to be the principal port for Indian merchandise. The conquest of Persia and Egypt by the Mohammedans later, however, deprived the European countries of the use of Alexandria for trade and access to Indian merchandise. Basra was founded at the head of the Persian Gulf and became as important a trading centre as Alexandria, controlling the movement of merchandise in both the easterly and westerly directions.

Trade Routes and Supplying of Indian Goods

The Arabs later gained control of the trade routes and stopped supplying Indian goods to the sea ports of the Mediterranean but the overland route to Constantinople provided the alternative for carrying Indian products to the European trade centres. In fact, Constantinople became the focal point for the movement of merchandise between Europe and India. The rise and fall of the Venetians, Genoans and Pisans, the bitter struggle between Venice and Genoa over the eastern trade and the Venetian supremacy over this trade for some time form but a small chapter in terms of time in our maritime history. With the annexation of Constantinople and trading routes to India by the Turks towards the end of the 15th century and with the continued piracy on the Alexandrian trade route by the Egyptians, a new pattern of rivalry involving South European, North African and West Asian countries over trade with the East emerged. Since mastery over these trade routes had a direct bearing on the power and prosperity of these nations, an alternative route to India was sought to be established by some of these countries which already had centuries of seafaring experience and expertise.

The quest for an alternative route hugging the coasts of Africa and Asia led to the sailing down the West Coast of Africa by the Portuguese Navigator, Bartholemy Diaz in 1487 and the discovery of the Cape of Tempests, later to be renamed the Cape of Good Hope. Vasco da Gama was deputed by King Manoel of Portugal in July 1497, five years after the discovery of the West Indies by Columbus, to complete the work done by Diaz. The King's astrologer, Abraham Ben Zakut, having studied his horoscope and having found it favourable for the discovery of the sea route to India, there were high hopes of success in the venture. Four ships, the *Sao Gabriel* (120 tons) commanded by Vasco da Gama, the *Sao Raphael* (100 tons) commanded by his brother Paulo da Gama, the *Berrio* (50 tons) under the command of Nicolas Coelho and a 200-ton store ship set sail from Belem on March 25, 1497. A violent storm was encountered while rounding the Cape and the crew, which wanted to go back, plotted a mutiny but Vasco da Gama succeeded in suppressing the mutiny by arresting the ring-leaders and threatening to throw them overboard. In March 1498, *Sao Gabriel* and *Sao Raphael* reached Mozambique, the store ship having returned to Portugal after transferring her stores and the *Berrio* having been found not seaworthy and broken up to repair the other ships. Vasco da Gama now needed a pilot to take him across the Indian Ocean and Arabian Sea to India and found one in the Moorish Broker, Davane, from Gujarat who was an experienced pilot and knew the seas contiguous to Africa, West Asia and India very well. His expert pilotage not only provided security from the jealous Arabs but also helped Vasco da Gama to proceed to Melinde from where the ships sailed on August 26, 1498. Had Davane not assisted Vasco da Gama, the Portuguese would not have reached India for some more decades which probably would have changed the course of India's maritime history.

While the discovery of the sea route to India by da Gama was of no great significance, especially when compared to the feats of Columbus and Magellan, the importance of his achievement lies in th fact that while the seas were regarded by the Arabs as a pathway for carrying out maritime trade, the Portuguese were the first to lay claim to sovereignty over these waters and using them as an instrument for the projection of their national policy. This claim was further sanctified by the Bull of Pope Calixtus III which considered the seas they sailed to be their possession. The Portuguese thus began considering themselves to be lords of the seas and thought they Were justified in confiscating the merchandise of all ships that sailed without their authority. K.M. Panikkar is fully justified in saying, "It may truly be said that India never lost her independence till she lost command of the sea in the first decade of the 16th century." The Portuguese claim to sovereignty of the seas and da Gama's strong attitude at the Court of the Zamorin of Calicut displeased the latter and the challenge to the ruler's limited sea power led to a series of indecisive skir mishes and sea battles off the coast of Malabar in the years that followed. The Portuguese intruders were detested by the Arab traders who joined hands with the Zamorin and in 1500 when Admiral Pedro Cabral bombarded Calicut, 80 ships of the Zamorin, manned by 1500 intrepid sailors and reinforced by the ships of a rich Arab trader, Khoja Amber, drove him away to Cochin. Two indecisive battles were fought off Cochin in 1503 and off Chaul in 1508. In 1509 the next battle of importance was fought off Diu when ships of the Zamorin, under the command of the courageous Kassim and reinforced by an Egyptian fleet under Admiral Mir Hussain, fought against a strong Portuguese force led by Den Francesco d'Almeida. This battle also produced no decisive result because of the treachery of the Sultan of Gujarat which led to the Egyptian fleet sailing away in disgust. The Indian Ocean was thereafter dominated by the Portuguese, and Albuquerque, the great commercial empire-builder and statesman, helped in firmly establishing Portuguese supremacy over the area.

Mention must be made here of the outstanding role played by the Zamo-rin's fleet which, under the leadership of the AH Marakkars, gave valiant battle to the Portuguese for well over 90 years. The Marakkars who had their headquarters at Ponnani, a natural harbour South of Calicut, held sway over the waters around Calicut. The most illustrious name in the family of the Ali Maraklcars was that of Kunjali Marakkar II who sank a number of Portuguese ships (the tally in a particular year being 50) and struck terror in the hearts of the Portuguese forces. For some reasons, however, Kunjali III (Mohammed Kunjali Marakkar) who was the last of the Kunjali Admirals and had won many a battle against the Portuguese, fell out with the Zamorin. This led to the weakening of the Zamorin's fleet and its capitulation to the Portuguese. The main contribution of the Kunjalis during the 16th century was that for over 90 years they kept the Portuguese at bay and harassed their fleet thus preventing them from carrying out incursions into the land areas of the subcontinent.

Having failed to defeat the Zamorin, Albuquerque seized Goa and its surrounding areas in 1510. Operating from Goa which occupied a commanding position in the prevailing scenario, Albuquerque hounded the Arab traders out of their favourite haunt, subdued the Sultan of Ormuz and relegated him to the level of a vassal of the Portuguese ruler, developed Socotra into a powerful naval base with a well-defended fort, established a strong government in Cochin after bypassing the Zamorin and brought immense power and wealth to his country by exercising 1513, he mustered a strong naval force and seized and fortified the Straits of Malacca. He also established amicable relations with the ruler of Pegu, who controlled the Arakan Coast, after prolonged negotiations with him.

Portuguese supremacy over the waters around India was thus established and reached its zenith during the days of Albuquerque. But in 1580, when Portugal joined hands with Spain and the Spanish Armada suffered a crushing defeat, it changed the course of events around the globe, one of its off shoots being the decline of Portuguese supremacy in the Indian region. It is a moot point that if the Spanish Armada had triumphed, the United States could in all probability have become a Latin American country and India a Portuguese dominion! '

The sudden change in the power equation was first exploited by the Dutch and the Dutch East India Company was formed at Amsterdam in 1592. The first merchant fleet of the Dutch reached India in 1595 but they did not challenge the Portuguese supremacy. Instead, they occupied Java and established a naval base at Batavia. Meanwhile, the British and the French also decided to benefit from fishing in our troubled waters and came to India during the earlier years of the 17th Century. It is thus apparent that while the Hindus controlled the trade routes until the beginning of the 15th

Century, the Arabs took over the main bulk of it from them for a while with a short period of overlap. But supremacy over these routes passed into Portuguese hands towards the end of the 15th Century. The Portuguese then reigned unchallenged for nearly a century till the defeat of the Spanish Armada and then the sun of the British maritime power rose over Indian horizons and the Indian Ocean during the first decade of the 17th Century.

The Mughal ruler, Akbar had a fairly strong Navy but its main component was a fleet of ships and craft based at Dacca which were used for operations in rivers and creeks for the protection of deltaic South Bengal from the *Magh* (Burmese) and *Feringhee* (half-caste) pirates who had the support of the Arakan rulers. He had an Admiralty which looked after the supply of ships and smaller craft, recruitment of suitable personnel for the ships and craft, security of rivers and waterways and collection of port revenue. The Mughals, however, did not appreciate the importance of building up a blue-water navy and developing sea-borne trade and commerce. Shipping and shipbuilding, ocean-going and riverine, however, flourished during the Mughal days in various parts of India such as Bengal, Kashmir, Lahore and Surat and there is evidence available to establish the high standard of technology maintained in the construction of these ships and craft.

Aurangzeb's navy was superior in size and efficiency to that of Akbar. Besides naval ships, he had four ships at Surat for carrying Haj pilgrims free of cost to Mecca but the lack of adequate sea-going naval ships caused the loss of some of his bigger ships to British pirates. By a Royal Charter of Queen Elizabeth I, the Honourable Company of the Merchants Trading to the East Indies, better known as the East India Company, was founded by the British on December 31, 1600 and a ship of the Company, the *Hector,* with Captain Hawkins as the Commanding Officer, arrived in Surat bringing a letter to Emperor Jehangir requesting for permission to trade with India. Hawkins reached Agra on April 16, 1610 and permission was duly granted and trading facilities promised by the Emperor but the Portuguese did not appreciate the British encroachment on their trade preserves. The British sensed this and sent a squadron of warships, the *Dragon, Osiender, James* and *Solomon,* under the overall command of Captain Thomas Best, which reached Swally, the roadstead of Surat, on September 5, 1612. This date is regarded by the British as the foundation day of the Royal Indian Navy, as the first arrival of their warships in India and the formation of the Indian Marine took place on this day.

A very interesting fact "discovered" by the late Commander (special) G.E. Walker, who was the Judge Advocate General of the RIN immediately before Independence, is that the Jack flown by the Indian Marine in 1612 was the flag worn by ships on the American side during the War of Independence when they rejected the Union Jack. The Jack of the Indian Marine was thus the first flag of the U.S.A. which over the years developed into the stars and stripes. The Indian Marine Jack had seven red and six white stripes and in the position occupied by the stars today, was displayed the St. George's Cross. This flag forms a part of the insignia of the existing RIN Association in the U.K.

Their monopoly over trade in the region having been challenged by the British, the Portuguese attacked the ships of the Indian Marine on October 29, 1612 with four galleons and forty other craft but had to admit defeat after a protracted battle. They then withdrew leaving the British as masters of the land and sea area around Surat who set up factories and formed a fleet of Indian small craft known as Ghurabs (the British called them Grabs) and Galivats for the protection of their sea-borne commerce from the Portuguese. The sobriquet "The Grab Service" by which the British Indian Navy was known for many years does not necessarily bracket it with the pirates of various nationalities who infested the Indian waters at that time.

The nucleus of the Indian Marine consisted at that time mainly of some warships built in England and a larger number of vessels built in India. The Ghurabs were heavy beamy vessels (about 300 tons) of shallow draft and were armed with six 9 to 12-pouiider guns while the Galivats were smaller craft (about 70 tons) mounting half-a-dozen 2 to 4-pounders. The crews of these craft consisted mainly of Hindu fishermen from the Konkan Coast.

The second major battle with the Portuguese took place in 1614 in which the Indian Marine emerged victorious and the East India Company was granted further trading rights by Jehangir. In the following year, Sir Thomas Roe was appointed Ambassador from King James I to the Moghul Courts. Merchandise manufactured at the Surat factories started moving by sea to the West for trade with the Persian Gulf ports in 1618. Having had the monopoly of trade in these ports for nearly a century, the Portuguese tried to block the passage of these ships across the Arabian Sea but were successfully thwarted from doing so by the British who annexed Ormuz from the Portuguese in 1622 and thus began their uninterrupted trade with Persia. This, however, did not deter the Portuguese from seeking another battle at Swally in 1630 where they were defeated once again and a truce was declared leading to the opening of some of the Portuguese ports to the East India Company's ships.

The Dutch had been keeping an eye on the balance of power in this region and in their efforts to consolidate their base at Batavia (now known as Jakarta), they captured the Straits of Malacca in 1641 and drove the Portuguese away from the Eastern gateway to the Indian Ocean. Realising the strategic importance of Colombo as a naval base for operation for the annexation of the Indian mainland, the Dutch then befriended the ruler of Sri Lanka which helped in driving the Portuguese away from Colombo also in 1654. Soon thereafter, they made inroads into the Portuguese bastions on the Malabar Coast. This was rendered even more effective by the main base of the Dutch at Batavia, their control of the Straits of Malacca and the advanced operational base at Colombo. Cochin was captured in 1663. This was further made possible by the British preoccupation with other problems but their friendly relations with Emperor Shahjahan prevented the Dutch from making any forays into the waters around Surat where the British factories were situated. A year later, however, Shivaji, the Maratha ruler, attacked Surat by land but the Britishers repulsed his attack.

Meanwhile, King Charles II of England had married Infanta Catherina of Braganza, the Portuguese princess, in 1662 and Bombay was ceded to him as a part of his dowry. The official version of the transfer document described the gift as "the Port and Island of Bombay in the East Indies, together with all the rights, profit, territories and appurtenances thereof whatsoever." Since, however, it was virtually impossible for King Charles II to administer Bombay successfully from England, he transferred it to the East India Company at an annual rental off 10 in 1668—one of the most significant events in the history of Bombay.

Despite the advice of his counsellors to the contrary, Sir John Child who was appointed the Admiral of the East India Company's land and sea forces between the Persian Gulf and Kanya Kumari in 1685, decided to adopt an aggressive policy towards the Mughals. Having taken on afar superior force, Child suffered an ignominious defeat at the hands of the Mughals who, with the support of the Sidis' fleet, captured most of Bombay island and besieged Child in the Bombay Castle which is now known as the Naval Barracks. Peace was, however, restored by redeeming Bombay on the payment of £ 15,000 in 1690 and some kind of a reconciliation having been effected between Aurangzeb and the Company. Meanwhile, in 1685 the Indian Marine Headquarters were shifted to Bombay and a year later the Service was rechristened the Bombay Marine.

In 1698, the Danes appeared on the scene and set up their trade after obtaining the permission of Prince Azimus-shan, grandson of Emperor Aurangzeb. By 1755, they had set up a factory and had hoisted the Danish flag at Serampore. In 1801, the British authorities forcibly seized Serampore but restored it immediately. In 1808, however, a detachment of British troops from Barrackpore occupied Serampore. The Danish East India Company recovered it later but in 1844 transferred all its assets to the British Government and left the country. The beginning of the 18th century saw the emergence of an Admiral of Shivaji's Maratha Fleet, Kanhoji Angre, whose name became a legend during these years and whose exploits are written in letters of gold in the annals of the navies of India. Shivaji was a firm believer in the doctrine "Jalaim Jasya, Valaim Tasya" (he who rules the sea is all-powerful) and Tukoji Angre, his Admiral and son, Kanhoji Angre and his descendents, put it to practice. In 1706 the fleet of Kanhoji, menaced and considerably reduced British trade between Bombay and the lower Malabar Coast and captured Colaba from the Sidis. A year later, maritime trade in the Indian Ocean was threatened by Arab pirates operating from Muscat who plundered a large number of ships. Equipped with a fleet of 10 Ghurabs and 50 Galivats, the Maratha Fleet, under the command of Kanhoji Angre, challenged the Arab fleet and drove it away from the Indian Ocean. Thereafter, Kanhoji began establishing mastery over the Konkan Coast by fortifying his base at Gheria (Vijaydurg). This fortress was manned by a specially trained garrison which had been armed and provisioned to withstand severe attacks from land and sea and prolonged periods of blockade. This was further reinforced by a dockyard built on a river front behind the fortress which was equipped to build bigger, stronger and better sea-going vessels for his navy.

SEA POWER IN PORTUGUESE TIME

The Portuguese by this time having been reduced to an insignificant sea power, along with the Sidis and the British faced a strong challenge from the Maratha Fleet. The size, manoeuvrability and fire-power of the Maratha Fleet continued to grow and hence the British Council decided to build corvettes for the Bombay Marine which would escort the merchant ships of the Company and protect them from Angre's wrath. This went on for some time and the Governor of Bombay, Charles Boone, decided to attack Gheria in 1717 with a strong fleet under the command of Captain Barleu. A bitter engagement followed and the Marathas forced the Company's ships to beat a hasty retreat after inflicting severe damage on the ships and killing a large number of the Company's soldiers and sailors. Uuderred by the near-catastrophe, Charles Boone carried out another attack, this time a surprise one, on Gheria on November 5,1718 and succeeded in silencing many Maratha guns after a ship-shore artillery engagement. The next day, however, when his forces landed, the Maratha guns which had been strategically positioned to cover the entire beachhead, mowed them down. The British fleet, with the handful of survivors hastily withdrew.

On receiving a petition from the Governor of Bombay for naval reinforcement, the King of England sent four warships under Commodore Mathews to provide support to the fleet of the Bombay Marine. British and Portuguese ships carried out an attack on Colaba, five miles from Gheria, in October 1722 but even this attempt was successfully repulsed by the Marathas and the attacking forces withdrew after having suffered severe losses of men, guns and ammunition.. Angered by the capture of some of their ships by the Maratha Fleet, the Dutch attacked Gheria in 1724 with a powerful squadron of seven men-of-war, each mounting 30 to 50 guns, but they suffered heavy losses and were beaten back.

The success of the Maratha Fleet against bigger and better equipped ships of England, Portugal and Hollalid and those of the Mughals and the Arabs stretching over several decades was mainly due to Kanhoji's tactics of using a large number of light, strong and fast craft, adequately equipped, which surrounded the heavier vessels of the enemy and simultaneously attacked them from all sides "thus overwhelming the crews of the enemy ships and then boarding them and putting them out of action by scuttling them or setting them on fire. Having had the unique distinction of maintaining naval supremacy over the sea area off the Konkan Coast for many years, Kanhoji suddenly passed away in 1729, survived by his sons, Sekhoji Angre and Sambhaji Angre.

The British treaty of alliance with the Sidi's to fight the Angres in 1733 was followed by Sambhaji's capture of some British merchant ships on December 16, 1735 which was a heavy blow on British trade. The Peshwas of Poona who were not quite friendly with the Angres, were then wooed by the British and a treaty was signed in 1739. By this time, Maratha control of the seas had extended from Kutch to Cochin and had severely hampered British trade. Meanwhile, in order *to* build ships at a site closer to the scene of action, the British had set up a naval dockyard at Bombay in 1735.

A combined operation by the British and the Peshwas by land and sea, led by Admiral Watson with his ships and 1400 sailors and Colonel Robert Clive with his army contingent, besieged Gheria and were successful in capturing it and reducing Maratha sea power to nought. It may not be out of place to mention here that Admiral Watson and 50 sailors of the Marine assisted Clive in the Battle of Plassey in 1757. Some merchants from Ostend, Antwerp and other Flemish towns arrived in Bengal on board a ship laden with merchandise during the second decade of the 18th Century. The Ostend Company was set up in 1722 with the blessings of Nawab Murshid Kuli Khan and a factory was set up in Banki Bazar, south of Chandernagore. They, however, faced considerable opposition from the other European trading communities and the Nawab's Charter was withdrawn in 1727 as a result. Soon thereafter, a naval engagement took place between the Flemish and Nawab's forces and the Flemish merchants, having been defeated, withdrew from India.

Entering the scene to challenge British sea power in the region in 1740 were the French and they began their operations by capturing Mauritius and converting it into a strong naval base and then sending a strong fleet into the Bay of Bengal to intercept and capture British merchant ships. The war of Austrian succession in Europe in 1744 saw the British and the French in opposing camps and Dupleix, the French Governor of Pondicherry, decided to act. Having already decided to capture the entire South Indian region, he used the French Fleet, which was under the command of La Bourdonnais, to launch an attack on the British Fleet which was led by Captain Peyton. The French Fleet succeeded in driving the British Fleet up the Hooghly and then, after a brief resistance, captured Madras. Dupleix, however, did not appreciate the importance of sea power as an essential factor in maintaining supremacy over land areas continguous to the sea. La Bourdonnais was thus allowed to return to France in 1747 and the British regained the command of the seas around India once again. They also brought six powerful ships and several small craft of Boscawan's Fleet to the Bay of Bengal in 1748 and beseiged Pondicherry. This siege, however, was not successful but the British continued to make their presence felt by annexing strategic and important regions. One of these was Chandernagore, a French possession, which was captured by Admiral Watson, assisted by Clive, in 1756. Watson died in 1757 and the British Fleet, under the command of Admiral Pocock, attacked Madras. Despite some reverses suffered at the hands of the French, the British land forces took the offensive and defeated them in the Carnatic War while Admiral Pocock defeated the French Fleet under D'Ache which was driven away from the sea leaving the British as the masters of the entire sea area around India.

Peace was, however, short-lived for after a few years of the British annexation of Pondicherry, Admiral Suffren, a redoubtable naval tactician, appeared on the scene with a reinforced French Fleet and attacked the British Fleet which was under the command of Admiral Sir Edward Hughes. A series of encounters ensued but following a treaty between England and France, Admiral Suffren and his Fleet left the area, converting the Indian Ocean into a British lake. The later half of the 18th century saw the extinction of Portuguese power in India, the British seizure of the island of Salsetta and other Portuguese holdings in India and the British victory over Haider Ali's navy at Honavar and Mangalore.

Both Hyder Ali and Tipu Sultan had maintained a fleet mainly to support their operations on land and protect their trade interests abroad. They were formidable adversaries who inflicted a severe defeat on the British and came near to breaking the power of the East India Company. But they were confined to the south and did not directly affect the fortunes of India as a whole. Haider Ali was a remarkable man and one of the notable figures in Indian history. He had some kind of a national ideal and possessed the qualities of a leader with vision. Continually suffering from a painful disease, his self-discipline and capacity for hard work were astonishing. He realised, long before others did the importance of sea power and the growing menace of the British based on naval strength. He tried to organise a joint effort to drive them out and, for this purpose, sent envoys to the Marathas, the Nizam, and Shuja-ud-Dowla of Oudh. But nothing came of this. He started building his own navy and, capturing the Maldive Islands, made them his headquarters for shipbuilding and naval activities. He died by the wayside as he was marching with his army. His son Tipu continued to strengthen his navy. Tipu also sent messages to Napoleon and to the Sultan in Constantinople. Haider Ali had, however, lamented that he could beat the English on land, but he could not dry up the sea.

One of the other little-known facts of our maritime history is that, over two centuries ago, the Germans too made an attempt to establish a footing in Bengal. In 1753, some merchants from Empden, atown in Germany, founded a company, popularly known at that time as the Bengal Company of Empden or the Royal Prussian Bengal Company. The British, the French, the Dutch and the Danes, who had already set up factories on the banks of the Hooghly, combined against the newcomers and orders were issued forbidding their pilots, masters and mates to render any assistance to the Germans.

The Moghul Nawab also issued orders to these foreigners asking them to prevent the setting up of a German establishment. The German ships, the largest of them being the Prince Henry of Prussia, however, arrived and set up a factory near Chandernagore and succeeded in getting the Nawab's approval for carrying on their trade after paying a "nazrana" (gift) on Rs. 5,000 to him. Faced with bitter hostility from the other European competitors, the Germans failed to expand their trade and could not make any headway toward constructing buildings and warehouses for the purpose. They decided, therefore, to wind up their trade and by 1760, returned to Germany.

Lord Nelson, when he was only 16, visited Bombay and Calcutta while on board the *Seahorse,* a twenty-gun ship, during its voyage to the 'East Indies' in 1775. The ship reached Bombay on the morning of August 17, 1775 and later visited Calcutta when Nelson contracted some "distressing illness and fevers." He was sent home on board the frigate, *Dolphin* and completely recovered before reaching England. The details of his journey from the Hooghly to Portsmouth are recorded in the book *Nelson* written by Carola Oman. The shipbuilding yard at Surat had been setup in 1635 during which year the East India Company built four pinnaces and other larger vessels, this being the first record of any of their shipbuilding activities in India. The shift to Bombay in 1735 was necessitated by its being safer and closer to the scenes of action. It was Lowjee Nusserwanjee Wadia, ancestor of along line of famous Parsi master-builders of ships, naval and commercial, who selected the site for the Naval Dockyard which during the course of the next 100 years, proceeded to build not less than 115 war vessels and 144 merchant ships including 84 gunships of a total tonnage of over 2,000 for the Royal Navy. The quality of construction of these ships was of such a high order that they were acclaimed by shipbuilding nations around the globe. It was the Wadias who proved to the world that Indian-built Malabar teak ships were far superior in seaworthiness and withstanding the detrimental effects of the elements than Britishbuilt oaken ships. *HMS Trincomalee* which was built by the Bombay Naval Dockyard in 1817 for the Royal Navy and which saw many battles during the period of her commission, is still in use at Portsmouth as *TS Foudroyant* for training school and college students in seamanship arid navigation and is the oldest sail-driven warship afloat today. Her Malabar teak hull and superstructure, despite several major modifications, damages suffered during battles and storms and continuous use for training purposes, is still as good as new and to quote a well-known shipbuilder, "good for another 300 years".

INTRODUCE OF NOMENCLATURE IN BOMBAY MARINE

The earlier decades of the 19th century saw the arrival in the Indian waters of pirates belonging to an Arab tribe called the Joasmis. They operated from the Arab side of the Persian Gulf covering the coast from Bahrain to Cape Mussendon and, with their headquarters at Ras-el-Khaima, they held sway over the entire Persian Gulf. Originally merchants and pearl-fishers, they now took to piracy. For many years they left the ships of the East India Company alone and attacked only small craft but since the Company ships took no action against the Arab pirates plundering ships and craft belonging to the others, this was interpreted by the Joasmis as a sign of weakness and later they stopped sparing the Company ships.

A fleet of 12 ships of the Bombay Marine, carrying 4,000 men and under the command of Captain Seaton, attacked Ras-el-Khaima in 1809 and bombarded this focal point of the Joasmis' operations but were beaten back by the well-entrenched Joasmi forces. The squadron of ships had, therefore, to return to Bombay and the Arab pirates continued to seize and plunder the Company's ships. Under the command of Captain Collier, the Company later despatched another fleet of II ships with 6,000 men under Major General Sir William Grant Keir. They blockaded the town of Ras-el-Khaima for four days as a result of which Sardar Hasan Bin Rehman, the Joasmi Chief, gave himself up and admitted defeat. The Arabs guaranteed safe passage to British ships in a treaty in 1820 and the East India Company was not subjected to harassment by the Arabs any further. An interesting fact recorded is that the Punjab Regiment of the Indian Army is probably the only example in the world of a land-based force, having a naval craft as its cap-badge with the motto "Sthal-wa-Jal" (earlier "Khushki-wa-Tari"). This regiment was permitted to adopt the galley as an emblem because it took part in many military expeditions overseas between 1796 and 1824.

Two important events took place in 1829. The Bombay Marine was assigned the new nomenclature, the Bombay Marine Corps, and *Hugh Lindsay,* a ship of the East India Company, was the first to be fitted with a steam engine. *Hugh Lindsay, a. 411-ton* ship of the Bombay Marine Corps, steamed out of Bombay on March 20, 1830 and reached the Suez after 21 days of actual steaming averaging a trifle under six knots. Thus began the gradual conversion of the Company's ships from sail to steam which was completed during the next 15 years. The year 1830 also saw another change in the name of the Service—this time to the Indian Navy.

All went well for seven years thereafter when in 1837 a pilgrim ship of the East India Company, whilst on passage to Mecca, with a number of rich pilgrims on board, was seized and plundered near Aden. A squadron of the Indian Navy's men-of-war, led by Commander Haines, was then sent to attack Aden but since the Sultan of Aden was in a repentant mood and ready to pay an indemnity of Rs. 3 lakhs, the ships spared Aden and returned to Bombay in 1838. The indemnity promised was, however, never paid by the Sultan and hence the ships returned to Aden in the same year and captured it.

In 1848, during the Anglo-Sikh War, the Indian Navy provided a contingent of 100 ratings and seven officers with their guns to participate in the siege of Multan. This would appear to be the second occasion when the Navy was actively employed for land operations. In 1852 a strong fleet of the Indian Navy, under the command of Captain Lynch, attacked and captured Rangoon. The Raja of Burma had refused to be cowed down by the naval might of Lord Dalhousie who was Viceroy of India and his defiance of the authority of the British resulted in his loss of the strategic city of Rangoon. Meanwhile, Persian and Russian seafarers in the Persian Gulf began harassing the Company's ships while they were on passage for maritime trade. A strong fleet of the Indian Navy under Sir Henry Leeke wasrsent to deal with the pirates and captured Bushire (Basra) after defeating the Persian Fleet in 1853. Ships of the Indian Navy also assisted those of the Royal Navy in suppressing piracy during the war in the Chinese waters in 1860.

The two highest decorations ever to be awarded to the personnel of the Indian Navy before Independence were earned during the 1857 uprising and on shore. An Indian Naval Brigade comprising 78 officers and 1740 men were assigned shore service during the uprising. Mister Midshipman Mayo of the 4th Detachment was awarded the Victoria Cross for his bravery at Dacca. This VC was later presented to the Service and was on display with a photograph of the young officer in the RIM (later RIN) Officers Mess at Bombay. The other recipient of the VC was Mister Acting Master GB Chicken of the 3rd Detachment in recognition of his desperate single-handed defence against an attack by a party of 20 armed men, five of whom were killed by him.

In 1863, a Marine Survey Department, manned completely by naval officers, was started in India which during the next 120 years has developed into a full-fledged Hydrographic Survey Department under free India's Navy. Before the formation of the Marine Survey Department, hydrographic survey was being carried out by the Bombay Marine/Indian Navy itself. In fact, survey work was started in 1772 and officers of the Service surveyed the coastal waters of not only India and the neighbouring countries and islands but also the Persian Gulf, the Red Sea, the East African Coast, the East Indies, the Philippines, the Pelew Islands in the Pacific, the Chusan Archipelago in the East China Sea and Tasmania in the Far South East? Considering the primitive instruments, the limitations of the ships used by these officers and the dangers of venturing into the unknown, the feats of eminent hydrographers like Captains McCluer, Ross and Blair would be comparable to the great Arctic explorers.

In 1863 the Indian Navy was reorganised as a non-combatant force with two branches at Bombay and Calcutta which were renamed the Bombay Marine and the Bengal Marine, naval protection of Indian waters having been taken over by the Admiralty. Their new role was transport of troops and Government stores; maintenance of 'Station Ship' duties at Aden, the Andaman Islands (Port Blair), Burma and Persian Gulf; the maintenance of gun boats on the Irawaddy and Tigris; maintenance of all Government light craft employed for military duties and in the maintenance of light-ships and lighthouses around the Coasts of India and Burma and in the Southern portion of the Red Sea and the Marine Survey of India. The nomenclature was to change again in 1871 when an Indian Defence Force with two ships was constituted and yet again in 1877 when the Government restored the combatant status to the Service and called it His Majesty's Indian Marine with two divisions at Bombay and Calcutta. The Service underwent yet another change in name in 1892 when it was rechristened the Royal Indian Marine.

From 1892 to the outbreak of World War I, the RIM did not make any significant contribution to the maritime history of the country. Before the War, the main tasks assigned to the RIM were marine survey, maintenance of lighthouses and transportation of troops. During the War, however, there were notable exploits of the RIM in various theatres of naval operations. Its ships transported troops, arms, ammunition and stores to Egypt, Iraq and East Africa. While on patrol in the Suez Canal, RIM ship *Hardinge* fought against the Turks and thwarted their efforts to block the canal. She suffered severe damage and lost one of her funnels but succeeded in preventing the blocking of the canal. RIM ships landed troops in Mesopotamia and its smaller ships, designed for operations in inland waters, rendered excellent service in the Euphrates and Tigris rivers. Three other ships, the *Northbrooke, Minto* and *Dufferin,* carried out patrolling duties in the Red Sea. While carrying out these duties, the *Minto* called at Jeddah and transported some Haj pilgrims safely back to India. The RIM was once again reverted to its non-combatant role when the War ended in 1918.

The international situation at the end of World War I, shortage of funds and extensive retrenchment adversely affected the RIM. With the task of naval defence of India once again entrusted to the Royal Navy, the combatant status of the RIM was lost. For the services rendered by the Royal Navy, the Government of India had to pay a staggering sum of £ 100,000 annually to the British Government. The RIM had, therefore, to be reduced to a small force entrusted with minor coastal duties. Most of World War I veterans were demobilised and no reservists were left for calling up during emergencies. This led to the mobilisation of Indian public opinion against the wilful eradication of the country's naval and maritime traditions and a number of committees were appointed to examine the future role of the Service and to make recommendations for suitable changes or expansion to be implemented. The Rawlinson Committee, the last such committee to be appointed, recommended the formation of a small combatant force to suit the needs of the country which was to be controlled by an administrative authority operating from the major port.

Very few Indians joined the Royal Indian Marine at that time though recruitment was open both to the Indians and the British. The first Indian to join the RIM as an officer was Engineer Sub-Lieutenant D.N. Mukerji who was commissioned on January 6, 1928. He rose to the rank of Captain and took premature retirement from service in 1950 and emigrated to England where he is still living.

The frozen continent of Antarctica which straddles the South Pole and where the environment is, literally and metaphorically, as clean and pure as driven snow, had always attracted adventurers and explorers from all parts of the globe. One of them was Lieutenant H.R. Bowers of the Royal Indian Marine who in 1910 had the distinction of being chosen to accompany the great explorer, Captain Scott, on his expedition to the Antarctic. Even though he was not an Indian, he was the first representative of this subcontinent to embark on an expedition to the South Pole. In the words of Commander G.E. Walker, RINVR, author of *The Historical Background of the Royal Indian Navy,* Lieutenant Bowers had the high honour of being selected as one of the party which made the last great journey to the South Pole itself. Scott wrote of him, "I believe he is the hardest traveller that ever undertook a Polar journey, as well as one of the most undaunted. Never was such a sturdy, active, undefeatable little man."

When only eleven miles from safety, the three survivors of that journey were compelled by a week-long blizzard and the exhaustion of their supplies to give up their march. Scott (one of the last acts of his life) wrote to Bowers' mother, "I write when we are very near the end of our journey, and I am finishing it in company with two gallant, noble gentlemen. One of them is your son. He had come to be one of my closest and soundest friends, and I appreciate his wonderful upright nature, his ability and energy. As the troubles have thickened, his dauntless spirit ever shone brighter, and he had remained cheerful, hopeful and indomitable to the end." Scott then wrote to his brother-in-law, "There is a piece of the Union Jack I put up at the South Pole in my private kit bag... send a small piece to the King and a small piece to Queen Alexandra.... A third piece is in the RIN Officers' Mess in Bombay, with the cups and spoons which Bowers carried with him on his journey, and which were found by his dead body in his last camp."

The cups and spoons of Lieutenant Bowers along with the piece of the Union Jack are now on display at the Naval Museum at Bombay. By sheer coincidence, the first Indian to set foot on Antarctica was also a naval officer, Lieutenant Ram Charan, an officer of the Navy's Education branch and a specialist in meteorology, who accompanied an Australian expedition to the South Pole in 1960. Unfortunately, he died in a road accident in New Delhi in 1961. The bulk of the personnel who took part in the first Indian expedition to Antarctica, Expedition Gangotri, in 1981 were also from the Indian Navy. Indian Navy also participated in the subsequent expeditions launched in 1982, 1983 and 1984.

The indomitable spirit of adventure of personnel of the Indian Navy has taken the Naval Ensign not only to the frozen continent of Antarctica but also to the top of the world's tallest mountain, the Everest. The intrepid and renowned mountaineer of the Indian Navy, Instructor Lieutenant Commander Manmohan Singh Kohli (later rose to the rank of Captain, Indian Navy) has had the distinction of not only climbing to the highest altitude without oxygen but also of putting nine men atop the peak and hoisting the Naval Ensign on it for the first time in its history.

Discipline Bill of Indian Navy

With the reconstitution of the RIM as a combatant force in 1928, the White Ensign was hoisted for the first time in its history on November 11, 1928. The Indian Navy Discipline Bill, based on the recommendations of the Rawlinson Committee, was also taken up by the Legislative Assembly in the same year and, after six years of deliberations, the bill was passed by the Assembly and the Council of States on September 5, 1934.

When the Indian Navy Discipline Bill was presented to the Indian Legislative Assembly on February 21,1928, it was presented as a non-contentious measure, of which barely a fortnight's notice was given, as no more was thought necessary. Mr. Mackworth Young, the Army Secretary, introducing the Bill, gave a brief history of the Service and pointed out that the intention was "to enable India to enter upon the first stage of her naval development and ultimately to undertake her own naval defence." He pointed out that Indians had always been eligible as officers of the RIM, but no qualified candidates had ever applied. One-third of the vacancies would be reserved for Indians in future, provided that suitable candidates offered. (He was asked whether 'one-third' meant only one person—which in fact it did, as there were only three vacancies a year—and he replied, "There will be more than one." It is difficult to understand why he said this.) Sir Shunmugham Chetty (later became finance minister in independent India) opened the opposition with brilliant speech saying: "My reason for opposing the present motion is that, without the consent of this House, the Government of India have decided to create an Indian Navy; necessary legislation was passed by Parliament, and what we are asked to do today is simply to legislate for the discipline of this Indian Navy, which has been created without our consent and without our approval. "The principles underlying the creation of a Navy are these: firstly, who will pay; secondly, who will officer the Navy; and thirdly what will be the control of the Legislature over the Navy.... The question, who will pay is very easily answered: the taxpayer in India will pay." He then pointed out that the "one-third of the vacancies" amounted to one officer per year, and after considering this in detail, went on, "We will-therefore have a Navy which for decades together will be officered entirely by British officers; and I ask the House to consider whether they will be willing parties to the creation of Indian Navy, which, though Indians may not be technically and legally excluded, will take several years to be officered by Indians."

As regards control over the RIN, he said, "I would ask whether the people of India desire to create an Indian Navy over which their control will be exactly identical with the control which this House has over the Indian Army." At this point Mr. Jinnah (later the first Governor-General of independent Pakistan) commented, "Which means nil". "In time of emergency the Indian Navy can be taken over by the British Admiralty with the consent of the Governor-General in Council, not with the consent of the Indian Legis lature, not with the consent of the Indian people; and the Governor-General in Council is a subordinate branch of the British Government."

Sir Shunmugham then dealt with the question of control in an extremely able manner, and finished up: "Fortunately for us, we are placed in this situation now: that without the passing by the Indian Legislature of the measure that is now introduced, the Indian Navy cannot come into existence.... I am sorry to use strong words, but I would conclude by saying that I would not touch the present measure with a pair of tongs."

Many later speakers elaborated and restated the points made by Sir Shunmugham Chetty without adding anything to them; his speech, however, determined the course of the debate. Munshi Iswar Saran opposed the saddling of India with the cost of a Navy whose expansion they could not control, and ridiculed the argument that at present the Navy "was only a little one," which he said, was like the nursemaid's excuse for her bastard, in *Mr. Midshipman Easy.* Sir Henry Gidney ridiculed the one-third reservation for Indians, pointing out ironically that the next step would obviously be to apply the communal rota to the one officer a year to be recruited. In replying for Government, Mr. Mackworth Young said that if Indian candidates were forthcoming in sufficient numbers, the proportion of the intake would be increased. He pointed out that even the old RIM could be taken over by the Admiralty in times of war—without even the consent of the Governor-General in Council. He said that it was absurd to suppose that H.M. Government would want to appropriate ships from the RIN in wartime and use them in the Atlantic (how oddly that reads, twenty-two years— and one world war—after it was said!) When the Bill came up again in 1934 Sir Shunmugham Chetty was the President ("Speaker") of the House; and although the question of Indianisation was again brought up, the Bill was passed without a division, everyone giving it his blessing at the "consideration" stage.

The Royal Indian Navy thereafter came into being on October 2, 1934 with its separate Naval Headquarters at Bombay under the Flag Officer Commanding Royal Indian Navy (FOCRIN).

The Scindia Steam Navigation Company was formed in the early twenties but its maritime activities were virtually limited to coastal trade as overseas contracts granted to the Company were very few. The training ship for cadets, *SS Dufferin,* was acquired by the Indian Mercantile Marine Department in 1926 and started training cadets for the Merchant Navy. A number of small shipping companies came into being during the early thirties which managed to capture a sizable chunk of coastal trade from foreign shipping companies but compared to the volume of exports and imports, the tonnage under the Indian shipping companies was virtually negligible.

Between 1934 and 1939, the Royal Indian Navy was developed into a small and efficient naval force and by the time World War II broke out, the RIN fleet comprised five sloops, a survey vessel, a patrol ship, a depot ship and a large number of small craft. Recommendations were made in 1939 for assigning greater responsibility for the naval defence of India to the RIN by the Chatfield Committee. In order to enable the RIN to carry out these duties, modernisation of the Service was also recommended.

The Chatfield Committee recommendations made in 1939 were based mainly on the proposals put forward by the RIN for the expansion of the Service which was to be completed in five years. The main features of the Committee's recommendations were the construction of four Bittern class escort minesweepers, development of depots and training establishments and acquisition of local naval defence equipment. Even though the recommendations were to be implemented over a period of five years, the outbreak of the War in 1939, greatly hastened the process of expansion. The annual sub vention of £100,000 to be paid to the British Government along with miscellaneous other charges ranging between £15,000 and £20,000 was also discontinued on the condition that it would be utilised towards expanding the RIN fleet and maintaining a squadron of six escort vessels which would, besides assisting the Royal Navy, carry out local naval defence duties.

Formation of reserves for the RIN was also resorted to before the War. The Royal Indian Naval Reserve (RINR) comprised serving officers of the Indian Mercantile Marine and had two branches, Executive and Accountant, to which the Engineering branch was also added at the outbreak of the War. The Royal Indian Navy Volunteer Reserve (RINVR) was constituted by inducting qualified members of the general public as commissioned officers and giving them six months intensive training at Bombay. This was also done for sailors, called ratings at that time. In addition to the regular service ratings, special service ratings were recruited who served for five years before being transferred to the Fleet Reserve for 10 years. These ratings belonged to the cadre of Royal Indian Fleet Reserve (RIFR). Personnel from the merchant marine were also recruited as "Hostilities Only" ratings for service during the War. The personnel strength of the RIN on October 1, 1939 was 114 officers and 1,732 ratings with only 16 officers manning the Naval Headquarters which was located inside the Naval Dockyard at Bombay."

When World War II broke out, the Royal Navy undertook the task of building, commissioning and wording up fast sea-going motorboats for coastal patrol and corvettes and minesweepers which were suitably armed and equipped for carrying out anti-submarine and escort duties in the waters around India. Magnetic mines posed a major threat to the merchant marine at that time and hence 263 merchant and naval ships were fitted with degaus sing cables made in India by June 1941. The first Basset class trawler, *HMIS Travancore,* was built at Calcutta and commissioned into the RIN in July 1941 and was followed by five more within a year and another six soon thereafter. The first Bangor class minesweeper built in India joined the RIN in 1943. Six sloops built in Great Britain and named after Indian rivers, Jumna, Sutlej, Cauvery, Kistna, Godavarl and Narbada, also joined the RIN to reinforce its fleet. In order to maintain effective control over the operational and organisational aspects of the RIN at Bombay, the FOCRIN could pay only occasional visits to New Delhi, the focal point of command and control: This led to considerable delay in obtaining New Delhi's clearance on important matters as the bulk of the exchanges between the capital and Bombay had to be by correspondence or by signal. A Naval Liaison Officer was positioned at New Delhi in October 1939 to reduce the time taken in processing important papers but even this proved unsatisfactory and hence the Naval Headquarters was transferred from Bombay to New Delhi in March 1941.

At the time of the outbreak of the War, all training establishments of the RIN were concentrated inside the RIN Dockyard, Bombay. These were the Seamanship School, the Signal School, the Gunnery School, the Mechanical Training Establishment, the Boys Training Establishment and the Antisubmarine School. There were no schools for training in torpedo, radar and electrical disciplines. There were also no facilities for training officers who were perforce deputed to the Royal Naval Establishments in the United Kingdom for basic and advanced training in all disciplines.

As the size of the RIN fleet increased and the tasks assigned to it multiplied, several new naval establishments came up at Jamnagar, Cochin, Mandapam, Madras, Coconada (Kakinada), Vishakhapatnam and Calcutta. To cope with the increased intake of sailors and requirements of equipping the fleet, the existing naval bases at Karachi and Bombay were expanded and modernised. The extremely rapid growth of the RIN in terms of the strength of the fleet and personnel posed grave problems of training personnel in the specialist and general tasks. For example, by June 1940 when Italy jumped into the fray, the RIN had doubled its strength and by 1942 it had expanded to nearly six times its pre-war strength.

The naval establishments also multiplied fast. To augment training boys at *HMIS Dalhousie* at Bombay, *HMIS Bahadur* was commissioned at Karachi. In addition, for training officers and ratings, two more establishments, *HMIS Himalaya,* the gunnery training establishment, and *HMIS Chamak,* the radar training establishment, where commissioned at Karachi. The other naval bases that came up about this time were *HMIS Shivaji,* the mechanical training establishment at Lonavla, *HMIS Akbar,* ratings'training establishment at Thane, *HMIS Talwar,* the Signal School at Bombay, and a mechanical training establishment at Pilani. Merchant ships were armed for defence At Karachi, Bombay and Calcutta and inspection organisations were set up at Vishakhapatnam, Madras and Cochin.

MERCHANT MARINE IN RIN

In order to make up for the wartime losses of the merchant marine, the need was felt for a major merchant shipbuilding yard and accordingly a site was located at Vishakhapatnam by the Scindia Steam Navigation Company but the first major ship, a freighter, could only be launched well after the War in 1948. The problem created by the inadequate supply of stores and supplies to the Allied forces owing to the United Kingdom's inability to send supplies in sufficient quantities was solved by the Indian mercantile marine who shouldered the responsibility of delivering stores to places as far as Malta and Hqngkong. Under the overall command of the Commander-in-Chief, East Indies, sloops of the Royal Indian Navy took part in the operations in the Red Sea, Gulf of Aden and the Persian Gulf in 1940. *HMIS Jumna* and *HMIS Sutlej* took part in the Battle of the Atlantic in 1941. In the same year, reoccupation of Berbera in the Gulf of Aden was made possible by the first combined operations, i.e. amphibious operations, by the Indian Army and the Royal Indian Navy. The RIN also played a vital role during the advance of the Allied Forces in Sudan. While *HMIS Clive* softened up the area between Port Sudan and Massawa with her armament and *HMIS Hindustan, Indus, Parvatiand Ratnagiri* led the attack, the minesweepers entered Massawa and annexed the port from the Italians.

HMIS Lawrence and *Lilavati* earned distinction in the operations in the Persian Gulf and two officers of the RIN were awarded the distinguished Service Cross. These were Lieutenant N. Krishnan for his act of gallantry while boarding and overpowering the crew of an armed tug belonging to the Axis during Operation Countenance for the capture of Abadan in 1941 and Engineer Lieutenant D. Shankar (later rose to the rank of Rear Admiral and became the Controller General of Defence Production) who, while boarding an Italian vessel, *Cabote,* during the Persian Gulf operation in the same year, went through the blazing bridge-deck at considerable risk to his life and captured the crew. One of the ships built by Australia during the War for the RIN was *HMIS Bengal* (733 tons), a Bathurst Class minesweeper. On November 5, 1942, she sailed from Fremantle as escort to *M.V. Ondina,* a Dutch tanker on passage to Diego Garcia. At 1145 hours on November 11, 1942, she sighted a vessel, about eight miles off, coming straight towards her. The newcomer could not be identified but, in any case, to adopt the safer course, Bengal sounded her action alarm, and the ship's company closed up at "Action Stations". *Bengal* altered course to starboard, and instructed the tanker to take station on her starboard beam. At this time, another ship appeared over the horizon, coming up at *Bengal's* port bow. Both ships were larger than *Bengal,* whose armament comprised one 12-pounder gun and a few close-range, anti-aircraft guns. By this time both the ships had been identified as Japanese. The *Ondina* was, therefore, instructed to act independently and to rendezvous at a certain position the following day.

Bengal then increased to full speed, and turned to engage the first raider. She hoped, in this way, to allow the tanker time enough to get away, but the Master of *Ondina* would not leave her to face the two raiders alone. Instead, with his four-inch gunmounted aft, he returned the fire. The action that followed is best described in the words of the Commanding Officer Lieutenant Commander W.J. Wilson, RINR: "The raider came up very fast and *Bengal* steamed straight ahead at her. The raider also increased speed, and opened fire at about 3500 yards with her forward guns. We retaliated, and hit first. At 3000 yards we must have hit the raider in the magazine because a great sheet of flame shot up astern, almost mast high. We then closed the range, and fought the action at about 2500 yards. The second Japanese raider never came closer than 8000 yards. Both fired at us continuously. The first ship we engaged carried on firing until, in a great sheet of flame, she blew up and sank. I estimate she fired over 200 rounds at us. At 1246 hours our ammunition was running short. We had very few rounds left, and our vessel was damaged fore and aft. The* ship that we sank was a large edition of the Kunikawa Maru class and was of approximately 10,000 tons. The second raider was slightly smaller, her tonnage being 8000. They were both firing 4-inch gun broadsides, and these appeared to be from 5.5 inch guns. We drew the enemy's fire, and acted as a screen, as long as possible, to allow the tanker to escape.

"The encounter lasted for over two hours, but really the first three minutes decided the issue. While shells were bursting all round them, the crew of, *Bengal kept* on firing one salvo after another. The sixth salvo made a direct hit on the first raider for, following a terrific explosion, flames leapt high in the air from her. This greatly enthused the RIN crew, we kept on firing steadily. By that time, the second raider had come within range, and opened fire. Within a quarter of an hour of action, a fire broke out in *Bengal's* officers baggage room. She had also been damaged fore and aft, and had only five rounds of high explosives remaining. The Commanding Officer accordingly decided to break off the engagement, and started to make smoke—but not before the first raider had gone down by the stern and sunk. "The *Ondina* had then opened the range at about seven miles, but the-second raider began to chase her and fire repeatedly. The tanker's ammunition was soon expended, and her Master, Captain H. Horsman was killed on the bridge. (He was posthumously awarded the Militair Willems Order-4-Dutch V.C.—by Queen Wilhelmina of the Netherlands.) The *Ondina* was then abandoned, whereupon the raider torpedoed her twice. The raider also machine-gunned the boat, killing the chief engineer and some of the Chinese crew. When the raider left the scene, volunteers boarded the vessel and, with some difficulty, got her under way. She eventually reached Fremantle, where she had been given up for lost.

"It was a matter of surprise, even to the ship's company, that the *Bengal* emerged from this action without serious damage. They had never been in action before, but when 'Action Stations' where sounded, everyone was perfectly calm, firm and disciplined, and all hands were, in fact, anxious to have a shot at the raider. The Captain's example was highly inspiring, and the tribute he paid to his men was fully deserved. He said, 'No praise is great enough for their magnificent conduct in face of the greatest danger. 'The FOCRIN Vice-Admiral Sir Herbert Fitzherbert spoke much in the same strain when in his message he said, 'We are all proud of you.' "When *Bengal* reached Colombo, every ship in harbour gave her an official and spontaneous reception. A band played on the jetty, and as the ship's company descended the gangway of their ship, they were greeted with loud cheers. The acme of the crew's joy however, was when they steamed into Bombay. While still outside the harbour, RIN ships which happened to be in the vicinity, saluted them. The 75 officers and men received a public reception, and were honoured at a lunch in the Sir Cowasji Jehangir Hall.

"Besides the Commanding Officer of the ship, Lieutenant Commander W.J. Wilson, RINR, who was awarded the Distinguished Service Order, two Indian ratings were also decorated. Leading Seaman Ismail Mohammed, one of the 12-pounder gun's crew, was awarded the Indian Distinguished Service Medal for gallantry and devotion to duty. Petty Officer Mohammed Ibrahim, captain of the 12-pounder gun, was awarded the Indian Order of Merit Second Class for setting an excellent example of steadiness and resolution and using his weapon to the very best advantage even after the *Bengal* had been hit by enemy gun fire."

The writer well remembers decyphering the signals from *Bengal* in the Navy Office in Calcutta that night and passing the news to the then Naval Officer-in-Charge, Calcutta, Captain L. Sanderson, C.I.E., RIN.

Operating from Chittagong and Koronge Island, ships of the RIN carried ^put sustained attacks on the Arakan Coast of Burma. They also provided close support to troops that had been landed by the RIN landing craft for driving the Japanese away from the area. Despite its success in operations in various theatres of war around the globe, the losses suffered by the RIN were negligible and when VJ Day arrived, ships of the RIN and their men were still raring to go. Nix ships of the RIN were lost during the War: *HMIS Pathan* (Escort Patrol Ship) 23rd June, 1940 off Bombay by explosion; *HMIS Parvati* (Auxiliary) 30th April, 1941 mined off Massawa; *HMIS Parbhavati* (Auxiliary) 8th December, 1941 off *Goa; HMIS Sophie Marie* (Auxiliary) 1st March, 1942 mined in Macpherson Strait; *HMIS Indus* (Sloop) 6th April, 1942 air attack at Akyab; and *HMIS Lady Craddock* (Auxiliary) 16th October, 1942 Cyclone in river Hooghly. ^The end to World War II was hastened by the nuclear holocaust perpetrated on the innocent residents of Hiroshima and Nagasaki in Japan and on August 15, 1945, Emperor Hirohito surrendered. At {he time of cessation of hostilities, the RIN fleet comprised seven sloops, four frigates, four corvettes, 14 minesweepers, 16 trawlers, two depot ships, 30 auxiliary vessels, 150 landing craft of various types, 200 harbour craft, several motor launches and harbour defence motor launches and over 25,000 officers and men. As the guns fell silent on August 15, 1945, exactly two years before we were to gain Independence, the stage was set for carrying out the post-war tasks, such as sanitising—sweeping large areas for mines and other sunken hazards in and around Indian waters; preventing any further repetition of the traumatic experience; decommissioning or assigning peace-time roles to a large number of ships and craft with the RIN which had been rendered redundant and refurbishing the Navy to meet the post-World War II requirements.

The 1939-45 global conflict also brought in the growing realisation of the after-effects of man's merciless and persistent assault on ecology which began with the Industrial Revolution and which has assumed monstrous proportions today, the rapidly dwindling energy, food and mineral resources of the earth and the vast potential of the living and mineral wealth in the oceans, on the ocean bed and below the ocean bed.

International rivalry over sharing the marine resources considerably delayed the adoption and coming into force of the Law of Sea Convention. This is likely to inexorably shift the theatres of future tensions from land to sea. The clouds of portent are already discernible over the distant horizon and how far man will succeed in striking a happy balance between his increasing needs and available resources without affecting ecology, only the future can tell.

INDIA'S MARITIME HERITAGE

UNLIKE the Atlantic and Pacific Oceans, the Indian Ocean is indented by the land mass of India, which lies in its centre. India has a vast coast-line running to nearly 3,500 miles. On its west coast is the Arabian Sea which stretches up to the Red Sea and is joined to the Persian Gulf. On the eastern side, the Bay of Bengal is connected with the South China Sea through the Straits of Malacca.

The Indian Ocean is a vast frontage facing India and is its natural highway. The centre of gravity of the Indian Ocean thus rests on the vast continental space of India. Geographically India occupies a strategic position in southeast Asia. However, the coast-line does not provide many harbours, and has only few good harbours. The chief of them before 1939 were Bombay, Calcutta, Cochin, Madras and Vizagapatam.

MARITIME ADVANCE FROM THE 3RD CENTURY B.C. TO THE 12TH CENTURY A.D.

This geographical position of India necessarily involved the maintenance of a navy, the history of which goes back to ancient times. From the time of the Mauryas we have definite information on shipbuilding and construction of men-of-war. Megasthenes informs us that the shipbuilders of India were salaried public servants and that the ships were built in the royal shipyards. The development of national shipping led to the creation and organisation of a Board of Admiralty (Nav Parishad) as one of the six Boards which made up the War Office of Emperor Chandragupta. In the time of his grandson Asoka, India was brought into systematic connection with the Greek kingdoms of Syria, Egypt, Cyrene, Macedonia and Epirus; and she became, through the efforts of the Emperor, the missionaries and the merchants, not only a spiritual centre but also a throbbing commercial spot of the Old World. Historian Smith observes: "When we remember Asoka's relations with Ceylon and even more distant powers, we may credit him with a sea-going fleet as well as an army."

In South India foreign trade and intercourse had developed under the Andhras with Rome between 200 B.C. to A.D. 250. R. Sewell, describes it thus: "The Andhra period seems to have been one of considerable prosperity. There was trade both overland and by sea; with Western Asia, Greece, Rome and Egypt as well as with China and the East. Embassies are said to have been sent from South India to Rome. Indian elephants were used for Syrian warfare. Pliny mentions the vast quantities of species that found its way every year from Rome to India and in this he is confirmed by the author of the 'Periplus'. Roman coins have been found in profusion in the Peninsula and especially in the south. In A.D. 68 a number of Jews, fleeing from Roman persecution, seem to have taken refuge among the friendly coast-people of South India, and to have settled in Malabar." South India also witnessed a spurt in naval activities again under the strong rule of the Cholas (985-1054 A.D.). These kings on the Coromandal Coast maintained a permanent naval fleet. The great Chola emperors Rajaraja I and his son Rajendra I pressed into service strong armadas for the extension of their power. The Chola power reached its apogee during the reign of Rajendra I. He invaded Ceylon and completed the conquest of the island begun by his father. He sent a large naval expedition against the kingdom of Sri Vijaya, a powerful maritime state which then held sway over the Malayan peninsula, Java, Sumatra and the neighbouring islands and controlled the sea routes from India to China. "Till the end of the tenth century, that is, for a period of nearly 500 years, the Sri Vijaya kings were the Lords of the Ocean. But in 1007 the Chola Emperor Rajendra fitted out a powerful navy and challenged the might of Sri Vijaya. He not only defeated the opposing navy, but captured Kedah and established the Chola power on the Malay Peninsula."

From 1498 to 1612

In later centuries, however, the naval superiority of Indian States seems to have declined, so that when the Portuguese appeared in the Indian Ocean, their progress could not be checked. Though from 1498 we have an unbroken record of naval and maritime history, the year marked the beginning of India's eventual eclipse from the naval and maritime field. When Vasco da Gama succeeded in discovering the oceanic route to India, he took a series of measures to oust the Indian sea power and commerce. The Portuguese claimed the monopoly of maritime trade for the Portuguese Crown and attacked vessels plying without Portuguese permits. These piratical activities and the attendant atrocities on the coastal towns and commercial communities by the Portuguese were vigorously opposed by the rulers of the Malabar Coast. Three naval battles were fought against the Portuguese—the first off Cochin in 1503, the second off Chaul in 1508 and the third off Diu in 1509. None of these was decisive and the supremacy of the sea slowly passed on to the Portuguese.

Though the Portuguese had thus established a kind of supremacy in the Indian Ocean, it was not undisputed. For well over 90 years the Zamorin's fleet under the family of Calicut Admirals known to history as Ali Marrakkars, with their headquarters and naval station at Ponnani, a naturally strong harbour to the south of Calicut, held its own in the home waters of Calicut. The most famous name in the house of Marrakkars is that of Kunjali Marrakkar II. He sank innumerable Portuguese ships (no less than 50 ships in one year) and his very name was a terror to them. But Mohommed Kunjali Marrakkar (Kunjali HI) the hero of a thousand fights and the last of the Indian 'sea-dogs' rebelled against the Zamorin of Calicut. The Portuguese benefited from this quarrel and succeeded in exterminating the famous Marrakkars. The exploits of these gallant Indian sea-dogs not only restricted the Portuguese power but also put an end to their inroads on the sub-continent.

Akbar, the Great Mughal, organised the Navy on sound principles. His Admiralty had four functions—supply of ships and boats, drafting of efficient seamen, watching of rivers and lastly the imposition and collection of port duties. The Mughal fleet was stationed at Dacca and its duty was to protect the Bengal coast from the Magh and Feringi pirates.

The Mughal Navy during the time of Aurangzeb was in a good standard of efficiency. According to Dr. Fryer, Aurangzeb had at Surat four great ships always in pay to carry pilgrims to Mecca free of cost. Some of the larger Indian ships at Surat like Fulteh Mahmood and Aurangzeb's own ship *Gunj Suwaie* fell a prey to a notorious English pirate called Every.

Running apace with the naval activity of Aurangzeb was the coming into its own of the Maratha Navy under Shivaji who believed in the doctrine of *'Jalamaiva Tasya, Balamaiva Tasya'* (whoever is powerful on sea is all powerful) and organised his Navy on sound lines. His genius was reflected in the creation of a navy, and the formation of a formidable fleet of 700 ships of various sizes. He was ably assisted in this task by Tukoji Angre and Daulat Khan. The whole of Konkan was brought under his sway with the help of his navy. The entire coast-line from Mandvi to Malabar was fortified and naval docks were built at several places. After the death of Shivaji and Tukoji, the latter's son Kanhoji Angre assumed charge of the Maratha navy. He reorganised and modernised it by the construction of several 300-ton ships with 30 to 40 guns. He strengthened his navy to such an extent that it could meet the attacks of the Portuguese and the English. His sudden death in 1729 however led to the decline of the Maratha navy. In the subsequent period, no indigenous power had any navy worth the name and whatever was left was extinguished by the emergence of the English East India Company as the supreme political authority in the country. Henceforth the history of Indian navy is the story of the maritime enterprises of the East India Company and of the organisation of the Indian Marine as the local instrument of sea power.

INDIAN NAVY FROM 1612-1939

Birth of the Modern Indian Navy

The English East India Company was founded in 1600 and the first squadron of ships, belonging to her arrived in India on 5 September 1612. Two months later the English forced the Portuguese to a battle off Surat and thereafter they set up their first factory at Surat. Captain Best of the John Company's first squadron cruised the west coast for three months and sailed off to Sumatra. With his departure, the Indian Marine was formally established. The Company obtained permission to open new factories, and a fleet of small craft known as 'grabs' and 'galivats' was formed to protect their commerce from the Portuguese and the pirates of the West Coast.

The grabs were vessels of about 300 tons, of shallow draught mounting up six 9-to-12-pounder guns. The galivats were craft of about 70 tons and usually carried about half a dozen 2-to-4 pounders. These craft were officered by volunteers from the Company's ships and their crews consisted mainly of Indian fishermen from the Konkan coast. From the early years of the East India Company, this force formed the nucleus of the Indian Marine, the larger ships coming out and returning to England as the Company deemed fit.

The East India Company had to fight battles with the Portuguese before getting a foothold on the country. In the second and third battles of Swally off Surat in 1614 and 1630 respectively, the Portuguese were overpowered by the English which enabled them to open more trading settlements in the country. After the acquisition of Bombay in 1668 by the Company and the transfer of their headquarters from Surat to Bombay in 1687, the Company's trade and administration tended to increase. About this time Sir John Child, Governor of Bombay, took a hasty step in attacking the Mughal fleet (the Sidis) which resulted in the loss of the island of Bombay and the Bombay Castle (the present Indian Naval Barracks) which was later redeemed after the payment of a huge sum. When the growing Maratha Navy under Admiral Kanhoji Angre spread its tentacles throughout the West Coast, the East India Company built corvettes to convoy their ships. In 1717 a strong English fleet under the command of Commodore Burlew attacked the Maratha garrison at Gheria but had to withdraw with severe losses. The task of suppressing the Marathas became easier only after the death of Kanhoji in 1729.

The English and the French

In 1740, a new power, capable of challenging British sea power entered the Indian Ocean. From their base in Mauritius, the French sent a strong fleet to intercept the British merchantmen. La Bourdannais commanding the French fleet scored a few good victories over the British but these were short-lived. The French were finally defeated and the English had undisputed control of the sea.

Shipbuilding

Great progress was recorded in shipbuilding during the Company's time. Four pinnaces and other larger vessels including the Queen were built in 1635. Bombay was a safer harbour and the present naval dockyard was selected as shipbuilding site by Nusser-wanji Wadia, ancestor of a long line of famous Indian shipbuilders. In a little over 100 years, no less than 115 war vessels and 144 mer-chantships were built in this dockyard including 84 gun ships of a total tonnage of 2,000 for the Royal Navy.

Nineteenth century saw the defeat of the Joasmis, the capture of Aden, Rangoon and Bushire and the Company's ships changing over to steam from sail. The first ship to be fitted with a steam engine was the Hugh Lindsay of 411 tons. She sailed from Bombay and reached Suez in 21 days. A Marine Survey Department was also started during this century. It was manned completely by Navy officers. In 1863 the Navy was reorganised on a non-combatant basis and renamed 'Bombay Marine'. In 1892, the Service was renamed the 'Royal Indian Marine'.

First World War

During the first World War (1914-18) the Royal Indian Marine ships carried troops and other war materials to Egypt, Iraq and East Africa. The Royal Indian Marine ship the *Hardinge* on patrol in the Suez Canal fought a gallant action when the Turks attempted to block the canal. She was badly damaged and one of her funnels was shot away but she prevented the blocking of the Channel. The R.I.M. also played a leading role in landing troops in Mesopotamia and their small river craft did very useful work on the Euphrates and Tigris rivers. The *Morthbrook, Minto* and *Dufferin* were in the Red Sea on patrolling duty. The *Minto* called at Jaddah and brought the Haj pilgrims safely back to India.

Retrenchment

At the end of the First World War, the Royal Indian Marine reverted to its peace-time non-combatant role. After the war, when Admiral of the Fleet Lord Jellicoe was on a visit to India, the Government asked him to draw up a scheme for the reorganisation of the Marine. He made proposals which were considered too costly to be implemented. The Esher Committee which reported on the Indian Army strongly recommended the reorganisation of the Royal Indian Marine as a combatant service. In 1920, the Government of India obtained Rear Admiral Mawby from the Admiralty, to draw up, as Director of the Royal Indian Marine, suitable plans for reorganisation, but his scope was limited and his scheme was finally rejected. Following the report of the Inchcape Committee, the drive towards retrenchment converted the service into a Yacht Squadron for high officials, with hydrographic, buoyage and lighting duties paid for by the local governments. The Indian Government did not like to spend money even upon these duties if the work could be done more cheaply by private contract. The Inchcape Committee recommended the scrapping of troopships, the carrying of troops by contract, and the virtual reduction of the Marine to a Survey Department and a Dockyard. In the final result, the Marine was left with the Clive for lighting and buoying duties on the Burma coast, where she also carried out political duties; the *Lawrence* carrying out similar functions in the Persian Gulf; the *Minto* acting as the Station Ship for the Andaman and Nicobar Islands; the *Cornwallis* lying in the dockyard unconverted, and two small ships, the *Pathan* and the *Baluchi*, for local training at Bombay. The *Elphinstone*, an old sloop of the Royal Navy was used as a relief ship until her loss in 1926. In this way, lack of appreciation by the Government of the necessity of building up a body of experienced officers and men by constant peacetime training and operations, was responsible for practically throwing away the sound body of experienced seamen ready at India's hand at the close of the last war, upon which a sound and flexible system capable of rapid expansion in an emergency might have been built. This was an index of official indifference to the development of an Indian navy and may be explained only by their complete dependence on the Royal Navy to guard the oceanic highway and the coast-line of India. The Royal Navy continued to guard the coast-line of India for which a sum of £100,000 was paid annually. It was not anticipated that the Royal Navy might some day be left alone to contend with the German and Italian fleets and to guard the seas of the world at the same time. It was also not foreseen that a war would threaten India from the east.

Rawlinson Committee

Following the rejection of his scheme of reorganisation, Rear-Admiral Mawby resigned his appointment as Director of the Royal Indian Marine and returned to the United Kingdom, where he registered a strong protest. Subsequent to this, in 1925, a Departmental Committee was appointed by the Government of India with Lord Rawlinson, the Minister of Defence and Member of Council in charge of the Defence portfolio, as its chairman, with the purpose of submitting a scheme for the reorganisation of the Service as a combatant force. The scheme put forward by the Committee was for (i) reorganisation of the Service as a purely combatant force with the title of the Royal Indian Navy, (ii) an initial strength of four armed sloops or escort vessels, two patrol vessels, four mine-sweeping trawlers, two surveying ships and a depot ship and (iii) the whole to be commanded at first by a Rear-Admiral of the Royal Navy on the active list. This was accepted by the Indian and the British Governments and an Act was passed through both Houses of Parliament to permit India to have a navy.

Recovery

The Royal Indian Marine was restored to combatant standing in 1928, but the full recommendations of the Rawlinson Committee could not be complete without the enactment of a new Indian Naval Discipline Act. Even then, the financial administration of the Royal Indian Marine left much to be desired. Proposals were required to be submitted to the Secretary of the Defence Department in the Government of India for inclusion of figures in the general Defence Estimates. These were submitted to a Committee consisting of the Commander-in-Chief in India and his Principal Staff Officers, but there was no Naval personnel among these or any representative of the Royal Indian Marine. The sum at the disposal of the Defence Department, moreover, was barely sufficient for the defence requirements, with the result that any proposals from the Royal

Indian Marine had to be considered not merely from the point of naval defence but in the light of the money available for the total defence of India in which the army played a major role at the time. Recruitment to the Royal Indian Marine at this stage was open both to the Indians and the British but, in practice, very few Indian officers joined the service. The first Indian officer to enter the Naval service was Engineer Sub-Lieutenant D. N. Mukerji, R.I.N. on 6 January 1923. The new Indian Naval Discipline Act was introduced as a Bill in February 1928, but failed by one vote to pass the Assembly. In February 1934, the Bill was introduced again with a few minor amendments, and was finally passed in August 1934 both by the Assembly and the Council of State.

On 2 October 1934 at Bombay, the Royal Indian Marine ceased to exist and the Royal Indian Navy was inaugurated. It was during this stage that the Service began to assume a form with Naval Headquarters at Bombay, under Flag Officer Commanding Royal Indian Navy (FOCRIN) and on paper the Royal Indian Naval Reserve (R.I.N.R.), the Royal Indian Naval Volunteer Reserve (R.I.N.V.R.), the Royal Indian Fleet Reserve (R.I.F.R.), Special Service and 'Hostilities Only' ratings and establishments at the outports. As will be seen in this narrative, progress in respect of various plans was painfully slow, and the outbreak of war found the Royal Indian Navy inadequate to meet the situation.

STEADY GROWTH OF THE R.I.N. BETWEEN 1934-1939

During the five years before the outbreak of the Second World War, the Royal Indian Navy was built up into a small but efficient combatant naval force. By 1939, it comprised five sloops, a survey vessel, a patrol ship, a depot ship and numerous small craft. The Chatfield Committee in February 1939 made far-reaching recommendations for taking over increased responsibility for the naval defence of India by the Royal Indian Navy and for her modernisation. Shortly before the outbreak of war, the navy began to establish reserves. The Royal Indian Naval Reserve was made up of serving officers of the Indian Mercantile Marine. The Royal Indian Naval Volunteer Reserve originally had two branches—Executive and Accountant. An Engineering Branch was added on the outbreak of war. R.I.N.V.R. officers were recruited from the general public and were given intensive training for six months at Bombay.

4

Marine Commandos Force

The Marine Commando Force (MCF) is a special forces unit, that was created by the Indian Navy in 1987. For many years, the Indian Navy wanted to establish an elite force for special maritime operations. Prior to this, Navy divers trained in explosive ordnance disposal and Army units were often assigned for maritime exercises. In 1983, the 340th Army Independent Brigade, which had a force of three infantry battalions at Trivandrum, was raised as a special maritime unit. They were assault operations in which both airborne and maritime forces participated. Since then, the Indian Navy has conducted various exercises as a show of force, notably in 1984 in the Andaman Islands and in 1986 off Goa.

In April 1986, the Indian Naval Staff created a plan for a special force which would be able to conduct recon, raids and even counter-terrorist operations in a maritime environment. Three Naval Officers were sent for training with the US Navy SEALS and further training was conducted with British Special Forces. These three Naval Officers formed the first nucleus of the Indian Marine Special Force (IMSF) which was formally raised in February 1987. In 1991, the IMSF had its name changed to the Marine Commando Force (MCF), but they are more familiarly known as MARCOS (Marine Commandos).

Operations

The IMSF first went into action a few months after its raising, in Sri Lanka, to fight against the LTTE (Liberation of Tamil Tigers Eelan). During Operation Pawan, a single battalion of the 340th Army Independent Brigade left the Naval base of Vizag for Jaffna and Batticaloa on board landing ships, together with a detachment of the IMSF which was to provide the beach reconnaissance party.

As one of the first IPKF units to be deployed, the 340th Brigade served until operations in the Tricomalee area were complete. Beside leading the beach landings, the IMSF also provided security patrols along the coastal road, west of Jaffna, until the Army's 41st Brigade was able to take charge. On 21 October 1987, a Indian Navy force conducted a successful amphibious raid against a LTTE base at Guru Nagar.

Then in November 1988, mercenaries of the People's Liberation Organization of Tamil Eelan (PLOTE), a party used by the India to counter the LTTE, attempted a coup in the Maldives. The Indian Armed Forces quickly began an operation to re-establish the former government. Under the codename Operation Cactus, Indian paratroopers on 04 November 1988, swarmed on the capital. However 46 mercenaries with 27 hostages, including the Maldivian Minister of Education, managed to escape on board a merchant ship.

The next day the merchant ship was detected by an Il-38 *May* MR aircraft and was then tracked by a Tu-142M *Bear*-F, another maritime recon aircraft, until two Indian Navy vessels were able to capture the absconding ship. Two Sea King Mk.42 helicopters, from the one of the naval vessels, dropped depth charges to deter evasion. Finally on the morning of 06 November 1988, IMSF commandos boarded the vessel and took control without any resistance from the mercenaries.

MARCOS is currently very active in Jammu & Kashmir as part of the army's counter-terrorist efforts. Their main task is to control the infiltration of terrorists from Pakistan to Jammu & Kashmir through Jhelum River and Wullar, a 65 sq. km freshwater lake. Clad in wet suits or BDUs and riding on inflatable raiding craft, they interdict arms supplies and fresh militants who are crossing over. Some MARCOS personnel have been seconded to Army special forces units conducting CT operations in the area. They operate similar to the Israeli Mistaravim units by sporting beards and wearing the *firan* (Kashmiri suit), thus making them indistinguishable from the locals. The unit has gained a fearsome reputation among nervous terrorists and are variously referred to as the *Dadiwali Fauj* (Bearded Army) since MARCOS are the only non-Sikh personnel allowed to grow them, *Jal Murgi* (Water Hens) for the speed in which they assault from the water and *Magarmach* (Crocodiles) for their amphibious capability.

Training

MARCOS trainees have to complete a two-year course, the first phase of which lasts one month, in which they undergo many rigorous physical tests of which only 50% pass. Then for the next nine months, they are taught how to use different types of weapons, conduct special warfare techniques and how to gather intelligence from the enemy. MARCOS also conducts operational reconnaissance training which includes a variety of external environments; beach, coastal, riverine and jungle. This part of training is conducted in sync with other Indian special forces at the Combined Commando School at Sirsawa. They also have to undergo a parachute training course and a diving course at Agra and Cochin.

Once trainees have completed their first nine months of these rigorous tests, they join groups-on a probational basis-where additional specialized training is carried out. This combat ready qualification takes another year. Most of the training deals with counter-terrorist operations, such as protecting oil platforms off Mumbai and also with anti-hijacking/piracy operations. All MARCOS personnel are static line parachute qualified and a number are freefall qualified (HALO/HAHO). MARCOS is one of only a handful of units in the world that is capable of para-dropping into the sea with full combat load and equipment. By the end of two years, only 10%-25% of the candidates remain. As with other Indian Special Forces units, all MCF personnel attend the four week high-altitude commando course run by the Parvat Ghatak School in Tawang, Arunachal Pradesh.

THE MARCOS TODAY

The strength of the unit is a closely guarded secret, however sources say that the number could be close to 2000 personnel, in 10 groups of 200 personnel each. Currently there are three main groups detached to the three naval commands; Mumbai (West), Cochin (South) and Vizag (East). INS *Abhimanyu*, in Mumbai, is where most of the specialised training is now done. The unit's quick rise has changed the unit's role-it was intended to be dedicated to special maritime operations, but a considerable part of the MARCOS is doubling as marine infantry, assigned to the 340th Brigade, with the usual flexibility of commando forces.

That means that they have the capability of conducting swift amphibious raids and co-operating with Indian airborne units, in joint assault operations. Each of the three main groups have smaller units within them known as the Quick Reaction Section (QRS), which is the size of a large platoon. They are given the task of counter-terrorism and specialized warfare. Unlike standard MARCOS units, which are armed with weapons like the 7.62mm assault rifle and the Sterling Mk.4 sub-machine gun, the QRS use AK-47 assault rifles and MP-5 sub-machine guns which are more suited to close-quarter engagements. Silenced pistols or crossbows with cyanide tipped, fibreglass arrows are used extensively for silent killing.

MARCOS training is far more rigorous, better than any standard Indian Army unit and even better than their Western counterparts, who are only given the task of amphibious assault. Although all MARCOS members are qualified parachutists and even undergo a combat divers course (which is not a common practice in other commando forces), only a few manage to complete the free-fall (HALO) parachute training and it is these few that are selected for operations with Cosmos CE-2F/X100 two-man subs. When the unit's role was expanded to include attacks on harbour facilities and the sabotage of enemy ships, the Indian Navy chose the Italian Cosmos CE-2F/X100 and eleven vehicles were bought in 1990. It has a length of 7 meters, a weight of 2100kg, and a maximum underwater combat range of 25 nautical miles. It carries two operators and is fitted with a forward compartment for carrying special equipment like heavy explosive charges or limpet anti-ship mines.

For the amphibious assault role, the Indian Navy relies on a small fleet based at Vizag. Two new 5600+ ton landing vessels of the Magar Class offer a good transport capability, thanks to the four Landing Craft Vehicle Personnel (LCVP) on davits, the beaching capability and a stern helicopter platform with hangar. Although locally built, the Indian Navy's original plan for eight of the class seem to have been shelved because of budgetary constraints. Eight smaller landing ships of the Polnochny Class are scarcely operational for lack of spare parts; they are 10 to 20 years old. The last four vessels support a small helicopter platform. Seven 500-ton landing craft utility (LCU), locally built between 1978-1987, are also in service.

The Indian Navy also shows great interest in air-cushion craft and a few are on order for fast, short-range assault operations. Although most of the naval inventory is of Russian origin and the Russians are the largest operator of air-cushion craft, the new hovercrafts are being procured in the West. The MARCOS is supported also by six Sea King Mk.42C and a few HAL Chetak helicopters. Because of the lack of midget submarines, whose delivery was denied by the Italian authorities, the Cosmos are transported close to the target on the back of parent submarines, most probably on Foxtrot Class submarines. The CE-2F/X100 can withstand a transit depth of 100 metres. Also surface ships like, surface combatants or naval auxiliaries, can be used for delivering these crafts, although with less discretion.

Future of Marine

The presence of a significant marine component within the Indian Navy fits very well with the declared intention of expanding the role of the fleet to establish a credible blue-water intervention force. An effective, yet dimensionally limited, capability of power projection is clearly available already and is coupled with a reasonable capability to conduct covert operations and specialized warfare. The armed forces have demonstrated an amazing quick-reaction capability and the willingness to establish an area of exclusive interest well beyond India's borders. That makes the Marine Commando Force (MCF) a flexible force for facing peace-time contingencies and making effective the intentions expressed by India's policymakers.

ARMY AND NAVY PLAN TO SET UP A MARINE BRIGADE

The navy and army have sent a proposal to the government seeking permission to transport a 5,000-strong armed infantry and special forces troops, tanks and weapons – an independent brigade group (IBG) – on foreign shores for active operations. This capability has both been controversial and strategically provocative. It has been learnt that after years of consultations, the army and navy have finally started seeing eye to eye on the modalities required to incrementally build up the capability to deliver a full brigade-strength contingent of troops – including two special forces units– with arms, ammunition, vehicles and weapons outside the Indian mainland.

"The need to move forces is in keeping with the expanded security focus on India's island territories and the ability to deliver forces expeditiously for humanitarian relief operations," navy spokesperson Commander PVS Satish said.

While the financial implications of such a capability are being worked out, they will involve integrated expenditure on larger amphibious assault vessels, equipment and joint training. The army has an IBG, the 340 Independent Infantry Brigade under Jodhpur-based 12 Corps, for amphibious assault operations. It re-raised the 91 Infantry Brigade early last year for amphibious warfare.

But the navy currently only has the capacity to transport a little less than two battalions on expeditionary missions. The move now is to crank up that capacity more than twice over for a full IBG. Former navy chief Admiral Arun Prakash said it was absolutely essential that the navy built up the capacity to transport a brigade-sized group across the seas. "We have 1,200 island territories. We have energy investments worth thousands of crores far from our shores. We have huge diaspora in the Middle East. If there was a Kargil-like situation on any of our island territories, we would need adequate boots on the ground for combat. There are also other liabilities such as piracy and potential hostage situations.

Being able to transport a couple of battalions isn't nearly enough," he said. Sources said the process to obtain approval from the government began under the previous navy chief Admiral Sureesh Mehta, currently India's high commissioner to New Zealand. The case is said to have been taken up afresh in February this year by the chiefs of staff committee for consideration by the defence minister.

While formal approval is yet to come, the government has indicated it is in principle inclined to approve the proposal. The capability received a cursory mention in an official technology roadmap document published by the defence ministry last month. Vice Admiral (retd) Madanjit Singh, navy's former western commander, said: "It is a major capability that the navy is looking at and will necessarily be a joint effort in consultation with the army. Such a capability is useful for operations, humanitarian relief and rescue operations." The Centre and South Block have always been wary about discussing expeditionary capabilities, considering the implications of such operations and India's carefully nurtured image of a country with no belligerent ambitions.

While the establishment has always guised amphibious capabilities as an imperative for more efficient humanitarian relief operations, there have been several recent signs that assault and combat are very much part of the plan. On April 14, a detachment of Indian soldiers conducted a landmark joint amphibious assault exercise with US Marines off the coast of San Diego on board the US Navy's landing vessel, USS New Orleans. In February last year – five months after the South Block formalised India's first joint amphibious warfare doctrine – the three forces conducted the biggest joint landing operation of troops (a battalion of the 91 Infantry Brigade re-raised in 2009 as an amphibious brigade) on Gujarat's Madhavpur beach after departing the navy base at Karwar, south of Goa.

Leaving little to the imagination, the South Block had announced then that the exercise proved that the forces could conduct "swift and intense conflict during military operations". Apart from being in the market for four-six more large amphibious landing ships to augment the American-built INS Jalashwa inducted almost three years ago, there are other items on order that indicate the desired amphibious assault readiness.

INDIAN NAVY REQUIRES MORE MARINE COMMANDOS

The investitature ceremeony held on 11th March in the Rashtrapati Bhavan saw two Naval Marine Commandos being decorated for bravery in action in the lakes of Kashmir — one received the Vir Chakra. Speak to any one who took part in OP Pawan in Sri Lanka and they will praise the Naval Commandos. In fact the Seaking 42C Helicopters of the IN are meant for Commando action and so the Indian Navy is definitely poised for increasing its Commando strength and like all big Navies should have a larger Marine Force. There is a realisation that marine commandos can perform very daring jobs in peace and war and in case of terrorism can be used ashore also.

The Indian Navy also organised a Seminar at the India International Centre on Marine Archeology and the seminar ended with the theme of Naval Future in the Indian Ocean and the speaker was the C in C Pacific. In the fifteen year plan of the Indian

Navy to go from 135 ships to 195, there will be need for its budgets to be supported and signs are that this will be the case.

The Defence Budget of 2003–04 has been comparatively favourable to the Navy, thanks to our Finance Minister. The Krivak class frigates will shortly be commissioned and the projected induction of 'Admiral Gorshkov' along with Type 971M Akula II class nuclear powered submarines and Tupolev-22M3 'Backfire' reconnaissance bombers will propel the Indian Navy to become a major power in and around the Indian Ocean.

It is good to note the presence of an area air defence SAM (Surface to Air Missile) system on the Krivaks and the projected 'Project 17' frigates, a tradition commenced by the Dutch 'Jacob Van Heemskerk' class and French 'Cassard' class destroyer/frigates. If this year's naval budget is some indication of "financial years to follow" it appears that the 'Cinderella' of Indian Armed Forces may at last get its due recognition. However the Navy should claim substantially more funds to raise a strong Marine Force similar in structure and strength to the United Kingdom Royal Marines, for undertaking extensive amphibious operations on enemy beachheads and to undertake Special Operations, as these activities are bound to assume great significance in years to come.

At least one dedicated multipurpose assault ship capable of embarking V/STOL (Vertical/Short Take Off and Landing) strike fighters and assault helicopters/gunships is required for sustained ship to shore offensive operations. In this context the possible sale of Royal Navy HMS Invincible V/STOL carrier makes sense. The ship also has extensive command and control facilities to act as the command platform of any amphibious operations. The Navy will additionally need at least two LPD (Landing Platform Docks) similar to Russian 14,000 ton plus Ivan Rogov class 'Mitrofan Moskalenko' or French 11,880 ton 'Foudre'. The objective should be to embark battalion-sized marines at various strategic points along with their equipment, armour and vehicles at a "short notice" and disperse them quickly from the landing or DZ (Dropping Zone) before any adequate enemy response. This nucleus force should be supported by an adequate number of landing vessels and platforms like "Roll-on Roll-off" vessels and LSTs (Landing Ship Tank). Political treaties should provide us access to distant bases for amassing propositioned stocks at strategic points.

Adequate forces of dedicated airborne platforms in support of amphibious operations need to be raised. This should predominantly comprise of V/STOL fighters, helicopter gunships in addition to assault helicopters. "Slower" IFR (In-Flight Refuelling) tankers capable of refuelling assault helicopters need to be inducted. In United States armed forces service this role is fulfilled by an IFR version of Lockheed Martin C-130 Hercules. The Marines of Indian Navy should receive higher level of training at par with Special Forces and should conduct frequent joint-exercises with the Marine Forces of United States and Europe. If possible, they should "invite" deployment to global "hot-spots" as part of multinational forces to gain combat experience. Notably the Italian small but efficient 'San Marco' Marine battalion has amassed huge reputation by following these procedures. It is logical to assume that if this force in terms of extensive equipment and capability was already existent during the Indian Airlines high-jacking/hostage crisis of December 1999 when terrorists were released in exchange of passengers, the outcome could have been much different.

INDIAN MARCOS

MARCOS (previously named as Marine Commando Force (MCF)) is an elite special operations unit of the Indian Navy. "MARCOS" is short for "Marine Commandos".

The force started off as the Indian Marine Special Force, the first batch qualifying in February 1987. It was later renamed as the *Marine Commando Force* (MCF) in 1991. The force has gradually acquired experience and a reputation for professionalism over the two decades it has been in existence. It is one of India's highest trained and best equipped forces.

The force was initially trained by the other special forces of the country, including those under the Home Ministry, the Army, Air Force, Police and paramilitary units. This was later supplemented by foreign training facilities, notably the SEALS of the U.S. Navy and further training was conducted with British Special Forces. Over the years, the force set up its own training facility, first as an adjunct of the operational company at Mumbai, later as the Naval Special Warfare Tactical Training Centre. Wide exposure to different forms of warfare have been obtained through field operations in counter insurgency and anti terrorist operations within the country, and joint exercises with more than a dozen countries across the world.

Strength and Operations

The MCF presently has approximately 2000 personnel, though actual strength remains classified.

Operations undertaken by MARCOS usually remains classified but some of the known Operations are:

- Operation Pawan (Hindi for Wind): Part of the Indian Peace Keeping Force (IPKF) in Sri Lanka in 1988.
- Operation Cactus: Part of the Indian Navy contingent defending the democratic government of President Maumoon Abdul Gayoom of the Maldives from a coup. The force played a supporting role in India's successful military aid in helping foil the attempted coup by Sri Lankan militants from the PLOTE and ENDLF. A group of 47 mercenaries attempted to escape by sea with 23 hostages, on a hijacked vessel, MV Progress Light. The MCF was pressed into service along with INS Godavari, a multi role frigate carrying Seaking helicopters, Alize aircraft operating from the Navy's base at Kochi. INS Godavari trailed the hijacked vessel for a couple of days, firing intermittently with her guns on the vessel's superstructure. An Alize anti-submarine aircraft dropped two depth charges near the vessel, causing the motley collection of militants to come up on the upper decks and surrender. A contingent of the Marcos operating from Ratmalana Airfield on the outskirts of Colombo, with some help from the Sri Lankan Army in terms of specialised equipment, thereafter boarded the ship and accepted the surrender of the militants and took them into custody.
- Operation Leech, which resulting in the slaying of a number of Burmese rebels at Narcondum Island in the North Andaman group of Islands. A small contingent of marcos was reputed to have been involved in the murky operation, which has found intermittent mention in various media.
- Operation Tasha, which was instituted after Operation Pawan wound up, and was more a coastal security operation on the Tamil Nadu coast to thwart operations

of the LTTE there, than something belonging to the realm of special operations.

- Operation Swan, which was a similar exercise on the Gujarat and Maharashtra coasts, after the December 92 blasts in Mumbai, wherein the MARCOS were used for patrolling.
- The MARCOS are presently deployed at the Wular Lake in Kashmir, one of Asia's largest fresh-water lakes, where they have achieved significant success in counter insurgency operations against terrorists and militants in Jammu & Kashmir. They have earned notoriety among the terrorists who have given the MARCOS the nickname gharial(Alligator).
- Kargil War. Covert operations behind enemy lines.
- Protecting offshore oil rigs and platforms. The MARCOS maintain a quick reaction team at Mumbai, to deal with threats to the offshore oil assets at Bombay High.
- Operation Black Tornado: MARCOS stormed the Trident and Taj Hotels at Mumbai during the recent terrorist attacks on 27 November, 2008 during the November 2008 Mumbai attacks, wounding one terrorist at the Taj, and sustaining two injuries.
- In its first ever action in the Gulf of Aden, MARCOS thwarted an attempt by pirates to capture the Indian merchant vessel *MV Jag Arnav* on November 11, 2008.
- On 13 December 2008 MARCOS units operating from the Indian Naval warship INS Mysore foiled a pirate hijack attempt of Ethiopian vessel *MV Gibe* off the Somali coast. In the process twenty three pirates were arrested

Training

Training includes the following:-

- Open and closed circuit diving.
- Basic commando skills including advanced weapon skills, demolitions, endurance training and martial arts.
- Para training.
- Intelligence training.
- Operation of submersible craft.
- Offshore operations.

- Anti terrorist operations.
- Operations from submarines.
- Skydiving.
- Various special skills such as language training, insertion methods, etc.
- Explosive ordnance disposal techniques.

Typical qualifying rates are very low, due to which the force is presently understaffed in relation to its sanctioned strength. The selection process is two staged.

Personnel wishing to serve with the MCF are first required to qualify a 3 day aptitude test of physical fitness, that screens out 80% or more of aspirants. Those reporting for selection then undergo an arduous five week screening process culminating in a 'hell's week' of sleep deprivation and grueling physical activity. Only about 20-25% of these trainees finally get to wear the MARCO badge.

Training lasts between a year and a half and two years, which sees the trainee pass through the basic diving and commando skills, which are conducted both at the in house training facility at the NSWTTC, and at various armed forces, para military, home ministry and civilian establishments across the country.

This phase prepares a marco for life as a general duty combatant in the force, and he has to undergo further training to take his place in a Prahar (the smallest independent section that can independently undertake operations). Basic training is followed by six months to a year of advanced training in specialised skills, that help the MARCO integrate into a Prahar with one or (usually multiple) responsibilities.

Activities

The Marcos are capable of undertaking operations in all types of terrain, but are specialised in maritime operations. They have been active in Jammu and Kashmir as part of the Army's counter-terrorist efforts. Their main task is to control the infiltration of terrorists from across Pakistan into Jammu and Kashmir through the Jhelum River and Wular Lake, a 65 square kilometer freshwater lake. Some Marcos personnel are also attached with the Army special forces units conducting counter-terrorism operations in the area. The Force has undertaken numerous joint exercises with special forces from around the world, including some of the best known naval special force units of the developed world. 2003 saw MCF participation in joint training exercises called *Exercise Balance Iroquois 03-1/Vajra Prahar*, with Special Operations Forces in Mizoram.

September 2005 again witnessed joint Indo-US naval exercises called Malabar 05, which had significant special operations content.

Bases

The MCF currently operates out of the naval bases at Mumbai, Visakhapatnam and Port Blair. Plans are afoot to shift the existing training facility the (Naval Special Warfare Training and Tactical Centre) to a new facility to be set up at the erstwhile Naval Academy in Goa on the lines of the Indian Army's Counter Insurgency and Jungle Warfare School (CIJWS) in Vairengte, Mizoram.

Equipment

Small Arms

- Browning Hi-Power 9mm Semi-automatic pistol
- Glock 17 9mm Semi-automatic pistol
- SIG P226 9mm Semi-automatic pistol
- 1A SMG 9mm Sub-machine gun
- Uzi 9mm Sub-machine gun
- HK MP5 9mm Sub-machine gun
- AKM Assault rifle and it's variants
- AK-103 Assault Rifle
- AKS-74U Compact assault rifle
- INSAS 5.56 mm NATO Assault Rifle
- Colt M16A2 5.56mm NATO Assault rifle
- Colt M4A1 5.56 mm NATO Carbine
- TAR-21 Tavor 5.56 mm NATO Assault rifle
- 1A SLR 7.62mm NATO Battle Rifle
- APS Underwater assault rifle

- Dragunov SVD Semi-automatic sniper rifle
- Heckler & Koch MSG90 Semi-automatic sniper rifle
- OSV-96 Anti-material rifle
- Cross Bow With Cyanide Tipped Arrow.

Support Weapons

- IMI Negev Light machine gun
- PK General purpose machine gun
- FN MAG 7.62 mm General purpose machine gun
- GP-25 40mm Grenade Launcher
- M203 40mm Grenade launcher
- AGS-17 Automatic grenade launchers
- RCL Mk III 84mm Recoilless rifle
- Shipon Anti-tank weapon
- 9K38 Igla MANPADS.

Transport

- H-3 Sea King transport helicopter
- Chetak Utility helicopter
- HAL Dhruv Utility helicopter
- Cosmos CE-2F X100 two-man submarines.

MARINE COMMANDO FORCE (MARCOS)

The Marine Commando Force (MCF) known as MARCOS is a special forces unit that was raised by the Indian Navy in 1987. The structure and size of the MCF is classified, however, speculation suggests that the force is comprised of approximately 2,000 personnel.

Modelled after the US Navy SEALs and the Royal Marines it was created to handle reconnaissance, raids and Counter-terrorism in a maritime environment.

American and British special forces assisted in its initial training, which now consists of a two-year course for new recruits. The training regiment includes: weapons, operational reconaissance, airborne, and diving courses. All MARCOS personnel are static line parachute qualified and a number are freefall qualified (HALO/HAHO). The MARCOS reputedly undergo the most strenuous training and dropout is more than 90%.

The Indian Navy's elite Marine commando (MARCOs) force can be launched from Ships, Aircraft and Submarines in full battle gear. The Marinc Commando cadre was createcd in 1987 with a complement of 38 officcrs and 373 sailors. These personnel were selected from clearance and ships divers of the Navy for meeting the threat to national off shore areas.

The Chariot cadre personnel are required to operate the submersible craft (CHARIOTS) during pre-emptive strikes in enemy harbours. In view of the rishy nature of their duties, personnel of the cadre are entitled to Marine Commando and Chariot Pay.

The Annul Forces have suggested continuance of the existing parity of the Marine Commandos and Chariot Pay with Submarine Pay in view of the increasing fresutncy with which they are called upon to perform. The salient features of the Sixth Pay Commission recommendations, which was approved by the Union Cabinet on 14 August 2008, include a provision that the rates of Special Forces Allowance for Army and Air Force are to be equated with Navy's Marine Commando Allowance.

The last time the Indian Navy bolstered its aviation arm was in the mid-1980s with a series of inductions that included the marine commando carrying version of Seaking helicopters from the UK. The utilization of HAL manufactured Dornier, mounted with modern synthetic aperture radar and electronic warfare equipment for coastal and short range surveillance, has proved to be a success. Induction of 11 more aircraft is in the pipeline and some are being configured to carry paratroopers for marine commando operations.

It's first action was against the LTTE in Sri Lanka as part of the Indian Peace Keeping Force (IPKF). In recent years, it has maintained a significant presence in Kashmir as a part of India's counterterrorist efforts. Major ports in the country would have their own elite marine commando units deployed on the lines of the National Security Guard, as part of their initiative to beef up security in the wake of the November 2008 terrorist attacks on

Mumbai. Army, Marine Commandos (MARCOS) and National Security Guard (NSG) commandos were involved in a fierce encounter with a group of terrorists inside the Taj and Oberoi hotels. MARCOS, the first team to enter the hotels, encountered stiff resistance from the terrorists who were heavily armed and well entrenched inside.

That the terrorists had landed in Mumbai by sea prompted the Shipping Ministry to lay out an elaborate plan to upgrade security levels in the ports. The Central Industrial Security Force (CISF), which is in charge of security at the major ports, will train its men to be commandos. The elite team, which will be trained by the marine commandos of the Navy and the NSG. Indian Navy Chief, Admiral Sureesh Mehta offered facilities for training commandoes, as it cannot spare Marine Commandoes for the National Security Guard or NSG.

5

The Growth of the Navy Till 1965

THE NAVY'S GROWTH DURING THE SECOND WORLD WAR: 1939 TO 1945

Prior to the Second World War, Britain's Royal Navy was responsible for the overall maritime defence of India. For this purpose, the Royal Navy maintained:

- a Fleet based at Trincomalee in Ceylon.
- a Fleet at Singapore.
- a Squadron at Bahrein.

The Royal Indian Navy (RIN) was responsible for coastal defence only. It had one naval base at Bombay and training establishments scattered in many regions of India.

In September 1939, when the Second World War started, the Royal Indian Navy had only five sloops, one trawler, one survey ship and one patrol craft. It had 114 officers and 1732 ratings (sailors were called ratings). All the six rating training schools were concentrated inside the Naval Dockyard in Bombay-Gunnery, Seamanship, Signals, Anti-submarine, Boys Training Establishment (BTE) and Mechanical Training Establishment (MTE). There were no rating training schools for Torpedo, Electrical or Radar. Officers went to Britain for basic and advanced training in all disciplines. Eighty percent of rating recruits came from the Punjab and from the Bombay Presidency-mainly Konkan, and of them, seventy five percent were Muslim and nine percent Hindu.

During the war, the Royal Indian Navy underwent a phenomenal expansion. Thirty one small vessels were immediately requisitioned to serve as minesweepers and patrol craft until newly built ships could enter service. The first Basset class trawler built in Garden Reach Workshop Calcutta entered service in 1941-it was followed by five more. The first Bangor class fleet minesweeper built in India entered service in 1943. Six new sloops came from Britain and were named after Indian rivers. Bathurst class minesweepers came from Australia. Numerous minor vessels like motor minesweepers, harbour defence motor launches and landing craft came from Britain, America and Australia. The naval base and Naval Dockyard at Bombay were modernised. Three new branches were created-Electrical, Education and Medical.

In 1945 when the war ended, the Navy had seven sloops, four anti submarine frigates, eight corvettes, fourteen minesweepers, sixteen trawlers, one survey ship, two depot ships, thirty auxiliary vessels, one hundred and fifty landing craft, two hundred harbour craft and forty five harbour defence launches. The number of personnel had risen to 3014 officers and 27,433 ratings, most of whom served in shore establishments. The recruiting pattern had changed noticably-there was a large increase from the Madras and Bengal Presidencies and a steep decline in recruitment from the Bombay Presidency and the Punjab. The intake of Hindus had risen to forty two percent and that of Muslims had fallen to thirty five percent. Several new naval base establishments and training establishments had come up all along the West and East coasts

PRE-INDEPENDENCE PLANS FOR THE NAVY'S DEVELOPMENT

British Strategic Perceptions in 1944

As Britain gradually reconciled itself to the inevitability of India becoming independent, the Commander in Chief India assessed that the vital strategic interests of the British Commonwealth in the Indian Ocean were:

(a) Oil supplies,

(b) Control of the eastern and western approaches to India.

(c) Air communications to Iraq, Ceylon, Burma and Malaya.

(d) Control of the seas and the island territories.

In his view, should India be unfriendly or liable to be influenced by a power such as Russia, China or Japan hostile to the British Commonwealth, Britain's strategic position in the Indian Ocean would become untenable and British communications with New Zealand and Australia most insecure.

The Plans for the Navy's Development in 1944/45. As the Second World War neared completion, three separate studies emerged sequentially on the future development of the Navy. The Godfrey Plan of 1944. This plan was prepared in April 1944 by Vice Admiral Godfrey, the Commander in Chief of the Royal Indian Navy, for submission to the Chiefs of Staff Committee. It had two phases. Phase I proposed the replacement of inefficient ships by modern frigates and sloops, acquisition of eight destroyers and training of personnel by 1947 to man a cruiser. Phase II envisaged the acquisition of aircraft carriers and submarines with associated training and maintenance facilities.

The Chiefs of Staff Committee Report of 1944 on The Size and Composition of the Post War Forces in India. This report assumed the only threat to be from Russia, that independant India would continue to remain in the British Commonwealth and that reinforcements would arrive from Britain and other parts of the British Empire to help India defend her frontiers. The Committee viewed the Royal Indian Navy (RIN) as a 'Dominion Navy', responsible:

(a) Primarily for the safety of Indian and 'Empire shipping in the sea areas contiguous to India's coastline, their approaches and the trade routes in the Indian Ocean.

(b) Secondly for the combined operational training of the Indian Army's specialist amphibious formations, providing escort and assault ships and craft for landing these formations on hostile shores, for which a nucleus force of assault ships and craft and a training organisation was to be maintained.

(c) Thirdly, in conjunction with the Air Force, the Navy was to ensure the timely neutralisation of any foreign invading force attempting a landing on the shores of India. It was therefore essential for the RIN to have an adequate air component for seaward reconnaissance and for air strikes in support of surface forces.

For these tasks, the Committee recommended a naval force of one Cruiser Squadron (3 cruisers), one Destroyer Flotila (8 destroyers), one Training Flotilla (8 Sloops), one General Duty Flotilla (8 frigates) and flotillas of minesweepers, motor torpedo boats and harbour defence launches, alongwith survey ships, assault ships and a depot ship for repairs.

COMMITTEE FOR PLANNING THE REQUIREMENT OF THE ARMED FORCES 1945

After the cessation of hostilities in August 1945, the Government appointed a Committee to plan the requirements of India's Armed Forces, based on the Chiefs of Staff Committee Report of 1944. The gist of this Committee's Report was that by the end of the War, Japan would have been completely subdued, the principal foreign powers in the East would be the USSR, the USA and China and that India would be responsible for maintaining sufficient forces to overcome a minor power and to hold out against a major power until Imperial Forces could arrive. It did not take into account an independent India after the War. It did anticipate that India would be a member of the British Commonwealth. Since no one part of the Commonwealth could, in peace or war, be self-sufficient or independent of supplies from other parts, the economy and defence of each nation of the Commonwealth would therefore, largely depend on the use of the sea and air routes and ports. While the main responsibility for keeping open these sea and air communications would rest with the Royal Navy and Royal Air Force under the orders of the British Government, each component part of the Commonwealth would need to be prepared to bear its share. India, in common with other countries of the Empire, would, therefore, need to maintain naval and air forces as necessary to ensure the defence of her bases and the security of shipping within her coastal waters from submarine, mining and air attack and to assist in the protection of trade in the ocean shipping routes.

India's central position in the Indian Ocean was likely to make her particularly sensitive to the need for an increased naval force and especially for larger warships than she at present possessed. Such ships, unlike the small units which the Royal Indian Navy had, would be capable of adequately representing India in other parts of the Commonwealth, foster better understanding of India and improve relations within the Empire.

Russia was viewed as the only major power likely to seriously threaten India. Aggression by Russia was therefore taken as the basis for estimating the forces which India would require for her defence against a major power. It was not possible to forecast the strength of the forces which Russia might be able to bring to bear against India. The scale of attack would depend on conditions which would change from time to time. As these conditions changed, the scale of enemy attack would need to be reviewed and defensive measures brought up-to-date.

So long as India was connected with Great Britain, either as a Dominion or by a treaty guaranteeing assistance, hostilities between Russia and India could only be either the cause of or the result of a war between Great Britain and the USSR. Such a war would, inevitably, sooner or later, develop into another world conflict. While India's contribution to a war of this nature would depend very largely on the defence policy of the British Empire as a whole, India was likely to bear the first brunt of such an attack and would need therefore, to be prepared at all times to defend her frontiers until Imperial reinforcements arrived.

The principal responsibility of India's Navy after the war would be the safety of Indian and Empire shipping in the ports of India and their approaches; India would also wish to take her share in the protection of this shipping on the trade routes within the Indian Ocean. It would be an important task of India's Navy to provide facilities for the combined operational training of the Army formations maintained in the country and to provide a share of the escorts, assault shipping and craft required to land these formations on a hostile shore, should this prove necessary. This implied the maintenance in peace of a nucleus force of assault shipping and craft and appropriate training organisations, as well as personnel possessing an expert knowledge of amphibious operations. In addition, the Navy, in conjunction with the Air Force, would need to be prepared to take its share in intercepting and attacking any foreign invading force which might attempt a landing on Indian shores.

The Army would be responsible for coastal defence and the Air Force for seaward reconnaissance, shipping protection and co-operation with the RIN. Naval units might be required to proceed at short notice to ports in occupied countries in case disturbances arose and to patrol the river approaches to such ports. As regards superpower aggression on Afghanistan, sufficient aircraft would need to be available to prevent the Afghans from being overawed by the Russian air strength on their border.

Naval forces to counter these threats, could not be quickly improvised in times of war. The main task of the Navy in peace, in common with the other Services, would be prepare for war but since the full strength of the naval force might be needed immediately on the outbreak of war and a long period was required both for the construction of warships and the training of naval personnel, naval forces, and air forces to co-operate with them, would need to be maintained in peace at a high standard of preparedness.

While for purposes of local defence, a number of small ships would need to be maintained, a proportion of large ships would also be necessary. The provision of such ships would produce a balanced naval force, form an added incentive to recruitment and increased pride in the service, besides assisting considerably in the training of personnel which could not be adequately carried out in small ships. In addition, great importance was attached to the formation of an adequate air component for seaward reconnaissance and a striking force and also to the maintenance of modern coast defences and material for local seaward defences such as booms, mines, nets and indicator loops.

The establishment of industries within India would tend to make her economy and prosperity more dependent on the security of her export trade and so maintain, and possibly increase, the importance of her ports and overseas communications. Therefore, India needed to maintain adequate naval forces and ensure that the ports on which she was dependent were kept up-to-date in accordance with modern requirements. The coastal trade of India was not only an essential part of her peace and war economy but was also an important factor in her transportation system. The requisitioning of the majority of her coastal steamers at the beginning of the present war for naval purposes had greatly increased the congestion on the railways. It was, therefore, important that encouragement be given to the development of the coastal trade and the shipbuilding industry, that sufficient naval force be maintained to avoid being obliged to requisition mercantile shipping immediately on the outbreak of war.

THE WANSBOROUGH JONES REPORT OF 1946

In 1946, an Interim Government was formed under Prime Minister Nehru. India's Independence was clearly foreseeable. The Prime Minister commissioned a British adviser, Mr Wansborough Jones, to recommend the scientific and organisational measures required to make India a self supporting defence entity. The Jones report outlined four basic roles for the Indian Armed Forces:

(a) To secure the land frontier against raids from border tribes or attack from a second class army.

(b) To support civil power.

(c) To provide a small expeditionary force capable of protecting India's regional interests.

(d) Within available financial resources, to develop a force capable of taking the field in a first class war.

Post Independence Plan for, "The Reorganisation and Development of the Indian Navy". After partition in August 1947, the RIN comprised:

- Four Sloops (KISTNA, CAUVERY, JUMNA, SUTLEJ),
- Two frigates (KUKRI, TIR)
- One Corvette (ASSAM)
- Twelve coastal minesweepers (Orissa, Deccan, Bijnor, Kumaon Khyber, Rohilkhand, Carnatic, Rajputana, Konkan, Bengal,Bombay, Madras). After the cyclone which hit Bombay in 1948, only Konkan, Bombay, Bengal and Madras remained in service. The remainder were so severely damaged that they had to be sold as scrap.
- One survey ship (Investigator)
- Four trawlers, four motor minesweepers, one motor launch, four harbour defence motor launches and landing craft.

In August 1947, Rear Admiral JTS Hall, RIN, was appointed as India's first Flag Officer Commanding Royal Indian Navy. His Chief of Staff (now called the Vice Chief of the Naval Staff) was Commodore Martin H St L Nott. These two farsighted officers, guided by Rear Admiral Lord Louis Mounbatten, then Viceroy of India, and assisted by Cdr (later Admiral) AK Chatterji the first Director of Naval Plans, the Staff Officer Plans Lt Cdr (later Vice Admiral) N Krishnan and Lt Cdr YN Singh, the navy's first aviator, prepared on "Outline Plan for the Reorganisation and Development of the Indian Navy". It visualised four essential roles for the Navy:

(a) To safeguard Indian shipping.

(b) To ensure that supplies could reach and leave by sea in all circumstances.

(c) To prevent an enemy landing on India's shores.

(d) To support the Army in sea borne operations.

The minimum force recommended was two aircraft carriers, three cruisers, eight destroyers, four submarines and miscellaneous small ships to be built up in 10 years. The plan envisaged gradual development of the Navy to form two fleets, each to be built around a light fleet carrier.

The plan clearly reflected the Indian Navy's aspiration for regional pre-eminence. Apart from several seminal recommendations to remedy the after-effects of the partition of the Navy, like shortages of manpower, constructing new training establishments, disposing of old ships and acquiring immediate replacements.

At the end of 1947, based on the above, a ten year plan for the expansion of the Navy was submitted to the Government and was approved in principle by the Defence Committee of the Cabinet in 1948 but without financial commitment.

THE PROFESSOR BLACKETT REPORT

Whilst these proposals were being discussed, Prime Minister Nehru in 1948 sought the advice of Professor PMS Blackett. He was a renowned British physicist who had pioneered naval operational research in the British Navy during the Second World War. Professor Blackett was asked to prepare a report outlining the measures necessary for India to become near self sufficient in defence production over a period of seven years.

Whereas previous studies had assumed that in the event of hostilities, the British and Commonwealth Navies would assist India, Prof Blackett's basic premise was that a newly independant India would wish to stand unaided where defence was concerned. In his view a Third World War was unlikely-the immediate need was to plan and prepare for a small scale war. Professor Blackett's report on how best India should meet her defence needs within available scientific, financial and industrial resources highlighted that:

(a) India was economically weak. To become self sufficient, a strong economy and industrial base was essential.

(b) The import of sophisticated defence equipment, though inescapable, had to be minimised to conserve foreign exchange for industrialisation and for improving agriculture, on which future rise in defence expenditure would be based.

(c) Front line platforms which depended upon state of the art technology for optimum performance during combat, like fighter aircraft, heavy tanks and aircraft carrier task forces, could not be afforded in the quantities required to confront a major power. The major powers were, in any case, unlikely to be drawn into a regional conflict as between India and Pakistan. On the other hand, both the USA and Britain had large stockpiles of weapons and material rendered surplus after World War II which did not require optimum performance in order to be effective.

(d) If India bought these surplus stocks, if India avoided expensive high performance weapons and chose low performance systems relevant to local scenarios, then self sufficiency was possible.

(e) The import of a new and improved weapon system should only be considered if its performance was so markedly superior to its predecessor as to justify the initial cost by reduced running and maintenance costs or to provide training schools with single models to keep the services in touch with weapon developments.

(f) In the long run, self sufficiency would create freedom of choice in foreign policy rather than strategic isolation.

Prof Blackett made specific recommendations regarding the composition of the three services. In his view, the Indian Navy's missions were:

(a) Protection of coastal shipping against mining, submarines, surface and air attack, with the capability to respond in kind.

(b) Escorting and protecting a small number of ocean convoys between Aden and Singapore but no further (merchant shipping was important for the development of trade and a valuable national asset).

(c) Co-operation with the Army and the Air Force in repelling landing operations and advances along coastlines, and to be able to undertake similar operations against the enemy.

DEVELOPMENTS 1948 TO 1952

In 1948, Vice Admiral Sir Edward Parry succeeded Rear Admiral Hall as Commander in Chief and Chief of the Naval Staff of the Royal Indian Navy.

He was able to tell the British Admiralty that India's Ministry of Defence did not want the Indian Navy to be just an adjunct of the British Navy but to be a real Navy capable of carrying out major operations of naval warfare (" Sea Power and Indian Security" by Rahul Roy Choudhary, Page 29).

In September 1948, a 69 ship Navy was proposed. However, because of budgetary constraints, the Navy had to recast its requirements. In October 1948, a revised plan proposed a 49 ship Navy. In December 1948, another revised plan spelt out the 'The Role of the Navy' and proposed a smaller 47 ship Navy comprising two aircraft carriers, three cruisers, eight escort destroyers, four fleet destroyers (British Battle Class/Weapon Class), four submarines, four A/A frigates, two A/S frigates, six fleet minesweepers, one LST, one survey vessel, five motor launches, seven minor landing craft and two squadrons of aircraft per carrier (one each for fighter and strike and one for SAR).

In 1949, Government approved only those proposals of the 10 year naval plan which related to the recruitment and training of personnel. The expansion of the Fleet, though restricted to one aircraft carrier, frigates, a survey ship and a landing ship, did not exclude submarines.

This setback was compounded by the difference in opinion between the Indian naval planners in Delhi and the British Admiralty. When Admiral Parry forcefully pressed the Admiralty to meet his plan requirements, the Admiralty told him that the primary function of the Indian Navy was the protection of the coastline and harbours of India and to perform specific functions in the defence of the British Commonwealth.

In 1951, Vice Admiral Sir Mark Pizey succeeded Vice Admiral Parry as the Chief of the Naval Staff. Since the Government was unable to afford large scale naval expansion and the British were not willing to give India what it wanted, Admiral Parry's plan had to be shelved. Instead, Admiral Pizey proposed a 10 year replacement program. It was carefully phrased to minimize opposition, both from the Government of India and the British Navy.

THE ARMED FORCES REORGANISATION COMMITTEE-1952

In 1952, this Committee was constituted to reduce the expenditure on the Indian Armed Forces during the period 1952/53 to 1954/55. The Committee recommended that two cruisers be acquired in addition to INS DELHI. In due course MYSORE was commissioned in 1957. The acquisition of the aircraft carrier was deferred. It was eventually sanctioned in 1956.

The number of ships to be acquired during this period were reduced. Since destroyers were not readily available, the newest available frigates were ordered from Britain.

DEVELOPMENTS 1954 TO 1962

In 1954, agreements were signed for the acquisition from Britain of eight new frigates (3 anti aircraft, 2 first rate anti submarine, 3 second rate anti submarine) and 6 minesweepers (4 coastals and 2 inshores).

As part of the Naval Replacement Programme, the Government also sanctioned two Fleet tankers. A second hand tanker had been purchased from Italy in 1953 and commissioned as SHAKTI in 1954. The Government sanction stipulated that the second tanker should be built in India.

In 1956, Vice Admiral Sir Stephen Carlill took over as Chief of the Naval Staff. By this time, Pakistan had joined CENTO and SEATO and had been promised substantial naval assistance. America committed to directly supply two destroyers and eight minesweepers and pay Britain for refurbishing and supplying a cruiser and four destroyers. Naval Headquarters, already preoccupied with pressing the case for the aircraft carrier, found itself compelled to propose:

(a) the acquisition of three destroyers from Britain to match Pakistan's acquisitions and

(b) the outright purchase of the three Hunt class destroyers which were on loan from the British Navy since 1952.

In April 1956 Government approved the development of combatant naval aviation. The light fleet carrier HMS HERCULES was purchased from the British Navy. In 1957, the Navy proposed to the Government the retention of existing ships in commission.

If approved, this together with the new acquisitions under construction in Britain would double the number of ships in the Fleet and enable it to cope with the increased size of the Pakistan Navy.

In 1958, the Government:

(a) Agreed to NHQ's proposal to keep the existing ships in commission till 1962/63 or expiry of life, whichever was earlier.

(b) Approved the outright purchase of the three Hunt Class destroyers that were on loan from Britain.

(c) Agreed in principle to the acquisition from Britain of three new destroyers in lieu of three of the six second rate A/S Type 14 frigates of the KHUKRI Class proposed in 1950. These destroyers were required to provide the aircraft carrier with anti submarine protection and at night act as VIKRANT's escorts in the event of surface action.

Pursuant to these decisions:

(a) The Navy floated informal inquiries to the British Admiralty regarding the availability of three Daring or Later Battle Class destroyers.

(b) Since the Bombay Dockyard would not be able to berth the envisaged size of the Fleet, the Navy proposed the setting up of a major naval base at Visakhapatnam and made plans for the immediate construction there of a 1120-foot jetty and a workshop.

(c) To establish a presence in the A & N Islands and to keep an eye on naval activity in the Bay of Bengal, the Navy proposed to Government the positioning of a Resident Naval Officer (RNO) at Port Blair.

(d) The Navy decided to dispose off the old minesweepers which were occupying precious alongside berths. RAJPUTANA, ROHILKHAND and two LCTs had already been disposed of in 1956. Action was now taken to dispose of BOMBAY, MADRAS and BENGAL. Only KONKAN was retained as a general-purpose vessel.

In 1958, Vice Admiral RD Katari took over as the first Indian Chief of Naval Staff. By this time, the first of the eight new frigates of Admiral Pizey's naval replacement plan had started commissioning and the aircraft carrier was being modernised. The Navy re-started its case for a submarine arm.

In 1959, Britain indicated that neither Daring nor Later Battle Class destroyers were available. The Navy then proposed to Government the acquisition from Britain of three Early Battle Class destroyers which were older than those earlier requested.

In pursuance of the decision to relieve the congestion of ships at Bombay and to ease the growing workload on the Naval Dockyard at Bombay, the Navy proposed to Government the basing of some ships at Cochin, Visakhapatnam and Calcutta.

In April 1960, Government acquired Mazagon Docks Ltd (MDL) and asked it to prepare a preliminary report on the facilities required to modernise MDL for building frigates. In November 1960, Government approved in principle that three frigates should be built in India.

The Navy's efforts to get the second fleet tanker built in India did not bear fruit. Government sanctioned the acquisition of a new Fleet Tanker to replace the old second hand tanker SHAKTI.

In January 1961, MDL submitted its preliminary report. Government deputed a team to discuss with the Admiralty, the collaborating shipbuilders and the armament suppliers the steps to be taken to execute the Frigate Project expeditiously and economically. The team recommended construction of three Leander class frigates in collaboration with Britain.

In December 1961, the Portuguese were evicted from Goa. The airfield at Dabolim was taken over by the Navy. In Delhi, there was difference of opinion between the Ministries whether Goa should be developed solely as a mercantile port or whether the Navy's requirement to have a naval base half way between Bombay and Cochin could be accommodated. This discussion continued until 1963.

Frigate Project

By 1962, in response to global enquiries, Sweden and Holland had also submitted proposals to build frigates in India. In mid

1962, a team led by the DCNS visited Sweden, Holland and Britain to make a final techno-economic assessment of the British proposal vis a vis the others.

The team recommended the British Leander frigate. In view of the difficult financial position and the shortage of foreign exchange, the final decision awaited the negotiation of credit on soft terms. When China attacked in the end of 1962, the age profile of the Navy's ships was as follows:

(a) Acquisitions After 1947. One aircraft carrier, two cruisers, six destroyers, one tanker and one stores ship, all of which were second hand. The new acquisitions were eight frigates, four coastal minesweepers and two inshore minesweepers.

(b) Old Ships Pre 1947. Six frigates and one LST.

DEVELOPMENTS 1963 TO 1965

After the military reverses during China's attacks in end 1962, India sought defence assistance from America, Britain and the Commonwealth. These countries asked for details of specific assistance. These details were sent. The requirements were phased in the form of a five-year plan and led to the formulation of the 1964-69 Defence Plan.

Meanwhile the American President and the British Prime Minister, who had met at Nassau in the Bahamas in December 1962, had decided that:

(a) America would not supply "lethal" equipment to India, except for equipping the Army's mountain divisions on the Indo Chinese border.

(b) Britain, the 'traditional supplier', would deal with the Navy's requirements.

(c) The envisaged aid to India of $120 million would be shared equally between America and Britain.

Immediately after China's attack:

(a) The first RNO Port Blair was appointed in November 1962.

(b) Government accorded sanction for the construction of the new 1120 foot wharf at Visakhapatnam.

The year 1963 was a major milestone in Indian naval planning. The Government initiated an exhaustive review of defence requirements. China was viewed as the primary threat. The Government decided that the Army's strength should be raised to 825,000 men and the Air Force's strength to 45 squadrons.

The resources required to achieve this meant that the Navy could not be strengthened. Whereas the Navy had proposed a force level of 130 ships, the Defence Plan for the Navy envisaged "a phased programme for replacement of over-aged ships".

During 1963:

(a) With a view to take up the construction of frigates in India, a team of officers headed by the DCNS visited Britain and Sweden to evaluate their offers of collaboration.

(b) The responsibility for Seaward Defence was entrusted to the Navy. The Coast Batteries which till then were manned by the Army were taken over by the Navy.

(c) The Navy was asked to garrison the A&N islands. INS JARAWA was commissioned as a naval establishment. A naval garrison was stationed at Port Blair and provided with vessels for moving between the islands.

(d) It was decided to set up at Visakhapatnam, the full fledged Naval Base and Dockyard which had been proposed in 1957.

(e) It was decided to develop Goa as a naval base. INS GOMANTAK was commissioned as a naval establishment. The Naval Air Station Daboim's facilities were updated to make them capable of operating jet aircraft.

By early 1964, the Defence Plan 1964-69 had crystallised. The requirements of the Plan were discussed by the Defence Minister's Delegations during their visits to America in May 1964, to Russia in August 1964 and to Britain in November 1964.

Neither America, Britain nor Russia perceived any threat to India from China's Navy. In their view, India's priority was to contain China on India's land borders by strengthening the Army and the Air Force. Russia however was willing to meet the Navy's needs.

In his book "Indian Navy's Submarine Arm", Admiral Chatterji states: "From the Soviet point of view, India's naval shopping list no doubt came at a propitious time. Following the victory of the

Chinese in the eastern Himalayas and Peking's sharp attacks on Soviet foreign policy in the Indian Ocean, Moscow's geo-strategic analysis of Southeast Asia welcomed a powerful Indian Navy that would associate and cooperate with the Soviet Navy to contain China in the region.

Whatever may be the reasons for the Soviet Union's prompt and positive responses to India's Naval requirements, it was certainly very helpful and timely in making up the various deficiencies in the Indian Fleet".

By 1965, collaboration agreements had been concluded with Vickers Yarrow of Britain for the indigenous construction of three Leander class frigates. Britain offered a special defence credit of 4.7 million pounds to cover the external cost of the Frigate Project for the first four years, as well as for the expansion of Mazagon Docks Ltd.

Negotiations were also finalised for the Navy's tanker to be built by a public sector shipping line in a foreign shipyard and on completion, for the tanker to be chartered to the Navy. When the Rann of Kutch incident occurred in April 1965 the position regarding the Navy's requirements was:

(a) America had said that Britain should deal with the Navy's needs.

(b) The British Navy had expressed its inability to spare either the type of destroyers or the type of submarines which the Navy wanted. British shipbuilders were willing to build a new Oberon class submarine which India wanted. India's suggestion for soft credit, as had been extended for the Frigate Project was being reconsidered by the British Government.

(c) Russia had offered a variety of ships and submarines to meet the Navy's needs.

In May 1965, soon after the Rann of Kutch incident, a series of events occurred with startling rapidity.

(a) In April, Pakistan intruded into Kutch.

(b) In May, Britain informed India that they were unable to extend financial assistance for an Oberon class submarine to be built in a Britain shipyard.

(c) In June, there was an increase in Indonesian intrusions into the Nicobar Islands. The Navy recommended to the Government an immediate increase in naval presence in the Bay of Bengal to deter further intrusions.

(d) The refusal of British credit to build the Oberon class submarine and the need for increased naval presence in the A & N islands combined to precipitate the decision to accept the Russian offer of ships and submarines which they had made in September 1964.

(e) In September 1965, an agreement was signed for the acquisition from Russia of four submarines, a submarine depot ship, five Petya class submarine chasers, two Landing Ships Tank Medium and five patrol boats, all for deployment in the Bay of Bengal and the A & N Islands.

In a letter to Rear Admiral Sridharan in November 1965. Admiral Mountbatten wrote: (Maritime History of India by Rear Admiral K Sridharan,) "I have a specially soft spot in my heart for the Indian Navy, having done so very much for it from the time I was the Supreme Allied Commander and had most of the Navy serving under me from 1943 to 1946 until I was Viceroy and then Governor General, when I took a great personal part in the division and reconstitution of the Navy.

"Ever since then I have been instrumental in getting almost all of the requirements of the Indian Navy met by the British Government, including the two cruisers, the aircraft carrier, the destroyers, the organisations for building the frigates at Bombay etc.

"I had even managed to get more favourable terms for the construction of a British submarine but alas it all took so long that this particular transaction fell through".

AN OVERVIEW OF THE NAVY'S GROWTH 1947 TO 1965

Viewed in retrospect, even though the allocations to the Navy were low, it was possible to gradually build up a modest force, using the sterling balances built up during World War II. Despite the disinclination to increase defence expenditure and even after meeting the pressing needs of the Army and Air Force, the Navy's percentage share of the defence budget rose from 4 per cent in

1950/51 to 9 per cent in 1956/57 and 12 per cent in 1959/60. From 1961 onwards, the Navy's allocation steadily declined to 4% in 1964/65, mainly because of the over-riding need to swiftly modernise the Army and Air Force after the Chinese aggression of 1962.

It is also interesting to note how the long awaited approval for the Submarine Arm resulted not only from a curious combination of several geopolitical and economic factors but also as part of a much larger decision to start acquiring the Navy's requirements from Russia.

As can be seen from the following table of ship acquisitions between 1947 and 1965, the Navy's growth was moderate, slow and steady, with new construction ships from the UK replacing those of World War II vintage and with indigenous construction gradually acquiring momentum.

6

Indian Navy: Challenges Beyond the Horizon

The Currency of Power

In the mid-1980s many commentators predicted the end of the role of military force as the "currency of power". Subsequent decades were however marked by global changes that significantly altered the distribution of international power. Radical shifts in the status of erstwhile subjugated states, the empowerment of newly developed and developing nations, and the displacement of totalitarian regimes across Europe, have altered the perception of the influence of military power in determining the course of global events. The freeing up of economies, which became the norm by the mid-1990s, resulted in a rise in expectations in many parts of the world. The spread of information made the disparities in living standards more glaring and national, political or ethnic groupings became assertive of their right to a share of the global wealth. As changing tectonic conditions result in periodic earthquakes which enable the earth's crust to adjust to the altered conditions, this instability created violent upheavals involving the use of military force to realign political or economic power. Predictions of the demise of military force as a currency of power were thus belied by the unilateral exercise of the military option in Central Europe and in West Asia. Far from the imagined era of stability (which is largely interpreted as the maintenance of the status quo) and the much vaunted "end of history" theory, the last two decades have been the most violent in history.

Apart from its being used as a means of forcibly redistributing political power within and between nations, military power is also being applied to further economic interests. The attack on Iraq by the US, and the current imbroglio in that unhappy country, had as much to do with the perceived energy requirements of the US as with any real or imaginary weapons of mass destruction. Similarly, it has been argued that Iraq's plans to trade its oil wealth in euros threatened the primacy of the dollar as the global currency, and the attack on Iraq was a measure to safeguard vital US economic interests. It is apparent therefore, that far from becoming irrelevant, or even waning in importance, military power is still considered a legitimate and viable option by countries that wish to impose their vision of the international order on recalcitrant lesser states. It is equally an unavoidable conclusion that states that wish to retain their freedom of manoevre in global affairs, must possess a sound economy, backed by a robust (even if defensive) military capability. Clearly the age has not yet arrived when nations can dispense with their armed forces. If anything, recent events would indicate the opposite-that failure to invest in national defence capability could cost a country dear.

The Nature of Future Wars

While it is fairly clear that nation states will continue to resort to military force, and we will need to maintain armed forces for the foreseeable future, it is much less clear, what size and shape and capabilities those forces will need to have. Warfare has begun to evolve away from the historical pattern, and massive wars on a global scale between evenly matched and industrialised opponents are generally accepted to be a phenomena of the past. Major influences on the nature of future warfare will be exerted by three main factors-economic interdependence and globalization, redistribution and realignments of international power, and technology.

With the collapse of the USSR, socialist economic doctrines were rapidly discarded by all countries and they have embraced the free market philosophies of the West. The resultant free flow of capital, the increase in global movement of labour, and the offshoring of industrial production have bound countries together in a variety of ways-economic, social and cultural. It would be impossible under these conditions for a country to inflict severe or lasting damage to another with which it has close economic ties without itself suffering in the process. Globalization has thus curtailed the freedom of the more powerful nations to act with impunity against weaker nations with well-developed economies, and with which they have economic relationships. The nature of conflict between such countries would necessarily be of brief durations and be focused on the achievement of narrow and specific (mainly economic) objectives.

The changed distribution and alignment of international power has various facets. The US, and under its leadership NATO, have resorted to military actions decisively against several countries in the last two decades. The object states of these actions are countries that are characterised by poor economic levels, political instability, and the absence of democratic forms of government. It is hard to see similar actions being taken against countries with a stable and democratic system in place, and which have well developed economic, social and cultural international linkages.

Although the US has emerged as the sole superpower, it has been forced to become increasingly heedful to international opinion. Thus, while the end of the Cold War resulted in the emergence of a single super power, the economic globalization that followed has swung the pendulum slightly back, resulting in a moderation of the superpower status.

The spread of satellite television brought distant wars to the homes of viewers, and the developed countries are finding it increasingly difficult to justify the loss of human life. The political cost of casualties in war has increased to the point where risk avoidance has become an important factor that impinges on war tactics in Western countries.

These factors permit the following conclusions:

- Wars of the future are likely to brief and focused on economic objectives.
- They will be more in the nature of specific operations against unequal and weak states with poorly developed and insular economic and political systems.
- They will not be waged with equally industrialised or advanced countries.
- They will be increasingly subject to world opinion and approval.
- Risk avoidance will result in the use of long range weapons and aerial bombardment with precision weapons.

The Future Navy

Specifically for the Navy, the current RMA will impinge on one of its basic traditional characteristics-the isolation of the naval commander at sea and the corresponding degree of freedom he had to make operational and tactical decisions. The published opinion is that the new scenario will enable rapid dissemination of operational information and decentralise decision-making, but there is another aspect which may have the opposite effect; the operational commander's superior too will have the total picture and will in a sense be alongside the fleet commander, which will considerably curtail his initiative!

Notwithstanding these areas of uncertainty, it seems inevitable that net-based war or network-centric warfare is the way naval warfare is headed, and our planners and designers will have to factor this into their template for the Navy of the future.

The US and NATO have recognised this and have embarked seriously on a programme of "transformation" of their Navies to make them conform to the new roles and warfighting trends. New organisations have been set up with the specific task of conceptualizing and implementing the process of transformation and many decisions have already been taken to make the force structure of the future navy correspond to its predicted role and missions.

It goes without saying that the strategic imperatives of all countries vary, and notwithstanding recent writings and pronouncements about shared strategic interests and natural strategic partners, those of the US and Western powers are bound to be at divergence with several aspects of our own strategic perceptions. It is necessary for the current trends to be seen through the prism of national self-interest, and to make plans for the future structure of the Navy accordingly. One fact does seem evident-there is a need for transforming the Navy to one that will meet our requirements of the future.

The Indian Navy has no time to lose in instituting such a process. The concept of network-centric warfare has already been studied for several years, but the task of making the navy of the future capable of it has to be addressed now if the current discourse is not to remain an academic one. A few major thrust areas could be:

- Design and production of an indigenous net platform on which the network-centric operations will be based. This would have two or three versions with differing capabilities for different classes of ships.
- Commonalisation of procedures between the Air Force and the Navy to enable joint operations followed by standardization of communication and sensor systems for networking compatibility.
- Reduction in the number of types of warships, to reduce logistic complexity and improve ship availability. The Quadrennial Defence Review of 2006 for the US Navy envisages four types of ships for a total of 143 major surface combatants. In contrast, the 21 principal surface combatants we have in the Navy today belong to seven different types.
- Institution of a programme for integration of the submarine force into the network; this will require a major effort to equip submarines with real time communication systems with minimal loss of stealth. It will also require a changed mindset in the operating philosophy of submarines wherein submarines are given the minimum essential operational intelligence and directives before deployment and thereafter left pretty much to themselves for the duration of hostilities.
- Institution of a development programme for precision guided weapons.
- Development of a modern and interoperable radar system network between all combatant units.

This is probably a minimalist approach, and it has not considered the major efforts required in associated areas, particularly in education and training. But the point to be emphasised is an often-stated truism: it takes a lifetime to build a Navy, and if we are to transform the Navy of today into one that meets the task of (say) 2025, then the time to act is already upon us. It is interesting to observe that in the US context, two of the most ship innovative design decisions, the Littoral Control Ship and the conversion of the Ohio class, were thrust from above upon the US Navy. The Indian scene is different, and the Navy will have to wage a long struggle to get approval for its every proposal. The scenario is complicated by the fact that technology is advancing at an exponential rate, and this increases the cost of upgradations, and brings in its wake the spectre of rapid obsolescence. The preparation of a blueprint for the future Navy, the setting in motion of the development of the technologies required, and the steering of the concept and its implementation will require a dedicated organisation at a high level. Such an organisation will need to study the problem in a comprehensive manner, and cover the entire range of issues from the analysis of technology to finance and design, construction and training. More importantly they will have to convince the Government and many within the Service itself of not only the need, but also the urgency of such measures.

Modernisation of warfare strategies and techniques, and adoption of technologically advanced concepts are futile exercises if the basic structure of the Navy is not given the timely attention that is due. The creation of a balanced maritime defence force is an essential aspect of any modernisation, and the shortfall in our fleet units and submarines has to be made good by the political commitment to a sustained building programme rather than by sporadic inductions. In conclusion it needs to be said that the entire premise in this chapter has been that the equipment and system needed for net-based warfare will be developed and built in India, as dependence on foreign sources for such crucial systems will create an unacceptable vulnerability.

It has also been based on the hope that the process of production and acquisition and for obtaining government approvals will also be modernised along with the equipment and systems for the armed forces.

INDIAN NAVY

India is a maritime nation strategically straddling the Indian Ocean with or substantive seaborne trade. The country's economic well being is thus very closely linked to our ability to keep our sea-lanes free and open at all times. Besides, India has other maritime interests as well. Our island territories situated on our Western and Eastern seaboards are at considerable distances away from the mainland. To ensure their sustained development, umbilical linkages with the mainland and maritime security protection are essential pre-requisites of our maritime security. Our offshore assets within the Exclusive Economic Zone (EEZ) of

2.02 million sq. kms, fisheries and deep sea interests, major and minor harbours and the overall seaward security of long coastline and island territories are other vital aspects of our maritime dimension and Navy's responsibilities.

Indian Navy has consciously taken the difficult route of indigenisation in consonance with the national endeavour towards self-reliance. The Navy embarked upon a programme for indigenous construction of ships and development of major sub systems, sensors and weapon systems with the help of Defence Research and Development Organisation (DRDO) and Defence Public Sector Understandings (PSUs). Commissioning of the indigenously built destroyer, INS Delhi on November 15, 1997, & commissioning INS Mysore on June 2, 1999 have enabled the Navy to become a builder's Navy and not just be a buyer's Navy. Self-reliance through indigenisation has been the Navy's guiding philosophy over the last half century.

The Indian Navy is organised into three regional commands:

- HQ Eastern Naval Command, Visakhapatnam;
- HQ Western Naval Command, Mumbai; and
- HQ Southern Naval Command, Kochi.

The Indian Navy is divided into the following broad categories

- Administration;
- Logistics and Material;
- Training;
- The Fleets;
- The Naval Aviation; and
- The Submarine Arm.

The origins of the modern Indian navy are traced to a maritime force established by the East India Company in the seventeenth century. This force had a variety of names—the Bombay Marine, the Indian Navy, and the Indian Marine. In 1934 the Royal Indian Navy was established, with Indians serving primarily in lower-level positions. After independence the navy was the most neglected of the three services because the national leadership perceived that the bulk of the threats to India were land-based.

The first efforts at naval rearmament emerged in the 1964-69 Defence Plan, which called for the replacement of India's aging fleet and the development of a submarine service. Between 1947 and 1964, fiscal constraints had prevented the implementation of ambitious plans for naval expansion. Consequently, many of the vessels were obsolete and of little operational value. As part of this expansion program, the British helped develop the Mazagon Dock shipyard for the local production of British Leander-class frigates. The Soviets, however, were willing to support all phases of the planned naval expansion. Accordingly, they supplied naval vessels, support systems, and training on extremely favorable terms. By the mid-1960s, they had replaced Britain as India's principal naval supplier.

During the 1980s, Indian naval power grew significantly. During this period, the naval facilities at Port Blair in the Andaman Islands, in the Nicobar Islands, and in Lakshadweep were significantly upgraded and modernized. A new line of Leander-class frigates was manufactured at Mazagon Dock in collaboration with Vickers and Yarrow of Britain. These frigates, redesignated as the Godavari class, have antisubmarine warfare capabilities and can carry two helicopters. During the 1980s, plans were also finalized for the licensed manufacture of a line of West German Type 1500 submarines (known as the Shishumar class in India). In addition to these developments at Mazagon Dock, the naval air arm also was upgraded. India purchased nearly two squadrons of the vertical and short takeoff and landing (VSTOL) Sea Harriers to replace an earlier generation of Sea Hawks.

In the mid-1990s, India was preparing for a major modernization program that was to include completion of three 5,000-ton Delhi-class destroyers, the building of three 3,700-ton frigates based on Italian Indian Naval Ship (INS)-10 design, and the acquisition of four hydrographic survey ships. Also to be built were an Indian-designed warship called Frigate 2001; six British Upholder-class submarines; an Indian-designed and Indian-built missile-firing nuclear submarine—the Advanced Technology Vessel—based on the Soviet Charlie II class; and an Indian-designed and Indian-built 17,000-ton air defense ship capable of carrying between twelve and fifteen aircraft. The air-defense ship will be, in effect, a replacement for India's two aging British aircraft carriers, the INS Vikrant, the keel of which was laid in 1943 but construction of which was not completed until 1961 and which was slated for decommissioning by 2000, and the INS Viraat, which entered service in 1987 and is likely to be decommissioned by 2005. The problems encountered with modernizing these and other foreign-source ships led India to decide against acquiring an ex-Soviet Kiev-class aircraft carrier in 1994.

In the spirit of international military cooperation, India has made moves in the early and mid-1990s to enhance joint-nation interoperability. Indian naval exercises have taken place with ships from the Russian navy and those of Indian Ocean littoral states and other nations, including the United States.

Naval headquarters is located in New Delhi. It is under the command of the chief of naval staff—a full admiral. The chief of naval staff has four principal staff officers: the vice chief of naval staff, the vice chief of personnel, the chief of material, and the deputy chief of naval staff. The total strength of the navy in 1994 was 54,000, including 5,000 naval aviation personnel and 1,000 marines (one regiment, with a second reportedly forming). Women were inducted into the Indian navy for the first time in 1992, when twenty-two were trained as education, logistics, and law cadres. In 1993 additional women were recruited for air traffic control duties. By 1994 there were thirty-five women naval officers.

The Indian navy is deployed under three area commands, each headed by a flag officer. The Western Naval Command is headquartered in Bombay on the Arabian Sea; the Southern Naval Command in Kochi (Cochin), in Kerala, also on the Arabian Sea; and the Eastern Naval Command in Vishakhapatnam, Andhra Pradesh, on the Bay of Bengal. Additionally, the navy has important bases in Calcutta and Goa.

The Southern Naval Command is responsible for naval officer training, which occurs at the Indian Naval Academy in Goa. Officer candidates are largely drawn from the National Defence Academy. After commissioning, officers are offered specialized training in antisubmarine warfare, aviation, communications, electronic warfare, engineering, hydrography, maritime warfare, missile warfare, navigation, and other naval specialties at various naval training institutions, many of which are collocated with the Training Command headquarters on Willingdon Island, near Kochi.

The Indian Navy is the naval branch of the armed forces of India. It currently has approximately 55,000 personnel on active duty, including 5,000 members of the naval aviation branch and 2,000 marine commandos, making it the world's fifth largest navy.

The Indian Navy currently operates more than 155 vessels, including the INS *Viraat*, the only full-deck aircraft carrier operated by a country in Asia or the Western Pacific, along with operational jet fighters.

Though the primary objective of the navy is to secure national maritime borders, India also uses its navy to enhance its international relations through joint exercises, port visits and humanitarian missions, including disaster relief. In recent years, the Indian Navy has undergone extensive modernization and expansion with an intention to increase its capabilities as a recognized blue-water navy. By 2020, the Navy is expected to operate three aircraft carriers and three nuclear submarines.

Role

The Indian Navy sees several principal roles for itself:

- In conjunction with other armed forces of the union, act to deter or defeat any threats or aggression against the territory, people or maritime interests of India, both in war and peace;
- Project influence in India's maritime area of interest, to further the nation's political, economic and security objectives;
- In cooperation with the Indian Coast Guard, ensure good order and stability in India's maritime zones of responsibility.
- Provide maritime assistance (including disaster relief) in India's maritime neighbourhood.
- To play a key role as part of 'a pluralistic security order' for a better world.

History

India has a maritime history dating back to 5,000 years. The first tidal dock is believed to have been built at Lothal around 2300 BCE during the Indus Valley Civilization, near the present day Mangrol harbour on the Gujarat coast. The Rig Veda written around 1500 BCE, credits Varuna with knowledge of the ocean routes and describes naval expeditions. There is reference to the side wings of a vessel called Plava, which give stability to the ship under storm conditions. A compass, Matsya yantra was used for navigation in the fourth and fifth century AD. The earliest known reference to an organization devoted to ships in ancient India is to the Mauryan Empire from the 4th century BCE. Emperor Chandragupta Maurya's Prime Minister Kautilya's Arthashastra devotes a full chapter on the state department of waterways under *navadhyaksha* (Sanskrit for Superintendent of ships). The term, *nava dvipantaragamanam* (Sanskrit for sailing to other lands by ships, i.e. Exploration) appears in this book in addition to appearing in the Buddhist text, *Baudhayana Dharmasastra* as the interpretation of the term, *Samudrasamyanam*.

Sea lanes between India and neighboring lands were the usual form of trade for many centuries, and are responsible for the widespread influence of Indian Culture on other societies. Powerful navies included those of the Maurya, Satavahana, Chola, Vijayanagara, Kalinga, Maratha and Moghul empires. The Cholas excelled in foreign trade and maritime activity, extending their influence overseas to China and Southeast Asia.

During the 17th and 18th centuries, the Maratha and Kerala fleets were expanded, and became the most powerful Naval Forces in the subcontinent, even defeating European Navies at various times. The fleet review of the Maratha navy took place at the Ratnagiri fort in which the ships Pal and Qalbat participated. The 'Pal' was a three masted fighter with guns peeping on the broadsides. The Maratha Kanhoji Angre and Kunjali Marakkar, the Naval chief of Saamoothiri were two notable naval chiefs of the period.

Colonial Era

The British Indian Navy was established by the British while India was a colony. The first Indian to be granted a commission was Sub Lieutenant D.N Mukherji who joined the Royal Indian Marine as an engineer officer in 1928. Indian sailors started a rebellion also known as the The Royal Indian Navy mutiny, in 1946 on board ships and shore estabilshments which spread all over India. A total of 78 ships, 20 shore establishments and 20,000 sailors were involved in the rebellion. When India became a republic on 26 January 1950, it became known as the Indian Navy, and its vessels as Indian Naval Ships (INS). On 22 April 1958 Vice Admiral R. D. Katari assumed office as the first Indian Chief of the Naval Staff.

Operation Vijay

The first involvement of the Navy in any conflict came with the success of *Operation Vijay* in the 1961 liberation of Goa. After Portuguese troops fired at commercial vessels and fishing boats passing near Anjadip Island, the decision was taken to militarily intervene to liberate Goa from Portuguese colonial holding. The Indian ships provided fire support to navy and army landing troops. During the operation, the *INS Delhi* sank one Portuguese patrol boat. The Portuguese frigate *Alfonso de Albuquerque* was also sunk after a brief fight.

Indo-Pakistan Wars

The Navy has been involved in two wars with Pakistan. While its activity in the Indo-Pakistani War of 1965 largely involved patrolling of the coast, it played a significant role in the bombing of Karachi harbour in the 1971 war. The name given to the attack was *Operation Trident*, which was launched on December 4. Owing to its success, it has been celebrated as Navy Day ever since. The attack was followed by *Operation Python* before the center of conflict shifted to the eastern India-Pakistan border and the Bay of Bengal.

To show solidarity with its ally Pakistan, the United States sent a nuclear carrier task force led by the *USS Enterprise* into the Bay of Bengal. A task force led by *INS Vikrant* was stationed to counter the *Enterprise* task force; Soviet Navy submarines also trailed the U.S. task force. A confrontation was averted when the U.S. task force moved towards South East Asia, away from the Indian Ocean.

The sinking of the Pakistani Navy's lone long-range submarine *PNS Ghazi* under unexplained circumstances, enabled an easy Indian blockade of East Pakistan.. The missile boats *INS Nirghat* and *INS Nipat* each sank a destroyer; the *INS Veer* destroyed a minesweeper. The naval aircraft, Sea Hawks and Alizés, operating from the *Vikrant* were also instrumental in sinking many gunboats and merchant navy vessels. There was one major casualty, the frigate *Khukri* (sunk by the *PNS Hangor*), while the *Kirpan* was damaged in the western sector of conflict. Ultimately, the naval blockade of Karachi Port and the complete blockade of East Pakistan's ports were successful in cutting Pakistani troops off from reinforcements, supplies, and evacuation routes. These actions proved decisive in India's victory in the war.

Operation Cactus

In 1988, the Indian Navy joined the Indian Air Force in successfully thwarting a coup attempt by PLOTE in the Maldives. A naval maritime reconnaissance aircraft detected a vessel hijacked by PLOTE rebels. One of the hostages on-board included a senior Maldivian minister and *Operation Cactus* was launched to secure the vessel. After military intervention by INS *Godavari* and Indian marine commandos, the rebels surrendered. In October 1999, a coordinated effort by the Indian Navy and the Indian Coast Guard led to the rescue of a hijacked Japanese cargo ship, MV *Alondra Rainbow*, from pirates.

Operation Talwar and Parakaram

During the Kargil conflict between India and Pakistan in 1999, the Western and Eastern fleet of the Indian Navy were deployed in northern Arabian Sea. Known as *Operation Talwar*, this was primarily done to not only safeguard India's maritime assets from a Pakistani naval attack, but also to deter Pakistan from initiating a full-scale war with India by blocking its naval sea-trade routes. Indian Navy's aviators and commandos also fought along side Indian Army personnel during the Kargil war. The Indian Navy took part in military exercises during the 2001–2002 India–Pakistan standoff. More than a dozen ships from the navy were deployed during the exercise, codenamed *Operation Parakaram*. Later in 2001, the Indian Navy provided escort to American warships traveling through the Strait of Malacca to take part in *Operation Enduring Freedom*.

Disaster Relief

During the 2004 Indian Ocean earthquake crisis, the Indian Navy deployed 27 ships, 19 helicopters, 6 naval aircraft and over 5000 Naval personnel in disaster relief operations. These deployments were a part of various area-specific relief operations including *Operation Madath* in the Indian states of Andhra Pradesh and Tamil Nadu, *Operation Sea Waves* in the Andaman and Nicobar Islands, *Operation Castor* in Maldives, *Operation Rainbow* in Sri Lanka and *Operation Gambhir* in Indonesia. This was one of the largest relief mobilizations that the Indian Navy had undertaken. Indian Naval groups were able to start large scale rescue operations in neighboring countries within 12 hours from the time of the tsunami, and was the first foreign navy to reach the affected areas. The quick deployment of forces during relief operations was a testing ground for the Navy's amphibious, as well as force projection capabilities. Deficiencies in the response led to modernization of the naval forces after the tsunami, including the acquisition of Landing Platform Docks (LPD) like the INS *Jalashwa* (formerly the USS *Trenton*), as well smaller amphibious vessels.

Operation Sukoon

During the 2006 Israel-Lebanon conflict, the Indian Navy evacuated 2,280 Indian nationals and people of various other nationalities, including four 436 Sri Lankan and 69 Nepali citizens, from war-torn Lebanon. This operation was named *Operation Sukoon,* meaning "Peace and tranquility". In the year 2006, ten naval doctors from India served for 102 days on USNS *Mercy* and conducted about 10 medical camps in Philippines, Bangladesh, Indonesia and East Timor. Indian Navy has also provided relief materials to survivors of cyclones in Bangladesh and Myanmar. Two ships from the Indian Navy carried the first international aid material for the victims of Cyclone Nargis in Myanmar.

IMPLICATIONS FOR THE INDIAN NAVY

During the past year, the only major ship acquired by the Indian Navy was an old Leander-class frigate from Britain for training purposes. This appeared consistent with the pattern of naval acquisitions in the past few years. For the past eight years, since the beginning of 1988, the Navy has not acquired a single principal surface combatant, either from abroad or the shipyards within the country. In terms of the sub-surface force, only four submarines have been commissioned into the Navy in the past six years. This situation is due primarily to the severe budgetary crisis faced by the armed forces, and particularly the Navy, since about 1990-1991. This will result in a massive decrease in the number of principal combatants of the Navy in the near future. According to a reliable estimate, this could be as much as a fifth of the total force of principal combatants; from 37 at present to 29 in the next four years by the year 2000, if no major warships are acquired from abroad.

Moreover, the scheduled decommissioning of the two aircraft carriers (the first towards the end of the year, and the second in six or seven years) in the absence of any replacement in place, will effectively end the Navy's balanced force structure, and capacity for blue water operations. In effect, a major change in naval doctrine and tactics will have to be thought out, prior to a major compensatory programme of naval acquisitions. The major trends in submarines and maritime reconnaissance/strike forces in the Indian Ocean point to the need to maintain a carrier arm in the Indian Navy for effective Anti-Submarine Warfare (ASW) and naval air operations. The modernization of the submarine arm is clearly another priority concer. While the recent statement of the naval chief is welcomed, it needs to be taken much further, in view especially of the emerging challenges to be faced from the Chinese Navy.

The interest displayed by China in the Indian Ocean, especially in terms of the construction and use of naval facilities in Myanmar, indicates the possibility of a Chinese naval presence in the area in the near future. Initially, the Indian Navy would primarily need to be prepared to deal with Chinese submarines in the Bay of Bengal. In the absence of any effective carrier-launched ASW force, this task would assume nightmarish proportions. The U.S. Fifth fleet in the Indian Ocean will remain a potential source of concern to the Indian Navy. While it may not directly attempt to influence Indian naval operations, the permanency of its presence signifies highly sophisticated weapon systems and far superior firepower in proximity to Indian waters. The nature of the political relationship between the two countries will determine the level of rhetoric to which the Fifth fleet will periodically be subjected to in public. Nonetheless, further developments in relation to it need to be watched carefully in India.

Transparency in the number and nature of warships in the fleet should be encouraged, and would be welcomed by the Indian Navy. The year ahead promises to be far more important for the Indian Navy than the past year. Notwithstanding the general elections scheduled for the year, major acquisitions for the Navy are expected to be decided, including that of a replacement aircraft carrier. The naval budget for 1996-1997 is correspondingly expected to rise even further in real terms than the budget provided the previous year. More important, the decisions taken during the year will have a critical bearing on the size and nature of the Indian Navy in the early part of the next century.

THE STRATEGIC VISION OF INDIAN NAVY

Indian Maritime Doctrine was formally announced in April-2004. However, the year-2006 'Navy Day' is considered to be as the day, once Indian Navy actually started, "transforming itself from a 'brown water' coastal defense force to a formidable 'blue water' fleet." Blue water navy has indeed two connotations: the technical and the political. Technically, a naval force having the capability to operate 200 nautical miles (320 km) from its sea shore into the deep sea on the longer ranges can be graded as the blue water navy. However, politically, it is the long range extension of the state's presence, as the former Indian Navy Chief of Staff, Admiral Jayant Nadkarni once said that, "legitimate use...of a Blue Water navy is power projection which is necessary" for a "power like India."

Indeed, India started expanding its naval fleet in early 1990s after conceiving the concept of blue water navy. Since 1998, India is regularly improving its naval doctrine. In 1998, Indian Navy issued; "The Maritime Dimension-A Naval Vision." This document set the mission for Indian Navy as, a force capable to operate in the open seas. In April 2004, a formal Indian Maritime Doctrine of 148 pages was proclaimed. The doctrine clearly lay dawn the future strategic vision of the Indian Navy with the subtitle as; The Maritime Dimension-A Naval Vision. Through the Vision Statement, Indian Navy gave a Roadmap to Transformation in October 2006. In 2007, with the mission to 'Freedom to Use the Seas': India's Maritime Military Strategy (IMMS) was issued. Since 1998, an Indian maritime vision has the dedicated support including the enhanced budget allocation from the successive governments; initially the NDA Government under BJP and later the Congress lead UPA Government.

Indeed, the Indian Maritime Doctrine-2004 has been formulated on the basis of strategic concept given by US Navy Admiral Mahan, to the United States President Roosevelt for the domination of oceans especially the Pacific Ocean to gain the status of a major power. Admiral Mahan had a vision that domination of Pacific would give US an edge over the other states geopolitically as well as geo-economically. According to Mahan, "the convergence there of so many ships...will constitute a centre of commerce, inter-oceanic encounters between states. It was one whose approaches will be watched jealously, and whose relations to the other centres of the Pacific by the (maritime) lines joining it to them must be examined carefully."

In the historical perspective, what Admiral Mahan had visualized for US Navy in the Pacific towards the end of 19th century, Indian Navy desires to achieve through the domination of Indian Ocean and surrounding waters by the end of first quarter of 21st century. India in fact desires the Indian Ocean to become 'India Ocean' and the way US entered the club of global powers in the beginning of the 20th century; India does the same in 21st century. Otherwise India considered the Indian Ocean as the part of its extended neighbourhood, where Indian Navy will safeguard its "diplomatic, security and economic interests".

Salient features of the Indian Maritime Doctrine-2004 include, controlling the choke points, significant islands and trade routes in the Indian Ocean, Arabian Sea and in the Bay of Bengal. The doctrine further lays down limits of the vision for the Indian Navy for the first quarter of 21st century as to; "look at the arc from the Persian Gulf to the Straits of Malacca as a legitimate area of interest." The doctrine also highlighted the Indian Navy as the "three-dimensional blue water force", having the potential to undertake significant assignments and roles "on the surface, underwater, and in the air." During the peace time, Indian navy will have to undertake the naval diplomatic assignments for the promotion of its cause. However, the proactive role of the Indian Navy would be the projection of its power beyond the limits of Indian shores. It has to counter the "distant emerging threats and protect extended 'Sea Lines of Communication' through and from the Indian Ocean."

In the regional perspective, as perceived Indian Navy has to operate against the navies of Pakistan and China. The doctrine however, "calls for a stronger deterrent capability against foreign intervention by non-littoral navies, not limited to China and Pakistan only. This strategic reach indeed call for procurement of more sophisticated diesel and nuclear capable submarines, establishing aircraft carrier and developing new cruise missiles. Indian Navy, currently operating in area of over 3.5 million square kilometres (extending from the Arabian Sea through Indian Ocean to the Bay of Bengal) is being modernized through the procurement of modern submarines, frigates and other naval vessels in collaboration with its Western allies, US, Israel and Russia.

With respect to the strategic designs of the Indian Navy, as 'Oceanic Navy', it has assumed for itself, "the primary responsibility lying on the Indian Navy to guard the steel ring created by Singapore, Ceylon, Mauritius and Socotra...the Indian Ocean must therefore remain truly Indian." With this strategic thought, the Indian Navy Vision Statement (2006), clearly laid down the role for Indian Navy as, "of safeguarding our maritime interests on the high seas and projecting combat power across (and around) the (Indian Ocean) littoral." Covering these wide ranging naval interests of India, Indian Premier Dr. Manmohan Singh said that, "our strategic footprint covers...to the far reaches of the Indian Ocean. Awareness of this reality should inform and animate our strategic thinking and defence planning."

In order to meet its energy needs and for its burgeoning economic drive as a great power status, securing the extended sea lines of communication from the Gulf to Southeast Asia is essential for the Indian Navy. In the wording of former Indian Naval Chief, Admiral Sureesh Mehta; "we are not only looking at countering threats but to protect the country's economic and energy interests. This task has extended our area of operations. This might necessitate our operating in distant waters. As the Indian economy grows, the country is making increasing investments in distant places to ensure the availability of energy flow to maintain this growth. This is gradually defining what may be called our secondary area of maritime interest."

Through yet another revised Maritime Doctrine of 2009, Indian Navy has made major changes in its 2004 doctrine. Indian Navy has revamped its existing policies to factor in maritime terrorism, piracy and coastal security as the matter of great strategic significance. The strategic designs of India as the blue water navy, capable to operate in the open seas, to pursue and safeguard Indian oceanic interests raise the question of "how far India has got the naval capability, the capacity, to match such strategic intentions".

7

The Indian Navy in 2020

Modernisation" of a Navy is a continuous process-and each major upgradation takes time and needs to be planned well in advance. The "Great White Fleet" which circum-navigated the globe in 1908-09, and announced to the world that the USA had arrived on the world scene, took twenty years to build. It took the FSU, under the dynamic leadership of Admiral of the Fleet Gorshkov, almost 25 years to build the Soviet Navy to a level where it could challenge the western allies. The Indian Navy of 2010-20 is already being built – the Air Defence Ship at Kochi, the Vikramaditya (Ex Gorshkov) at Russia, along with its complement of MiG 29K, the Naval LCA at Bangalore, the Scorpene submarines at MDL, and at last count about 22 Destroyers, Frigates, corvettes, LSTs, OPVs, and FACs at various shipyards around the country. We must, therefore, look at what is needed, and what is possible, for the time frame of 2020-2030, and what else is needed to fill the voids prior to 2020. In arriving at the final figures we must take into account the probable security challenges and maritime threats that we will need to counter and the maritime interests that we will need to protect, preserve and indeed promote; India's stature and position in the comity of nations; our economic potential; and finally our design, industrial and ship-building capability. A little "crystal ball gazing" is, therefore, an essential part of the planning process – never an easy thing to do at the best of times.

Security Environment and Challenges Geo-strategic Location. Geography, they say is the handmaiden of strategy – and geography has indeed been very kind to us. It has bestowed on India many strategic opportunities, options and indeed advantages some of which are:-

- A coastline of 7516 Km, which includes the mainland as also the Island territories.
- 12 major, 21 intermediate and 164 minor ports.
- A total of 1197 Islands, which provide Defence in Depth and also give us a huge EEZ. At 2.01 million sq km our EEZ is 2/3rds of our land area. After demarcation of the continental shelf our EEZ is likely to be 2.54 million sq km.
- A very favourable geo-strategic location astride the vital East-West trade routes, which enables us to control, when necessary, this energy/trade lifeline. Position matters – on land as on the Sea.
- Moreover, the ocean that laps our shores is itself unique. Unlike other oceans, it is not "open-ended". It is closed to the North by the Indian sub-continent and has a few "choke points" that afford entry into it.

Unregulated Ocean Space. Speaking to the press at Singapore on 12 Nov 2003 I had described the Oceans as "the largest unregulated space in the world", a quote that has appeared in the editorial of the 2005 edition of "Jane's Fighting Ships". As the editorial points out, this may seem strange considering that the UN Convention on the Laws of the Sea is now in place. But the fact is that while the UNCLOS has given various rights to nations, the right to freedom of navigation has not changed, nor have the attributes and essential characteristics of the oceans that constitute 70% of the surface of the globe. These attributes are:-

- Large parts of the Oceans remain Unowned. While nations have sovereign rights over their territorial seas and commercial rights to all the resources in their EEZ, no nation "Owns" the "High Seas".
- Because the High seas are largely unowned, they are uncontrolled. It's a case of "No Policeman-No Law". On the high seas there is nobody, but nobody, to control your movements.
- Because the High Seas are unowned, there are No Boundaries at Sea. This is what makes the Navy different to all other Services, which work within the confines of national boundaries. The Navy works in an International arena on a daily basis. Twelve miles out of port and we are in International waters.

- Because of these attributes of the Oceans, the Sea is One.

Thus, all nations with a coastline are maritime neighbours.

Maritime Terrorism. The new scourge of terrorism has taken the world by storm. So far major acts of terrorism have by and large been restricted to land areas. But as security on land is tightened, the ease of access and movement across the world's ocean areas will tempt terrorists to take their "trade" to sea. The war on terror at sea cannot be fought by individual nations. It will have to be a worldwide effort that will require Navies of the world to work together – as countries are doing ashore.

Nuclear Backdrop. We are now a declared nuclear weapon state (NWS) and, after some hiccups, the world has accepted this reality. Our nuclear doctrine clearly states that we will maintain a "Credible Minimum Deterrent" based on a triad of weapon delivery systems. We are also a declared "No First Use" (NFU) NWS. Any country with an NFU policy must ensure that it has an assured second-strike capability. Missile silos, airfields and aircraft are easily detected by satellites and are hence easy targets. A nuclear submarine is very, very difficult to detect. Even if detected, it is extremely difficult to target, as it is constantly on the move at speeds of twenty knots or more.

Territorialisation of the Seas. Maritime powers have always wanted (as they still do) as much freedom of the seas, as possible; whereas non-maritime powers want as much ownership of the seas, as possible. With the UNCLOS, both have got much of what they wanted. Almost 40% of the ocean areas have become the Exclusive Economic zones of countries. The full claims for the world's EEZ have yet to be submitted by many countries and agreed to by the UN, and more important, by neighbouring states. Earlier we had neighbours and boundaries only on land. Now we have them at sea as well. The more the neighbours, the more are the problems. The larger the EEZ, the greater is the area of responsibility of the maritime Services.

Global Governance. Globalisation has made countries more inter-dependent and States will increasingly work together to ensure their economic development, as also to promote peace, stability and combat common threats. In future, therefore, one sees a form of "Global Governance" slowly but surely creeping to seaward to ensure that the "Freedom of the Seas", that the west holds so dear, is not misused by terrorists. The ISPS code, the Container Security Initiative and the Proliferation Security Initiative are manifestations of this trend. This will require the Indian Navy to patrol its area of interest, and work with other Navies, much more than it has done in the past.

Strategic Frontiers. What then is The Indian Navy's "area of interest"? Our land frontiers are well known. So also are our maritime boundaries with our immediate maritime neighbours. But our current area of interest lies far, far beyond our territorial sea and the EEZ. It extends all the way to the choke points that afford entry into the North Indian Ocean as shown in the map below.

Extra-Regional Presence. Any nation with the capability can traverse the Oceans and arrive in force at the doorstep of another maritime state-no matter how distant it may be. Powerful Navies have indulged in "Gun Boat Diplomacy" in the past. While the phrase may be out of fashion these days, Navies continue to be used for the same purpose, by whatever name it may be called. It is well known that the strategic focus of the world has once again shifted to the North Indian Ocean, due to a combination of Terrorism and world energy reserves. The presence of extra-regional powers in the Indian Ocean is bound to last well into the foreseeable future. The Indian Navy consequently has to operate in the same waters as are being patrolled by the world's most technologically advanced nations.

Defence of Trade. Trade is the lifeblood of any economy–and so it is with India. Our economy is booming and this trade will continue to soar. Today 90% of the crude oil we use comes from across the oceans – be it imported or produced in our offshore oil fields. Our dependence on natural gas is increasing by the day. Over 95% of our trade by volume comes across the oceans. Any disruption of this trade lifeline, particularly any disruption in the flow of oil, will endanger the economic prosperity and security of the country. Defence of trade has always been a major mission of the Navy and this will continue to be so.

Maritime Diplomacy. The Navy works very closely with the External Affairs Ministry to further the interests of the country around the world. Towards this end it sends ships on overseas deployments to show the flag and build "Bridges of Friendship"–

which was also the theme of the Navy's very successful International Fleet Review in 2001. Towards this end the Navy also trains a considerable number of foreign Naval personnel in its many training institutions. With many small nations on the Indian Ocean rim now getting huge EEZs there is a growing demand for assistance and suitable vessels to patrol these areas. It is in India's interest to meet these demands and supply equipment as and when requested. Since many of these countries cannot afford to buy such vessels we must be willing and ready to supply them at short notice, and free of cost. Budgetary provisions must be regularly made for such assistance.

Regional Naval Expansion. The Naval development plans of maritime states in the Asia-Pacific region clearly indicate that all are giving greater importance to maritime security then ever before– a trend that we must take note of. The Threat. Very often I have been asked to identify the "Threat" that the Indian Navy is going to face. The immediate threat is well known, but I have always desisted from identifying others because "to name an enemy is to make one". But more important is the fact that in this respect the Navy has to think and plan differently than the other two services, which can clearly identify the threat across our borders. Because of the unregulated ocean space, ease of access and movement a threat can develop from the sea very quickly. So, unlike the other two Services, Navies are not built purely to counter known threats but to protect maritime interests. The larger a country's dependence on the oceans, and the larger its interests at sea, the larger its Navy has got to be.

FLEET MODERNISATION

Availability of Funds. The Navy is a capital intensive Service and it takes a long time to design, develop and build ships. The larger the ship, the longer is the time taken to design and build it. Taking a typical destroyer/frigate (The work horses of any Navy) it takes around 10 to twelve years from Government approval to commissioning, if the ship is to be designed and built in India. Assured funding over three plan periods (i.e. 15 years) is absolutely essential for any planned modernisation. Historically, the fate of Navies has been linked to the fate of their country's economy. Fortunately for us the Indian economy is doing very well and modernisation of the Navy (and indeed of the Armed Forces) can be easily funded over the next three plan periods in particular, and for the future in general. This statement is supported by published/ stated figures for the Indian economy and the assumptions at sub-paras (d) and (e) below:-

- The GDP in 2004-05 was around Rs 2658750 Crores.
- The GDP has been growing at an average rate of 6.35% and very recently the PM announced that this year it will grow at 7% (for the first time the GDP growth in the first half of the fiscal year has been over 8%) and there is every possibility that it could touch 10% in the future.
- The percentage of GDP allocated for Defence during the latter 1980s varied from 3.08 to 4.24%. Since then this has gradually dropped, and from 1991 to 2005 the percentage has varied from 2.77 to 2.24. This was quite inadequate to fund the modernisation of the armed forces.
- We have been able to afford 3 to 4% of GDP for defence in the past and we can easily do so in the future. It must become stated Government policy that we will spend 3% to 4% of GDP for defence;

Besides making adequate money available for defence, it will also enable planned modernisation which has not really been possible in the past as, more often than not, the Budget has driven the "Plan" rather than the Plan driving the Budget. Assuming a modest 6.35% growth rate, the expected GDP at five yearly intervals is likely to be:

- 10-10 Rs 36,17,137 Crores
- 15-15 Rs 49,20,989 Crores
- 20-20 Rs 66,94,835 Crores
- 25-25 Rs 91,08,091 Crores
- 30-30 Rs 123,91,243 Crores

Share of the Defence Cake. How much each Service should get from the allocations for Defence has always been somewhat contentious. The Navy being the smallest of the three Services, has always received the least. As early as in 1988, General Sundarji had stated that by 2000 the Navy should get 20% of the Defence budget. He realized the value of a Navy in World affairs. Regrettably, this has not happened and it was only in 2002-03 that the Navy crossed the 15% mark and received the highest ever allocation of 17.6% in 2003-04. Since then it has hovered around the 17% mark and this should gradually be increased to 20% as India will certainly need a powerful Blue Water Navy as it takes up greater responsibility in world affairs. The peace process currently underway will ultimately give us a Peace Dividend that will allow us to reduce troops on the border. (Sub-continental Armies are perhaps the only ones that are amassed on the borders. The rest of the world takes boundaries for granted and respects them) For planning purposes, however, let us assume an allocation of 17%. Even with this, the expected allocations to the Navy as shown below (assuming only 3% of GDP is allocated for Defence) would be adequate to fund the projects/modernization being recommended :-

- XI Plan 2007-08 to 2011-12 Rs 92586 Crores
- XII Plan 2012-13 to 2016-17 Rs 125960 Crores
- XIII Plan 2017-18 to 2021-22 Rs 171366 Crores

Aircraft Carriers. For many years now the Indian Navy has been stating that it needs a minimum of three aircraft carriers to fulfill its missions. One is required to be operational on each coast and the third will normally be under maintenance. After much delay (it took over 15 years!), the Government finally approved the construction of the Air Defence Ship to replace the INS Vikrant, which was phased out in 1997. It took 8 years to get government approval to induct the Ex-Gorshkov (now christened Vikramaditya), which will replace Viraat in 2008/09. It is time now to place the order for the third carrier, which should really be a repeat of the ADS. Batch building of ships and standardization greatly reduce the life cycle costs of a ship. Moreover, for the third carrier we will not have to invest in a separate carrier air wing, as the intention and requirement is to have only two carriers operational at any one time. If approved now, we will have three carriers in the 2020s.

Strategic Forces. Now that India is a declared Nuclear Weapon state with a No First Use Policy it is absolutely essential that we put our second strike capability in Nuclear Submarines as soon as possible. There are many advantages in doing so and the actions of existing NW States are good indicators of the direction in which we should go. The Government should approve, start and fund such a programme at the earliest, as it is vital for the security of the country. The ultimate aim should be to have at least four such submarines so that at least one, if not two, are on patrol at all times.

Destroyers and Frigates. These ships are really the workhorses of the Navy, both in peace and war. Today, we have 11 destroyers and 11 frigates, which are far too few. In fact, after the 1962 war a study had recommended that the Navy should have 28 such warships – a target that the Navy has never been able to achieve. Forty years down the line much has changed and the responsibility of the Navy has increased manifold.

In the next 20 years this figure must go upto at least 20 of each type. Five Leander Class frigates are already well past their prime and need immediate replacement. (One was earlier decommissioned without a replacement) Three project 17 Frigates under construction will replace the first three Leanders. The three Godavri class frigates will need to be replaced between 2010 and 2015 by which time they will be between 25 to 30 yrs old. Thus there is an immediate need to place orders for at least six more P17 frigates, just to maintain the current force levels of Frigates. Additional orders will need to be placed on MDL and GRSE to take the frigate numbers to twenty by 2025.

As far as destroyers are concerned, the first of the Kashin class destroyers will be 25 years old this year and the youngest (Ranvijai) will be 17 years. They will all need to be replaced between 2010 and 2020. Three Project 15A destroyers are already on order and it would be cost effective to increase this order to five so that they replace the five Kashins.

It will thus be seen that Mazagon Docks, the shipyard building both the P17 Frigates and the P 15A Destroyers, must deliver 9 x P 17 frigates and 5 x P15A destroyers between now and 2020 i.e. almost one ship a year – assuming that orders are placed well in time and no delays are introduced. Going by their past performance they will not be able to meet this target and so the only option to maintain present force levels will be to exercise the import option and a repeat order for the Talwar class destroyers recently imported from Russia is a very attractive option. A minimum of four should be immediately ordered to maintain force levels. Additional orders for the Talwar class and/or the Delhi Class must be placed a little later to take the destroyer fleet upto 20 by 2025.

THE INDIAN NAVY-A PERSPECTIVE VISION UPTO 2020

Geo-Economic Situation

The closing decades of the twentieth century witnessed sweeping changes in the security perceptions of most nations. There have also been major changes in the security environment in the Indian Ocean.

Albeit, India has made great strides towards economic progress and is continuing to do so. The momentum achieved cannot be sustained unless a certain measure of internal and external security is ensured. Traditional state-centred geopolitics of the past was too narrow and parochial in conceptualising, both, geography and politics, and, appreciating the impact of the oceans on politico-economic forces.

As politics becomes more civil society oriented, transcending state-centric concerns and as geography becomes more humanised and ecocentric, the interaction between the two would result in geo-economic and geo-strategic factors replacing geopolitics. More than ninety five percent of India's trade is sea borne, in addition to which, the country has a huge EEZ with enormous reserves of minerals, energy and food. Protection of India's maritime interests, which form a major chunk of the country's economic interests, is therefore vital.

It is necessary to plan ahead and prepare for this inevitable metamorphosis, in which the maritime element will become more and more important. Potential threats interfering with our maritime interests will have to be overcome, firmly and resolutely and efforts made to coax regional players into maritime co-operation for mutual protection of economic interests. In view of the above there is a need to take stock of the situation and formulate a perspective vision of the Indian Navy during the period up to 2020. India's intended nuclear stance and technological developments enveloping defence forces worldwide would have to be judiciously catered for.

Aim

The aim of this paper is to examine the role of the Indian Navy during the next two decades vis-à-vis India's maritime interests, and suggest, a viable force structure and outline plan of action for attainment of the same.

INDIA'S MARITIME POWER POTENTIAL

Continental Outlook. During the last fifty-one years, India's attention has been deliberately diverted to its land frontiers. The attempt is to prevent its strategic gaze from focussing on the maritime surge enveloping the country from the East and West. India cannot be a great power unless it is willing to shift to the doctrine of sea-air-land battles with primacy in the Indian Ocean, Bay of Bengal and the Arabian Sea. Historical evidence indicates that a nation, without a commitment to build a world class Navy, cannot be a world class player.

Influences in the Indian Ocean

India deserves to aspire to play the role of a regional power in South Asia and a facilitator for regional cooperation. Since independence, India has made substantial progress in establishing its pre-eminence in the Indian Ocean region. Its involvement in the liberation of Bangladesh, peacekeeping operations in Sri Lanka and suppression of the coup in Maldives are some examples of its superior power status in the region. Although, not at the receiving end of the dictates of other powerful nations of the world, it also does not have the leverage to influence international affairs substantially.

India's potential lies in its geo-strategic location, size and distribution of its island territories in the Indian Ocean. It has vast natural maritime resources, both, living and nonliving of which, only a limited amount have been exploited. It has a large reserve of human resource in terms of professionals and technically trained persons. Its economy is growing, specially with liberalisation and relaxation of governmental controls. Though the response from the developed countries is that of caution, the potential of the Indian and other ASEAN markets would continue to lure foreign investors. India has achieved a high degree of self-reliance in the field of science and technology, however, has yet to exploit its complete potential.

Considering its power potential, its relationship with its neighbours and its pre-eminence in the region, India is likely to establish itself as a regional power in the Indian Ocean in the coming decades. This would be in consonance with India's anthem for the future, professed by Dr APJ Abdul Kalam, which reads, "A developed and strong India by 2020, or even earlier, is not a dream. It may not even be a mere inspiration in the minds of many Indians. It is a mission we can all take up and accomplish".

Indian Parliamentary Maritime Group

Although the political class has continually cast a blind eye towards the sea, a step in the right direction was taken on 12 Nov 1999, when the Indian Parliamentary Maritime Group, was launched. The group comprises an all party forum of members from the Lok Sabha, Rajya Sabha and maritime organisation representing naval, merchant naval shipping, shipbuilding and marine environmental interests of India. The group is expected to raise issues of maritime interest, which will enlighten and force our politicians to look towards the sea. The presence of such a group in parliament is bound to give much wanted impetus to the harnessing of our maritime potential and is expected to formulate a maritime policy for the nation.

PERCEVIED CONFLICT AREAS

Exploitation of Undersea Resources

The conflicts over the use of ocean space arise principally from two developments. The first, an explosion of technological advances in exploiting mineral resources in the sea bed, and second, the rising influence of developing countries in asserting their claims to the benefits of such exploitation.

Delimitation of Maritime Boundaries

Indian is yet to settle its maritime boundaries with Pakistan and Bangladesh.

Ownership of Islands

The increasingly broad coastal state jurisdiction would lead to disputes over islands which can increase the area coming under a states control by acting as an anchor point from which to draw base lines. The discovery of resources in nearby ocean space would act to exacerbate the situation. Dispute over the Sprately islands, New Moore Island or Rockall etc, typify this potential.

Environmental Concerns

The environmental concerns of coastal states have been strenuously opposed by states with shipping interests who fear that pollution regulation by coastal states may meddle with freedom of navigation.

Oil Flow from the Gulf

In the context of oil and energy dependency, the Persian Gulf-Arabian Sea is becoming increasingly critical to India's vital interests. Pakistan in recent years has been expanding its naval forces. It has developed ports Gawadar, Pasni, etc, which are abeam of our oil flow from the Persian Gulf and very close to the choke point of Hormuz. At the same time India's offshore installations in the Arabian Sea face a potential threat from the expanding Pakistani naval forces.

Chinese Presence in the Indian Ocean

China did not hesitate to occupy the Paracel Islands in 1971 and declared her intention to recover the Spratleys as well as the Senkaku islands which are presently under Japanese control. Beijing intends to further improve the Karakoram highway to Pakistan, which will eventually connect China to seaports in the northern Arabian Sea. Her interest in Myanmar is similarly to revive the famous Burma Road. Beijing appears keen to modernise ports at Sittwe near the Bangladesh border and Mergil on the Thai border as also Haingyi Island in the Bay of Bengal for facilitating Chinese trade and commerce. In addition, radar installations have been upgraded in the Great Coco Island. Reports have emanated from China wherein a General of the PLA navy stated that they would extend operations into the Indian Ocean to prevent India from dominating these waters. The Indian Ocean becoming India's ocean is something they aren't prepared to accept.

ROLE OF THE INDIAN NAVY

Fallout of India's Draft Nuclear Doctrine

With an overt nuclear capability and intent of building up a 'credible minimum nuclear deterrence', India is on the probable and logical path of weaponisation and of achieving unclear stability with a mutuality of deterrence against potential adversaries.

India has voluntarily imposed upon itself a principled and moral 'no-first-use' clause. However, the ability to rapidly retaliate would be necessary. India's nuclear forces would have to be organised and deployed, to ensure survival and the ability to endure repetitive attrition attempts with adequate retaliatory capability.

Safeguarding National Interests

With the country's economic reform programme gathering momentum, protection of trade, defence of our territory, islands and offshore maritime interests would no longer be sufficient, however, would perforce have to include defence of national interests. India would, therefore, be forced to relook at the role of the Indian Navy, keeping in mind factors associated with its changing nuclear status. Important aspects to be paid attention to, would be as follows:-

(a) Capability to protect overall economic development, interests in our EEZ and our sea trade.

(b) Non-allowance of any outside interference.

(c) Maintenance of adequate influence over regional competitors.

(d) Development of adequate influence to deter outside states from lending support to regional competitors.

(e) Shift to view the islands in the Indian Ocean, as platforms, to dominate the region and exercise influence over the neighbourhood.

(f) Ability to create a massive intervention from the sea, as part of the naval contribution to the overall war effort to terminate a continental war.

(g) Capability to adapt to littoral warfare.

(h) Capability of executing the nations eventual second strike. However, this is still seen as a deterrent and would not be usable in the strategic sense.

Facilitating Regional Co-operation

A multi purpose and resolute sea force could cost effectively deter, negotiate and persuade opposing parties to amicably settle their differences by sitting across the table. Nations in the Indian Ocean, in particular, are keen to develop their economies and enhance bilateral and multilateral co-operation, and further, to promote stability in the region. Hence the ocean could be transformed to be an area falling under the rubric of 'cooperation' rather than 'conflict' as maritime activities would tend to be located in a less emotive environment. Broadly, the specific areas of naval co-operation and initiatives are envisaged as under:-

(a) Conduct of joint exercises and manoeuvres.

(b) Striving for greater transparency and provision of advance information about exercises and manoeuvres above an agreed threshold.

(c) Setting up of a joint task force to cater to natural calamities.

(d) Initiating a dialogue to establish an Indian Ocean forum that could draw upon SAARC and ASEAN, for example, and such littorals not part of any association as also the extra-regional navies.

(e) Pooling the expertise/experience of nations in specific areas, such as ship design, shipbuilding and hydrography.

(f) Establishing of common training facilities where high capital expenditure is involved such as missile ranges, submarine training escape school and underwater ranges.

(g) Making joint efforts to tackle maritime pollution, conservation of maritime environment, sea based traffic in narcotics, piracy, global smuggling, poaching (beyond the capability of Coast Guards) and rescue at sea.

(h) Ensuring the safety of sea lances in specific areas by establishing 'presence' in mutually acceptable manner.

(i) In short, these proposals envisage the perfect cocktail of international relations, wherein Balance of Power, Balance of Interests and a Respect for Sensitivity for each nation state is maintained.

TRENDS IN NAVAL WARFARE

Future Ship Design

Fleet Combat Ship: The fleet combat ship, eventually replacing today's guided-missile cruisers and destroyers, would designed to engage in anti surface, anti air and anti submarine warfare and it could carry out power projection missions. Its weapon suite design would emphasise the sensors needed for these missions, including surface radars, sonars, and aerial early warning systems. It would be able to operate Helicopters for anti submarine and mine warfare, and unmanned aerial vehicles (UAVs) for reconnaissance and targeting. It would have all the necessary links and nodes for C4I2 within the overall naval force combat system. If missile technology advances meet expectations, such a ship may not need guns except for self-defense. Close-in defences using laser weapons for defense against antiship missiles, wherein the incoming targets could be illuminated from the side, would mature in time to be included in these ships' weapon suites.

Ship Building

Naval ships take roughly ten years from the drawing board stage to commissioning and have a life expectancy of around 30 years. 'The rapid rate of obsolescence of naval weapon systems has to be catered for, by planning built in reserves. We have already experienced such situations and must be ready to accept that designing the 'silver bullet' may not meet up to future contemporary systems and would thus bely many an expectation. Advanced surface combatant designs would incorporate and extend many features currently in experimentation on today's ships. Indeed, once these features are developed to the application stage, many of them could be retrofitted to greater or lesser extent in today's ships at major maintenance and overhaul milestones during their service lives to increases survivability, system reliability, and ship service life.

The philosophical approach to shipbuilding would have to change if the price ration of ship construction are to be taken care of. The hull accounts for about one third the cost of the ship, whilst weapons, sensors and navigational aids account for another 42 percent or so, leaving machinery and auxiliaries the balance 25 percent. A ship would become current if the 42 percent were to be replaced every 10 to 15 years for a mid life update. To make this worthwhile the remaining 58 percent would have to be of quality to ensure the backup endurance. To illustrate this, a generator with a lesser horsepower to weight ratio may sound more advanced compared to that with a greater ratio, however, with a longer running hour limit between overhauls, the latter would be a more important factor in building a longer lasting platform.

Instrumentation. Instrumentation would be fully integrated and automated using distributed and networked sensors, actuators, and microprocessor controls to minimise crew size and maximise efficiency. This would include damage control, a very sensitive area that is currently a major determinant of crew size.

Ship Signatures and Vulnerability

The active and passive signatures of ships would be managed in all aspects, viz., wake reduction, noise reduction, hull and superstructure shaping, and electromagnetic and infrared emission control. This would help acoustic and electronic countermeasures function much more effectively to mask ships under combat conditions and to make detection and tracking difficult for opponents.

Ship vulnerability to hits will always be a problem. Signature reduction and active defence would help reduce the chances of hit. The chances of surviving a hit could be greatly improved by known design features such as separation of critical, redundant system elements (such as fiber-optic lines and instrument networks), and by automation in damage control that reduces response time and more accurately focuses damage control efforts. Finally, armour could be applied selectively to critical areas such as magazines and combat direction centers. All such measures are in the pipeline today, in the design of modern warships, with serious attention to automation in damage control being the newest addition to the list.

Speeds

As the speeds of ordnance delivery increases and with superior computational speeds as well as faster missiles, the significance of higher combat speeds will disappear. Speeds will be relevant to effect quick deployment and to maintain the high flexibility of naval forces. These speeds are not obsolete in number, but a figure on the basis of which naval forces are expected to re-deploy. This would be in the region of 23-24 knots, sustained. Higher combat speeds would be irrelevant to achieve tactical superiority.

Aviation Platforms

Tactical naval aviation would grow, as indeed it must, if navies strive to increase ranges by taking sensors up into the sky. Aircraft are likely to be the biggest beneficiaries of miniaturisation; the effect of which has already been felt in the 'Sidetrack' concept where a pod carried by a Harrier provides an immense airborne early warning (AEW) picture from 45,000 feet, through data-link, albeit temporarily. Aircraft innovation, like the tilt rotor (already capable of 230 knots and a ceiling of 22,000 feet) and Advanced Compound Helicopter would enable large ship smaller than carriers to operate aircraft. Manned navel aviation would grow as the AEW and ELINT package becomes smaller. So would the Joint-STARS package come into the Indian navy in the same way that the smaller version has now been fitted into a commercial jet for the British forces?

UAVs. The function of AEW would be rapidly taken over by UAVs whose only limitation would be the antennae size. UAVs would be developed for general targeting, AEW, and providing communication relays.

Sub-surface Platforms

As the surface of the ocean becomes more hazardous, the change to AIP and nuclear propulsion would become more urgent. The incorporation of submarines into the overall tactical picture by means of a satellite based system would remove the shortcoming the submarine currently suffers in being unable to see the big picture with own sensors. The entry of submarines into the field of tactically coordinated operations, special operations, reconnaissance and land attack would see this platform depart from its traditional role of sea-denial into finding its place as a capital ship of any navy. Besides, the submarine, without doubt would be the second strike capability of the future nuclear scenario. Submarines would have to undertake the entire spectrum of land-attack missions. It could be argued that surface ship vulnerability may favour the submarine as a forward-positioned missile launch platform for ballistic missile defense.

REVOLUTION IN MILITARY AFFAIRS

The extraordinary technological advances currently taking place in satellites, sensors, communications and computers, coupled with new ideas about navel tactics and force structures, would lead to, what military planners regard as, one of the most sweeping revolutions in warfare. The world is entering into one of those rare historic periods, when new capabilities would combine with new doctrines and tactics to produce unprecedented revolution in military affairs, sparked by the exploitation of Information

Technology. In future, military commanders would talk about, the need to obtain 'Information superiority', akin to Aerospace Superiority.

Communication Technology

Today, naval communications are primarily accomplished via low-bandwidth voice, text and data. The operational use of technology such, as video teleconferencing is uncommon. Higher-bandwidth communication via satellite would enable video teleconferencing among ships and shore assets. Operational effectiveness and personnel efficiency could come about with seamless communication at sea and ashore. This would imply compatibility of operational procedures and physical interfaces onboard and ashore for switching form satellite communications to PSTN and data networks. It should be kept in mind that communication technology is driven and would continue to be driven by the commercial sector, which is more advanced. With the growing use of optic fibre cables, increased channel rates and channel bandwidths would increase in much the same ways, the shift from HF to SATCOM in the past two decades.

Command and Control

Higher-bandwidth interaction would enable widely distributed Tactical Commanders to meet online, and understand time-critical information in a shared electronic environment that would provide an adequate illusion of shared presence. Future command centers would exploit a range of technologies that are now under development in both commercial and military sectors, including speech recognition and synthesis, high-resolution projection displays (two-and threedimensional), shared information visualisation, resource and mission planning, simulation, etc. These technologies would be integrated in a cohesive system that would provide the means for groups of individuals to understand complex situations. Future system effectiveness would depend on human-centered-system approaches that would enable commanders to interact, using systems in more natural ways with threedimensional vision, hearing, speech, gestures, and touch.

Information Warfare

Rapid access to appropriate knowledge at all levels would

optimise war-fighting and crisis response capabilities. Instead of massive forces and fire power, we would have to rely, increasingly, on information technology, This would be necessary to outsmart adversaries by knowing enemy positions more precisely, attacking them more quickly and fighting more decisively, while having to put fewer lives to risk. Safeguarding of own and exploitation/ disruption, of the enemy's information spectrum respectively, would constitute information warfare and would comprise the following major elements:-

(a) Command and control warfare.

(b) Electronic warfare.

(c) Psychological warfare.

(d) Cyber warfare.

COTS and Dual Use Equipment

So far warfare has always looked to technology to provide more 'bang for buck'. The rapid pace of advancement of technology would continue, if not increase, in the coming decades. In quantitative terms, it is accepted that more technological advancement took place in the last quarter century than in the previous seventy-five years. With the adoption of COTS and dual use technology, the navy would be forced to take advantage of and keep pace with technological developments in the commercial world.

Software

Software would be dominant in almost every type of system, from administrative software for payroll, inventory control to command and control, fire control and weapon imbedded software, etc. General use software would be governed by and would have to keep pace with commercial trends. Planning and decision-aids would be used for logistics, resource allocation, inventory planning, mission planning, force structures selection.

THE FORCE LEVEL MIX

Defining the Task

Strategic deterrence would have to be based on a mix of nuclear weaponry, delivery means and strong conventional forces. The need to maintain a conventional edge to prevent subsequent conventional conflicts would form a key element of deterrence. The area of operation of the Indian Navy is about nine million square miles.

Closer home India would need to exercise total sea control, however around the sea-lanes the level of dominance could be allowed to degrade a little. While routine surveillance of these areas could be carried out by satellite, investigative surveillance would require manned aircraft.

Ships of around 3000 and 6000 tonnes, aircraft carriers, submarines and long range patrol aircraft would be preferred to act in such a large area without any whistle stops. Small combatants packaged to deliver the largest punch in the smallest hull would have no place in our environment. Long legged ships, not requiring frequent fuelling and maintenance would be necessary. From the technical and maintenance point of view, also, it would it would make eminent sense if the machinery, equipment and main sensors were to be standardised between two kinds of ships, of around 3000 and 6000 tonnes with aircraft carriers built around the same propulsion and auxiliary machinery.

Influence of Technology

Technology advances in recent years have introduced new concepts in navel strategy. To the navy's primary role of sea control, they have added two new dimensions of strategic deterrence and projection of sea power ashore. India already has a base level in all the fields mentioned. The navy will have to move forward in all the areas talked about so far or, else, expose herself to serious degradation of her combat efficiency levels below that of some of the smaller but better funded navies.

More 'Bang for Buck' Owing to the enormous surge in costs of funding the naval strategic component of national nuclear deterrence as well as investing in the assets that create information dominance, the Indian Navy would have to give up all frills. Even if the naval budget were to increase dramatically to offset the cost of building nuclear submarines, the cost of individual platforms would require an economising of numbers to offset the spiralling costs of technology. Frills could be given up in the following manner:-

(a) Transfer of all preventive duties of a patrol nature to the Coast Guard.

(b) Activation of all minesweepers and maintaining a containerised mine hunting capability to be carried out onboard hired Off Shore Vessels. This would be possible owing to the change to mine hunting instead of minesweeping.

(c) Transfer of major sealifts and amphibious lifts to merchant ships of the SCI.

(d) Exit from all brown water operation.

Simultaneously, whilst affecting the above trimming, the Navy would have to cater for the following:-

(a) Judicious update of the punch of her existing fleet to match current technology in weapons, sensors and other equipment.

(b) Design of new ships to evolve from the Fleet Combat Ship concept, and capable of operating UAVs from onboard. Concentrate on two types of surface vessel of approximately 3000 and 6000 tonnes displacement, aiming to build 12 of each to stabilise at 24, and supported by large fleet tankers.

(c) Decommission progressively all patrol aircraft not capable of 15 hours flying time and raise the numbers of four engine aircraft to achieve a 1:1 ratio with surface vessels.

(d) Maintain a mix of diesel and nuclear submarines initially; however progress towards an all nuclear force of SSBNs and SSNs by 2030.

(e) Build a carrier group comprising two CVBGs capable of sustained operations of 100 days at a time with necessary auxiliaries.

(f) Build an amphibious group capable of landing one reinforced battalion in the first wave, including helicopters, landing ships and landing craft, retaining a brigade lift capability with STUFT.

INFRASTRUCTURE

Research and Development

The changes envisioned in this paper cannot be brought about, without, first and foremost, encouraging and supporting the research and development efforts by our DRDOs and other research organisation. In the light of sanction they would form the backbone for our continued and uninterrupted advancement in technology to keep abreast with, if not, to forge ahead in their respective fields.

The navy must therefore, constantly identify and indicate technologies of interest, for research and development by these organisation.

Space Applications

Satellites would play a major role in future information systems, remote sensing, etc, and their potential would have to be tapped to the fullest.

The Indian Space Research Organisation is well accomplished and has carried out pioneering work in many areas. The navy must forward a white paper indicating its specific areas of interest, for developmental work by the organisation.

Intellectual Resources

The incessant brain drain from our Indian Institutes of Technology should be curbed with offers for more rewarding perks in our own country akin to what management graduates are receiving. Channelising this immense potential resource pool towards DRDO and ISRO efforts would give an envigorating boost to the research efforts.

Shipbuilding Yards

The backbone of the ship building industry is the public sector shipbuilding yards. Close liaison with these yards would ensure that our specific requirement for the future is met, including STUFT.

Dockyards

Personnel infrastructure in the Navy, today, consists of about 50,000 uniformed personnel and 50,000 civilians. The Major portion of the civilian strength is taken up by the two dockyards, whose personnel strengths were based on the absurd and irresponsible union rules of the sixties and seventies. With the shake out in all industries facilitated by clubbing jobs, it would be possible to reduce dockyard strengths to about 6000 each from the present 12000. Heavy specialised works could be off-loaded to trade and private dockyards.

HUMAN RESOURCE MANAGEMENT AND DEVELOPMENT

Operational Personnel

The personnel and recruitment patterns would have to undergo major changes with the executive branch having to be downsized or taking on technical responsibilities that it is currently incapable of. New rates or new emphasis on qualification in electronic warfare, satellite photo interpretation, unclear engineering, airborne ASW operations will have to be freshly created and built up.

The ND and communication branches will have to merge to become the operations branch in the first phase and later on to absorb the RC and UC rates with their sensor control functions. The hardware group will have to be built around a new rate similar to the now defunct QA rate. Many of these changes have already been attempted by other navies years ago and we shall not be pioneering any new steps in this regard.

Specialised Personnel

Rapid advancements in technology would leave a generalist groping in the dark. It would be necessary for technical personnel to be vertically specialised in a specific field; be it missiles, gunnery, anti submarine warfare, navaids, communications, software or hardware development, system interfacing, action information systems, airborne ASW.

Technically non-proficient sailors have no place and it is interesting to note the acrimony that arose recently in the pages of US Naval Institute Proceedings where an American author stated that the expertise of most European Petty Officers was below that of US junior rates.

Harnessing Human Resources

Human resource is an intangible factor, which, if harnessed, has the potential of a force multiplier, Careful thought most, therefore go into cultivating it, for optimum results.

Recruitment Philosophy

By virtue of India's population, there would never be a shortage of volunteers to join the navy. However, the navy would have to compete with the civilian market for quality personnel. Among the many factors in this competition would be:-

(i) The need to provide working and living conditions that would encourage personnel to embark on a naval career ahead other careers in the civilian would.

(ii) In terms of both economics and force effectiveness, it would be important to keep personnel in the forces longer. There would be advantages in recruiting people who are, on an average, better qualified than today's recruits. Recruiting would have to be more aggressive and may have to tap people in the personnel pool, such as college graduates or individuals in mid-career, before they are usurped by the civilian market.

(iii) Research confirms that people feel more satisfied with their lives if they are satisfied with their jobs, and that good matching of people to jobs leads to better job performance and greater job satisfaction. The well-known psychological tests and associated techniques for accomplishing such matching must be honed and adapted to changing environment.

Training Philosophy

The future navy would comprise both, male and female personnel, who would hail from a variety of cultural and education backgrounds to which the training systems would have to be sensitive and adaptive.

(i) All major navies are being designed to operate with fewer people who have more technical capability at their disposal. Technology, in the form of elaborate, networked instrumentation, automated machinery controls, and integrated information and communication systems that can generate fast responses. The functions affected will very from shipboard damage control and system maintenance to target acquisition and weapon firing, all of which will be performed with fewer personnel in future naval systems. Personnel would have to be considered as integral parts of the overall system, from its inception.

(ii) More emphasis would have to be laid on simulators to speed up training and improve job performance, thereby shortening the time required for more expensive training with actual systems and forces in their real environment.

(iii) It is close to impossible for an individual to keep pace with the proliferation in electronics and wide spectrum of evolving digital applications. Vertically specialised training would be essential to ensure in depth knowledge of systems for optimum exploitation, upto junior officer level.

(iv) Although much debate has been generated on a single operator maintainer concept, the same would not be feasible due the preceding argument.

(v) Computer and communication networks would allow distributed training, so that one expert instructor could train people simultaneously at widely dispersed locations, with a consequent reduction in travel costs and time away from assigned stations.

(vi) Training costs are never lost and it is extremely important that individuals be made to undergo regular training updates to keep abreast with the rapid changes in technology.

(vii) Well qualified and trained personnel are the wealth of any organisation and therefore would have to be retained for maximum period thereafter to enable obtain optimum returns.

Quality of Life

Military careers would find it increasingly difficult to compete with civil careers in terms of pay packets. However, quality of life, which is the forte of the defence forces, would have to be maintained by way of improvements in services offered.

(i) Policies of the navy that value and support their personnel should be seriously and effective implemented.

(ii) Special attention would have to be paid to promotion prospects to ensure that stagnation and consequent frustration does not take place.

(iii) Technology can also improve the work environment in many ways, from enhancing comport to providing adequate and suitable tools and machinery to get jobs done.

(iv) Personnel at sea, perform better if the security of their families is ensured. Personalised attention would have to be given to the quality of housing, education, medical care, work opportunities for spouses and elder children, and all the other tangible and intangible factors that lead families to feel satisfied or dissatisfied with their daily lives.

(v) Personnel on deployment also wish to keep in touch with their families; a need that is possible to meet with today's worldwide communications networks. Shipboard routines must provide for is, and must do so without compromising ship or base security. Technical means must be devised to support a policy of keeping in touch with families without jeopardizing the force or its operations.

(vi) There is also evidence that personnel feel benefited if they can use their spare time to advance their education and technical skills, leading either to better promotion prospects or better job prospect on leaving the navy.

OUTLINE PLAN

Formulation of maritime Policy

National Security. Protection of geo-strategic and geo-economic interests would present the navel forces with operational challenges that could best be met through the development of deterrent capabilities derived from the wide spectrum of rapidly advancing technologies.

Regional Co-operation. The situation in the Indian Ocean is undergoing positive changes with most of the regional hotspots turning in the direction of political solution. The focus would have to be on creating an environment of regional cooperation for mutual facilitation of economic development and thereby protection of own economic interests.

Creating Political Awareness

The Indian Parliamentary Maritime Group would have to take on the onus of educating and enlightening our politicians on maritime philosophy and developments, to enable framing of a visionary maritime policy based on national security and regional co-operation.

Jointmanship. A convergence of major financially, technically, and operationally driven trends would require that naval forces increasingly operate jointly with other services and national forces and resources. Extensive equipment and mission sharing are implied, as would be needs for multi-way compatibility and interoperability, task sharing, and information sharing among all the elements of the joint operating and war fighting systems.

Adoption of Technologies.

Commercial Technologies. The world of technology is advancing at a blistering pace. Many advanced technologies are now available globally and to future adversaries. To maintain technological superiority and dominance of the battlefield, the naval forces would have to be agile users and adapt these 'commercial-of-the-shelf'technologies, rapidly, for military use.

Sustained Research and Development. Sustained and focussed indigenous research and development would be necessary for self-reliance. The nation may tend to dilute the thrust in this area due to budgetary strains post globalisation. Budgetary constraints would continue in the future as well, however, resources would have to be efficiently and effectively allocated to R & D, unique to the navy, army and air force, and in a timely manner.

Fusion of Military and Commercial Technologies. The navy would have to inter-operate evolving commercial technologies in knowledge extraction, data management, and data presentation, conjointly with unique military technologies in data linking and target acquisition to deal with the increased complexity and tempo of warfare.

Countering the Digital Battle

Computers. Computer technology would be a major enabler of future naval operation. Computers would enable enhanced situational awareness, realistic modelling and simulation, faster war fighting decisions, more effective weapons, lower-cost platforms, and more efficient and effective use of people. The navy should exploit the continual evolution of commercial computer technologies into robust computational systems.

Communications. The navy would have to engage in early exploitation of the rapid growth in commercial communications capabilities, including satellites and fiberoptic communications, to acquire the necessary increased bandwidth and diverse routing for future networking needs. The navy should also prepare for graceful degradation of these systems in times of warfare.

Information Warfare. The naval information systems would have to be protected against increased software and electromagnetic information warfare attacks and other vulnerabilities. The navy should develop offensive information and electronic warfare technologies to find, identify, and attack adversary systems and to strengthen own systems.

Arriving at the Right Force Level Mix

Force Structure. After trimming the tasks of the navy, the force structure should look at platforms that convey combat power to the location where it is needed and weapons that deliver the requisite combat power against opposition targets. The weapons would strongly influence the design of the platforms. It should then examine the design of ships, aircraft, and submarines that would use those and other weapons. Mid life updates of existing ships and judicious design of new ships, should be planned, so that the navy is able to protect the country's maritime interests despite budgetary constrains which would remain a nagging factor.

Infrastructure. It would be necessary to encourage and tap the country's immense research, development and intellectual potential, along with expertise in shipbuilding in order to meet our future requirements, without having to get bogged down by external pressures.

Human Resource Management

Recruitment and Training. Recruiting would have to be more aggressive as well as selective. The overall intellectual capability of personnel would have to be of a higher order from the inception stage itself and would later have to be honed with superior and efficient training methodologies, to handle advanced and complicated systems.

Quality of Life. Constraints with offering lucrative pay packets would have to be made up for by improvements in the quality of services provided to personnel, in order to attract quality personnel and keep them satisfied.

Specialisation. All persons would have to be technically trained and vertically specialised in a particular field for maximisation of the force multiplication effect.

Planning

Adept planning and a sound amalgamation of the above factors would enable the Indian Navy to build the right force level mix, intrinsic to protection of the geoeconomic and geo-strategic factors that would affect the country's national security policies.

Geo economic and geo-strategic factors would soon gain significance in our national security environment. Protection of maritime interests, which forms a major part of the country's economic interests, would therefore be necessary. Potential threats that would tend to impinge upon our maritime interests would therefore have to be deterred. A strong and resolute naval force would not only ensure this but would also facilitate co-operation in the region, thereby promoting overall stability.

With the revolution in military affairs and advancements in technology, the navy would have, but no option, than to constantly keep abreast with these trends. In order to overcome budgetary constraints, some of the superfluous tasks undertaken by the navy would have to be trimmed and all frills cut whilst carefully planning mid-life-updates of its existing fleet and judiciously designing new incumbents to arrive at the best force level mix. Infrastructure existing and the intangible human resource element would have to be harnessed and exploited to the fullest. 63. Framing of a suitable maritime policy, on the initiative of the Indian Parliamentary Maritime Group would offer a framework for the Indian Navy, to work towards building the right force level mix capable of protecting the country's maritime interests.

PLANS FOR THE DEVELOPMENT OF THE NAVY

Plans for the RIN made daring the 'Forties'

Towards the end of World War II, it was decided to appoint a Committee for planning the requirements of India's Armed Forces after the cessation of hostilities. The Committee's primary role1 was to assess the size and composition of the Post-War Armed Forces in India, which included the future Royal Indian Navy arid the tasks it was going to share with the Army and the Air Force. This Committee's proceedings were to be based on the 'Report on the Size and Composition of the Post-War Forces in India' prepared by the Chiefs of Staff Committee.

This report makes significant reading; it was, of course, based on the assumption that by the end of the War, Japan would have been completely subdued, the principal foreign powers in the East would be the U.S.S.R., the U.S.A. and China and that India would be responsible for maintaining sufficient forces to overcome a minor power and to hold out against a major power until Imperial Forces could arrive. It didn't take into account an independent India after the War.

In the course of discussing the parameters on which the framework for the report would be based, the report states, "The British Commonwealth of Nations comprises many countries and communities linked together by the sea and air. No one part of the Commonwealth can, in peace or war, be self-sufficient or independent of supplies from other parts. The economy and defence of each nation and community of the Commonwealth must, therefore, largely depend on the use of the sea and air routes and ports. While the main responsibility for keeping open these sea and air communications must rest with the Royal Navy and Royal Air Force under the orders of the British Government, each component part of the Commonwealth should be prepared to bear its share. India, in common with other countries of the Empire, should, therefore, maintain such naval and air forces as are necessary to ensure the defence of her bases and the security of shipping within her coastal waters from submarine, mining and air attack and to assist in the protection of trade in the ocean shipping routes.

"India's central position in the Indian Ocean is likely to make her particularly sensitive to the need for an increased naval force and especially for larger warships than she at present possesses. Such ships, unlike the present small units of the Royal Indian Navy, would be capable of adequately representing India in other parts of the Commonwealth and might do much to foster better understanding of India and thus improve relations within the Empire." The Committee described the principal task of the Navy thus: "The principal responsibility of India's Navy after the war will be the safety of Indian and Empire shipping in the ports of India and their approaches; India will also wish to take her share in the protection of this shipping on the trade routes within the Indian Ocean. It will be an important task of India's Navy to provide facilities for the combined operational training of the Army formations maintained in the country and to provide a share of the escorts, assault shipping and craft required to land these formations on a hostile shore, should this prove necessary. This implies the maintenance in peace of a nucleus force of assault shipping and craft and the appropriate training organisations, as well as personnel possessing an expert knowledge of this subject. In addition, the Navy, in conjunction with the Air Force, must be prepared to take its share in intercepting and attacking any foreign invading force which may attempt a landing on the shores of India."

The report considered the Army responsible for coastal defence and the Air Force for "seaward reconnaissance, shipping protection and co-operation with the RIN." It was also considered essential that "naval units may be required to proceed at short notice to ports in occupied countries should disturbances arise and to patrol the river approaches to such ports." Concern was expressed for superpower aggression on Afghanistan, "We must also ensure sufficient aircraft being available to prevent the Afghans from being overawed by the Russian air strength on their border"—an appreciation which is of interest even today!

On the state of peacetime preparedness and inter-Service cooperation: "It is necessary to bear in mind that naval forces, to counter these threats, cannot be quickly improvised in times of war. The main task of the Navy in peace, in common with the other Services, is to prepare for war but since the full strength of the naval force may be needed immediately on the out break of war and a long period is required both for the construction of warships and the training of naval personnel, it follows that the naval forces and air forces to co-operate with them must be maintained in peace at a high standard of preparedness.

"While for purposes of local defence a number of small ships must be maintained, we consider that a proportion of large ships will also be necessary. The provision of such ships will produce a balanced naval force, form an added incentive to recruitment and increased pride in the Service, besides assisting considerably in the training of the personnel which cannot be adequately carried out in small ships. In addition, we attach great importance to the formation of an adequate air component for seaward reconnaissance and a striking force and also to the maintenance of modern coast defences and material for local seaward defences such as booms, mines, nets and indicator loops." As regards possible aggression from major powers, the report states: "Apart from a possible long term threat from China, Russia is the only major power from whom a serious threat might be likely. So long as

India is connected with Great Britain, either as a Dominion or by a treaty guaranteeing assistance, hostilities between Russia and India could only be either the cause of or the result of a war between Great Britain and the USSR. Such a war would, inevitably, sooner or later, develop into another world conflict. While India's contribution to a war of this nature will depend very largely on the defence policy of the British Empire as a whole, she is likely to bear the first brunt of such an attack and must, therefore, be prepared at all times to defend her frontiers until Imperial reinforcements arrive."

The appreciation of possible threat is evident: "Russia is the only major power which appears likely to be in a position seriously to threaten India for some years after the present war. For this reason, aggression by Russia has been taken as the basis for estimating the forces which India would require for her defence against a major power. It is not possible to forecast with any degree of accuracy the strength of the forces which Russia, by the time she is likely to become an enemy, may be able to bring to bear against India. The scale of attack would depend on the conditions which obtain at present or those which appear likely if normal preparations were made, and on the assumption that Russia will evacuate North Persia at the end of the War. As these conditions change, so must the scale of enemy attack be reviewed and our defensive measures brought up-to-date; at the same time, it will be necessary to consider the possibility of a threat by any other major power."

In July 13, 1946, a despatch from Lord Wavell, the then Viceroy to Lord Phick Lawrence, the then Secretary of State for India, *inter* alia said, ".... the greatest danger is that an independent India may come under the domination of Russia. It is very difficult to estimate how likely this is to happen. An independent Indian Government could hardly be unconscious of the length of its seaboard or of the fact that 90 per cent of its trade is seaborne. The defences of the country are so much stronger by land than by sea that India would naturally look first for a naval alliance, especially at a time when a steady flow of imports is so vital to the development of the country. And it must surely be many years before Russia can become a formidable naval power in the Indian Ocean. Again communications by land with Russia are so bad that Russian help would be no substitute for British or American help in developing the country. It seems, therefore, that the future Government of India will not of its own choice go for Russian protection.

"Russia might however try to employ her usual tactics of giving support to a revolutionary party. Conditions in India are not unfavourable. A few capitalists and princes have enormous fortunes, while labour is still exploited, has genuine grievances, and has begun to feel its power. Maladministrationcan easily cause local scarcity and famine. The nucleus of a Communist organisation already exists and is making itself felt. It would not be difficult for Russia to gain a foothold in the country by its usual methods if the Government is weak and if the gateway of Afghanistan is not effectively barred."

The Navy's case was effectively put in the following words: "The establishment of industries within India will tend to make her economy and prosperity more dependent on the security of her export trade and so maintain, and possibly increase, the importance of her ports and overseas communications. It follows, therefore, that India must maintain adequate naval forces and that the parts on which she is dependent must be kept up-to-date in accordance with modern requirements. The coastal trade of India is not only an essential part of her peace and war economy but is also an important factor in her transportation system. The requisitioning of the majority of her coastal steamers at the beginning of the present war for naval purposes has greatly increased the congestion on the railway which might have been impossible had India been threatened from the outset. It is, therefore, important that encouragement should be given to the development of the coastal trade and the shipbuilding industry, that sufficient naval forces should be maintained to avoid being obliged to requisition mercantile shipping immediately on the outbreak of war."

Even the naval air element was thought of as is evident: "Provision must be made for naval defence both as regards the development of the Royal Indian Navy and the formation of an air component to work in co-operation with it."

It is obvious, therefore, that the British strategy for an allied or commonwealth future did consider independent India as a vital link between the East and the West. To sustain their interests in the Indian Ocean Area, Indian maritime strength was given an important place. "Discussion on the future Royal Indian Navy" in the report was based on the premise that the Naval forces after the war would be limited to those needed only for local naval defence and to assist in the protection of trade in the Indian Ocean. It also included maintenance of sufficient assault craft for training the Indian Army in amphibious warfare during peace.

It was based on the assumption that the Royal Indian Navy was already capable of limited coastal defence and had adequate seagoing strength. It, therefore, required provision and development of a balanced naval force which could be further developed in case of a future war.

The Committee, therefore, recommended the generation of a complete force consisting of one squadron of three cruisers, a destroyer leader with a flotilla of eight destroyers, one eight-ship training flotilla of sloops, one eight-ship flotilla of frigates for miscellaneous duties, eight Bangor/Bathurst class minesweepers and eight motor minesweepers. As regards smaller," amphibious and auxiliary craft, a total strength of eight motor torpedo boats (MTB), eight motor launches (ML), eight harbour defence motor launches (HDML), two marine survey vessels with auxiliaries and trawlers, a 'nucleus' of assault ships and craft and one repair ship was recommended.

These recommendations made in 1944 envisaged a two-stage development of the Royal Indian Navy. Stage I had a time frame of two years from 1945 to 1947 for replacing "existing inefficient ships" by frigates and modern sloops, acquisition of eight destroyers and training of personnel for cruisers.

The time-frame for Stage II was a four-year period after the war with Japan ended during which the rest of the recommended force levels had to be provided. It was perceived that the Royal Indian Navy would require about 1,500 regular officers and 15,000 ratings who would gradually be trained to man the RIN ships to replace the Royal Naval personnel then serving in the RIN. It was also stated that "His Majesty's Government" would lend these ships to India, which would subsequently be maintained and repaired in England at the cost of the Indian exchequer. Further, it recommended that "His Majesty's Indian Dockyard" at Bombay continue and there should be base establishments and repair facilities on both the west and the east coasts.

FLAG OFFICER COMMANDING IN RIN

On April 12,1944, Vice Admiral Godfrey, the Flag Officer Commanding the Royal Indian Navy, submitted a detailed paper to the Reorganisation Committee on the 'Future of the Royal Indian Navy' much on similar lines and also keeping in view what the Royal Navy could possibly provide or spare. His plan also was divided into two stages, each comprising several phases. His recommendations elaborated on larger ships than those that existed with the RIN at that time and included aircraft carriers and submarines in the final stages of development. His plan also emphasised the organisation of the RIN to generate an in-house capability for maintenance and training (such as adequate requirement of bases, dockyards, depots, training and additional shore establishments).

In the preparation of various reports and papers prior to and after the War, evidently the Royal Indian Navy was envisaged to develop into a full-fledged Dominion Naval Force towards the late 'forties' and be deployed as a vanguard of Commonwealth interests. It appears that even after Independence our planners continued to remain influenced by what was said earlier.

That the Indian Navy did not quite develop on these lines could possibly be attributed to the "land-frontier-threat only" concept that continued to occupy Indian minds at the highest levels for decades that followed. This resulted in the inadequate funds made available for developing the maritime force in the years that followed.

The guns finally fell silent on August 15, 1945 and the time had come to assess the requirement of future weapons and platforms in the light of the post-War environment. Before, however, this could be done, the RIN had to undertake large-scale demobilisation of personnel (no longer required for war) as well as decommissioning of many old ships and craft which had mushroomed during the war. Toe Service had also to handle a mutiny in February 1946 and to transfer a sizeable part of its assets to Pakistan in August 1947 In as early as October 1944, the then "Viceroy of India, Viscount Wavell, in a secret telegram to the then Secretary of State for India Mr. Amery, suggested a number of measures which would help "to change the atmo sphere in India" at that time. One of the major suggestions was a declaration by the British Prime Minister himself that it is the definite intention of the British Government to give India self-government as early as possible and it was suggested that the declaration should also say that "the greater measure of cooperation that political parties in India give, the earlier the change over is likely to be." A significant suggestion in the same telegram mentioned that in the same declaration a "promise of modern ships for the Indian Navy at the end of the war" should also be made.

At a meeting of India and Burma Committee held on May 28,1947, the then Viceroy Viscount Mountbatten is recorded to have said, "The Interim Government was very anxious to obtain a British cruiser for service with the Indian Navy. It was, in his view, essential to the efficiency of the Indian Navy that this request should be met; this would have the further advantage that the Indian Navy would for years be dependent on the British Navy for active help in maintaining in service a naval unit of this size. He thought that it might be possible for a British cruiser to be loaned to the Indian Navy under arrangements similar to those recently made with the Norwegian Government."

In the first Plans Paper brought out after Independence on August 25, 1947, the role and the force requirements of the Navy of free India for the next ten years were given a concrete shape for the first time. To quote from Chapter V of the Plans Paper, "The eventual role of the Navy of India is to safeguard her shipping on the high seas from interference in war; to ensure that supplies can both reach and leave India by sea in all circumstances; to keep open her ports and coastal shipping routes; to prevent any enemy landing on her shores; and to support the Army in any operations which may be required in the furtherance of the national policy." It was stated, "So long as India remains within the British Commonwealth of Nations, her task will be very much lightened by the assistance she will receive from the Royal and other Dominion Navies. But even in these circumstances, she will be expected, and indeed she will wish to, contribute to the general Naval Defence of the Commonwealth in accordance with her status as the principal sovereign state in the Indian Ocean."

The Plans Paper preceived the building in the shortest possible time a completely Indian manned balanced task force consisting of two light fleet carriers, three cruisers, eight destroyers, four submarines and "such smaller ships as were necessary for training and auxiliary purposes." The plan emphasised on the induction of air and submarine elements in the Indian Navy with an aim "to build up such a force" within a definite period of the suggested 10 years. The Plans Paper was prepared by the Royal Indian Navy's Chief of Staff, Commodore M.H.St. L. Nott, a regular RIN officer at Naval Headquarters. His service continued to be loaned to India for developing the Navy even after Independence. He unfortunately died in an aircrash in Italy in March 1948. Those who worked with him speak highly of his knowledge and foresight.

ACQUISITION OF SHIPS

Based on the recommendations of the first Plans Paper, negotiations were initiated with the British Government for acquiring the first cruiser for India, *HMS Achilles* (of the famed Battle of the River Plate of World War II), which was to be commissioned on handing over as *HMIS Delhi.* Arguments favouring the acquisition of three such cruisers (Leander class) were put up as Plans Paper 2/47 which deliberated on the build-up of the RIN as a balanced naval force, getting out of the sloop stage and for contributing towards India's image in the region. Based on these considerations, Naval Headquarters recommended to the Government that the acquisition of the first cruiser be given overriding priority.

HMIS Delhi

This cruiser, costing £736,500,* which was inclusive of the cost of normal outfits of armament and naval stores and any modifications required to be made for habitability in tropical conditions, was to be manned by 24 Indian Commissioned Officers, four British Commissioned Officers, two Indian Warrant Officers and 16 British Warrant Officers besides 756 ratings of various specialisations and branches. Twelve officers were to be deputed to the U.K. for training and specialisation in Navigation and Direction and attachment to various ships and establishments. Several ratings were also to be sent to the U.K. for training and specialisation in various disciplines including Part II Qualifications' in gunnery, radar, torpedo and antisubmarine warfare, communications, engineering and electrical technology and store-keeping. The first Commanding Officer or the cruiser was Captain H.N.S. Brown of the Royal Navy with Commander R.D. Katari as his Executive Officer. (Commander Katari rose to the rank of Admiral and took over as India's first Indian Chief of the Naval Staff.) About this time, it was decided not to acquire the other two cruisers, the Ajax and the Leander.

The plans took more concrete shape when Plans Paper 10/1948, wherein the details of the composition of the Navy of the 'fifties', as envisaged at that time, were given. As it was appreciated that it may be impractical to accord Government approval to the complete development programme at that stage, it was proposed that sanction be initially accorded for the first six years of the development programme only. The ships and aircraft to be acquired during the period 1949-54 were, one light fleet carrier, three cruisers, seven destroyers, six submarines, one survey vessel, one landing ship tank and some other supporting craft. While negotiations were going on for the finalisation of plans for the other ships, action had already been initiated to finalise the manning, equipment and-training plans for *HMIS Delhi.* The main bulk of the crew for the cruiser had to be carried on board naval ships to the U.K. well in time for working up the various departments of the cruiser before its commissioning. *HMIS Kistna* and *HMIS Cauvery* were assigned this task. The officers, ratings and essential stores and equipment were embarked on these two ships which were prepared for a cruise to the U.K. Calling at Aden, Port Said, Malta and Gibraltar, these ships headed towards their respective destinations—*Cauvery* to Plymouth and *Kistna* to Portsmouth.

During passage, Commander Katari, the Commanding Officer of *Kistna,* received orders appointing him the Commander (officially designated 'Executive Officer', i.e., the seconding command) of the *Delhi.* On arrival in the U.K., Commander Katari underwent a few precommissioning courses at Davenport and Portsmouth. He then joined the *Delhi* which was undergoing refit at the time at Chatham. His first lieutenant was Lieutenant Commander S.M. Nanda, his navigator Lieutenant K.L. Kulkarni, and his gunnery officers Lieutenant Commander V.A. Kamath and Lieutenant Kirpal Singh. All these officers later rose to flag rank. July 5, 1948 was a red-letter day for India when the Indian Navy's first cruiser *HMIS Delhi* was handed over by the Commander-in-Chief of Nore to Shri V.K. Krishna Menon, the then Indian High Commissioner in the U.K. Notable among the guests present on the occasion were Admiral Sir Harold Burrough, under whose guidance the ship had been refitted and Vice Admiral W.E. Parry, Commander-in-Chief designate of the Royal Indian Navy. The 'work-up' programme for the Indian crew began immediately. A few days before *HMIS Delhi* sailed for India, Lord Mountbatten who had by then relinquished his appointment of India's Governor-General and returned home, visited the ship. He was highly impressed by the way the ship was being handled by its fresh complement of officers and ratings. The ship sailed from Sheerness on July 6, 1948 and, on her way to India, called at Portsmouth Portland, Gibraltar and Malta for a few weeks for a further spell of 'work-up' which was facilitated by the presence of the Mediterranean Fleet at Gibraltar. At Malta, the ship was visited by Admiral Sir Arthur Power, Commander-in-Chief of the Mediterranean Fleet.

The *Delhi* had a standard displacement of 7030 tons while the full load displacement was 9740 tons. Her length was 554.5 feet, and her beam, a little over 55 feet, her draught, 16 feet forward and 20 feet aft. She was powered by Parsons' geared turbines delivering a specified horse-power of 72,000 on four shafts. Her maximum speed was 32 knots. Her armament package comprised six six-inch guns for surface operations and eight four-inch guns, fifteen 40 mm guns and four three-pounders for anti-aircraft defence. The ship had eight 21-inch torpedo tubes. The oil fuel capacity was 1800 tons while the bunked accommodation was for a complement of 680.

The *Delhi's* crest was a caparisoned elephant carrying a ceremonial umbrella with the logo "Sarvato Jayamichchhami" (may you be a victor every where) and the ship was to be the first in the series of cruisers that were to be acquired for the Navy and named after major Indian cities. As *Achilles,* her pentagonal crest portrayed the head of a knight-in-armour. On the ship's arrival in India on September 16, 1948, the officers and ratings were accorded a tumultuous welcome. Shri Jawaharlal Nehru, and many other civilian dignitaries visited the ship immediately on her coming along side. The Prime Minister addressed the officers and ratings and expressed his pride in the floating fortress and the men on board who would, if the occasion arose, effectively defend the country's shores with all their might.

Lieutenant Commander V.A. Kamath (later to become a Vice Admiral), INS Delhi's first gunnery officer, reminisces "My direct association with *Delhi* perhaps goes back longer than any other officer past or present in our Service, as I was sent to the Whale Island Gunnery School at Portsmouth in as early as March 1947 to train Indian ratings in the Gunnery System of the cruiser. At that time, it was still the pre-partition Navy and the idea was that we would eventually commission all three Leander class cruisers then remaining with the RN, of which *HMS Achilles* (later *Delhi)* was to be the first. While at Portsmouth I had frequently to visit *Achilles,* then refitting in Chatham, to progress the gunnery aspects of the refit, as the RN complement on board did not have a specialist 'G' Officer."

"Partition came in August 1947, and the only Gunner I had with me at Whale Island, Sharif Khan, and all the Muslim ratings who opted for Pakistan, were returned to Karachi. Unfortunately, those who opted for Pakistan formed the bulk of the gunnery ratings and we had to wait a few more months before fresh batches of ratings who had opted for India were sent to England to start all over again the training that had been going extremely well until August 1947. This obviously put back the commissioning date of the ship, which eventually took place at Chatham on July 5, 1948.

"At the reception held on board alongside Ballard Pier on the ship's arrival at Bombay, I remember we were honoured by the presence of our then Prime Minister, Pandit Nehru. He was, unfortunately, completely lost in this large drinking gathering of uniformed officers and men and the smart set of Bombay. He spent most of the time standing morose by himself in a corner of the quarterdeck hardly talking to anyone. It was then that Lieut enant Percy Simmons, who was the Senior Watchkeeper on board, who, I vaguely remember, tried to make conversation with Pandit Nehru. It appears that when he was told by the P.M. that he was planning a visit to Indonesia on board *Delhi,* Percy Simmons took upon himself to give the Prime Minister some sound financial advice on how best to go about the exchange of Indian Rupees into Indonesian Rupiahs. This incident may well explain why Pandit Nehru left the ship in a huff earlier than expected."

MAGAR JOINS THE FLEET

About this time, these were four Landing Ships Tanks (LSTs), Class 3— *HMS Smiter, Thrasher, Bruiser* and *Avenger,* in various Indian ports. These ships had been borrowed from the British

Government by the Quartermaster General of the Indian Army on behalf of the Government of India for dumping surplus ammunition into the sea. Due to lack of trained personnel, however, only one ship had been in continuous use and this was manned by the Royal Indian Navy. Each landing ship had a cruising speed of 12 knots and bunked accommodation for 18 officers and 150 men in addition to the normal ship's company. It could also carry 2,000 tons of stores or, alternatively, a varied combination of lorries, landing craft and tanks. These ships were essentially ocean-going tank-landing ships capable of landing tanks, vehicles and men directly on beaches during amphibious operations or for disaster rescue purposes.

Communication links between Bombay and Cochin were very poor and a train journey took more than three days. Cochin was at that time being developed as the Navy's premier training establishment while the Naval Dockyard was located in Bombay and thus there was an immediate need to transport large quantities of stores and equipment from Bombay to Cochin. The LSTs were considered best-suited for this purpose. These ships could also be used to transport steel from Calcutta and cement from Bombay to Vishakhapatnam and Cochin for construction purposes.

However, the plans had to revised owing to many reasons and it was later decided to acquire only one LST and thus *HMS Avenger* was acquired for the RIN from the British Government. The ship was renamed *HMIS Magar* and was commissioned into the RIN on April 11, 1949.

Three Destroyers Join the SIN

Naval Plans Paper 1/47 had envisaged, besides building up a cruiser squadron of three ships, the development of a destroyer flotilla of eight ships concurrently with the acquisition of a Fleet Air Arm and a submarine flotilla. In Plans Paper 5/48, however, the number of destroyers required was reduced to five, out of which three were to be acquired by the end of 1948 and two early in 1950-51. Plans Paper 7/48 dated June 4, 1948 stated that as a result of negotiations with the British Government, the Admiralty had agreed to transfer three destroyers, *HMS Rotherham, Redoubt,* and *Raider* to the Government of India. It was anticipated at that time that these ships, which were undergoing refit at various Royal Naval Dockyards, would be ready for handing over to the

Royal Indian Navy by January 1949. At that time there was an acute shortage of ratings with Part II qualifications, i.e. professional specialist qualifications in different disciplines. It was, therefore, considered necessary to firstly, train these ratings in their respective qualifications before appointing them to the destroyers, and secondly, depute a certain number of key officers and ratings for training in sea-going destroyers of the Royal Navy before they became proficient to carry out their specialist tasks on board these destroyers. It was also hoped to complete the training schedule of these officers and ratings well in time for their being available for commissioning the destroyers in March 1949. All three destroyers were planned to be commissioned together as they would then be able to 'work-up' as a team and it was considered that two months' working up with Royal Navy's Home or Mediterranean Fleet, would be sufficient before the ships sailed for India. The ships were expected to arrive in India by June 1949.

In case an adequate number of billets could not be made available on board the Royal Navy's destroyers, it was alternatively planned to depute officers and key ratings only for the first destroyer for sea training with the Royal Navy, besides a few engine-room personnel for the second and third destroyers; the bulk of officers and ratings were to be trained on the first destroyer after it was manned by RIN personnel. To give these officers and ratings sufficient sea training to commission a new type of ship on which the majority had no experience, it was considered necessary to commission the ships at intervals of two months so that the three destroyers would be commissioned in a period of four months and be ready after a further period of two months to allow for the working up of the third destroyer. All destroyers were to be ready to sail for India in company. The complement of three ships varied as the *Rotherham,* being the senior ship of the squadron, was to be commanded by a Captain and he would carry his staff in addition to the normal complement of the ship. The *Raider* and the *Redoubt* were to be commanded by a Commander and a Lieutenant Commander respectively so that a definite order of seniority within the squadron could be maintained. Including the specialists in gunnery, torpedo, anti-submarine, communications and navigation and direction, the officer complement of the three ships was to be 17, 14 and 13 while the complement of ratings, 229, 208 and 205 respectively.

The total non-recurring expenditure involved in the acquisition of these destroyers was Rs. 1.548 crore^ and the annual recurring expenditure was estimated at Rs. 75.39 lakhs. This expenditure was to be met by debiting it to the unreleased portion of the sterling balance. These destroyers were expected to have a life-span of 15 to 18 years when they were to be replaced for which it was also proposed to make an annual contribution of Rs. 10 lakhs for each destroyer, besides building up a reserve stock of ammunition to be kept ashore. The non-recurring annual expenditure of Rs. 25.13 lakhi per destroyer included Rs. 1.74 lakh$ for pay and allowances of officers, Rs. 3.39 lakhs for pay and allowances of ratings, Rs. 10 lakh for stores and the sinking fund of Rs. 10 lakhs towards replacement after 20 years.

The formal request for the transfer of the three destroyers was made when Shri H.M. Patel, the then Defence Secretary, addressed a letter to Mr. John Lang, Secretary to the Admiralty, on November 15, 1947. This was followed by a formal letter addressed to the Secretary, Military Department (Defence Staff), Commonwealth Relations Office, London, which also sought facilities for the training of the ship's crews, prior to their commissioning in the Royal Naval destroyers and training establishments. The formal sanction for the acquisition of the three 'R' Class destroyers was obtained in July 1949. It was also decided that the ships, *HMS Rother-ham, Redoubt* and *Raider* were to be respectively renamed *Rajput* (Flotilla Leader), *Rana* and *Ranjit.* The actual cost of the three destroyers, paid on March 25, 1949, was £ 700,800 while the cost of reconditioning these ships worked out to £ 344,200. *HMIS Rajput,* with Captain A. Chakraverti (became a Rear Admiral before retiring) as its Commanding Officer and Senior Officer of the 1 the Destroyer Squadron, the Indian Navy's first destroyer squadron was commissioned with pomp and eclat at Portsmouth on July 28, 1949. *HMIS Ranjit* with Commander G.S. Kapooras its Commanding Officer had already been commissioned at Chatham on July 4. The third destroyer, *HMIS Rana,* whose Commanding Officer was Commander S.N. Kohli (later an Admiral and Chief of the Naval Staff) was commissioned at Devonport on September 9, 1949.

The standard displacement *of HMIS Rajput* was 1,750 tons while that of the other two ships was 1,705 tons; the full load displacement of *Rajput* was 2,510 tons with the other ships' full load displacing 2,425 tons. The overall length of this class of ships was 358.25 feet with a beam of 35 feet eight inches, the maximum displacement being 16 feet. The armament consisted of four 4.7-inch guns which could be used against surface and serial targets and four two-pounder pompoms. Besides, *Rajput* had six 20 mm anti-aircraft guns while the other two ships had four 40 mm anti-aircraft guns each. Each ship was fitted with eight 21-inch torpedo tubes on quadruple mountings and four depth-charge throwers. The propulsion machinery of each ship comprised Parson's geared turbines delivering a specified horsepower of 40,000 on two shafts giving it a maximum speed of 32 knots.

The crests were shaped after traditional shields and depicted different types of mediaeval Rajput weapons; the *Rajput* crest displayed a Rajput helmet and two crossed spears, *Rana's* crest had a broad-based knife with a petagonal blade and a cross-grip, and *Ranjit's* crest carried two crossed curved daggers enclosed in a ring.

8

The Mine Warfare Problem

Naval mines can be used strategically, channelling or denying passage through restricted waters and in and out of ports needed for sustenance by littoral nations. They can shape the naval battlespace, the approaches to it, and routes of commerce, setting the conditions of a campaign. Used tactically, they can slow or stop movement to and through narrow straits and to landing zones on beaches, and in so doing can also make a slowed or stopped force more vulnerable. Yet despite the many instances in which mines were important in past conflicts, the U.S. Navy historically has underrated mine warfare as an element of naval warfare.

During the Civil War the Confederate forces at the Battle of Mobile Bay, unable to meet the Union fleet on equal terms, used mines as a defensive barrier. In that battle Rear Admiral David Farragut, the Union commander, using techniques involving surveillance and reconnaissance followed by mine hunting and avoidance of the located minefield—techniques that are similar in concept to those in use today —penetrated the barrier losing only a single ship. This action perhaps helped establish an attitude that has persisted to this day: that mine warfare is principally for the use of weaker naval forces to defend against, and to be overcome by, stronger ones. It was nevertheless at great expense, 80 years later, that German and Japanese minefields had to be overcome both to allow merchant shipping to move in and out of allied ports and to clear the way for offensive landings in both the Atlantic and Pacific theatres of war.

Less noticed, mining by the allies had some notable successes in World War II. In the Atlantic war, the Royal Air Force (RAF) flew 20,000 mine-laying sorties over a period of 5 years, sinking

638 ships with the loss of 450 aircraft. This compares with 366 ships sunk directly by RAF torpedoes and bombs over the same period with the loss of 857 aircraft. Only 196 Axis ships were sunk by British submarines and surface ships. Similarly, in the Pacific theatre mines dropped by U.S. B-29s in the spring of 1945, together with American submarine warfare, effectively isolated Japan from all overseas sources of food and resources for the rest of the war.

In the more recent past, the United States has not been averse to using sea mines. During the Vietnam War, in May 1972, thousands of magnetic-acoustic mines were dropped in Haiphong harbour and in other harbours along the North Vietnamese coast, virtually stopping the delivery of war materials by sea. Within 3 days, 27 foreign merchant vessels were trapped in port. When peace talks broke down the area was reseeded in November 1972. For 2 more years, without loss of U.S. life, this mining campaign continued to stop shipping into and out of Haiphong and other North Vietnamese harbours, thus interdicting 95 percent of the seaborne logistics resupply to North Vietnam.

A limited attempt to employ mines during the Persian Gulf War proved less successful. On January 18, 1991, four A-6 aircraft dropped 42 mines, but the Iraqis shot down one A-6. Based on the continued Iraqi naval activity following the U.S. mining, it appears that the minefield, which was not reseeded, had no discernible effect on Iraqi operations. This experience highlights the importance of developing survivable means of delivery (and reseeding) in hostile areas such as by standoff aircraft or submarines. Despite the successes of naval mining both by and against the United States, the U.S. Navy has generally held its use in relatively low regard. Although there was some continuing attention to the Soviet mine warfare threat during the Cold War, the U.S. Navy planned to rely primarily on NATO allies for countermine warfare in the event of maritime hostilities. To help counter the Soviet submarine threat, the Navy did field sophisticated CAPTOR homing mines in the 1970s.

MINE WARFARE FOR OPERATIONAL EFFECTIVENESS

Countermine Warfare

More recently, the U.S. Navy's interest in mine warfare took a strong turn upward when the Chief of Naval Operations directed, in a 1995 white paper, that mine counter-measures (MCM) —a critical element of countermine warfare— should receive much more attention and should become organic to battle forces at sea rather than remain exclusively the domain of a separate supporting force. This increased Navy interest grew out of the Gulf War experience and the growing realization that sea mines are readily available to potential U.S. opponents and are relatively inexpensive. Russia, Italy, Sweden, and others are major suppliers of modern mines to the more than 50 countries that today possess a sea mining capability. Potential U.S. Navy and Marine Corps contingency regions have significant mineable waters, including the Persian Gulf, the Strait of Hormuz, the Taiwan Strait, the Red Sea, the Adriatic Sea, the Yellow Sea, the Korea Strait, and the coastal margins of the Sea of Japan. During the "Tanker War" in 1987–1988, the USS *Roberts* was heavily damaged by a drifting mine, leading to the embarrassing image of U.S. warships following, rather than leading, the tankers they were nominally protecting. During Desert Storm, Iraqi mines impeded U.S. amphibious assault planning and heavily damaged two U.S. warships—the cruiser *Princeton* and the amphibious carrier *Tripoli*—effectively removing them from further support of the operations.

Mines are particularly valuable to hostile "asymmetric" forces that cannot engage U.S. naval forces directly. Naval mines are more widespread and in many ways more difficult—and certainly more time-consuming—to counter than the likely air and missile threats. Since World War II 14 U.S. Navy ships have been sunk or damaged by mines, whereas only 2 have been damaged by missile or air attack. In all the time since World War II, no U.S. ship has been damaged by submarine action. Of the 14 mine hits on ships, 10 occurred during the Korean War, and North Korea remains a potential antagonist today. Countermine warfare is much more than mine countermeasures. In the mine warfare framework used by the Commander, Fifth Fleet, countermine warfare involves five phases:

1. Intelligence collection and surveillance,
2. Notification of imminent mining,
3. Interdiction, both on land and at sea,
4. Post-interdiction intelligence evaluation and dissemination, and
5. Mine countermeasures.

The first four phases emphasize measures intended to prevent mines from entering the water. Current carrier battle groups and amphibious ready groups deploy with capabilities to plan and execute the first four phases of countermine warfare. The fifth phase—mine countermeasures—addresses localizing the threat posed by mines already laid or thought to have been laid. Because they have very limited MCM capability, today's carrier battlegroups and amphibious ready groups depend on the specialized support provided by the dedicated MCM forces.

Mining

While the threat of sea mines to U.S. interests is now receiving increased U.S. Navy attention as a significant part of potential antagonists' "asymmetric warfare" arsenal, mines are also an important element of naval power available to the United States. This is particularly true at a time when the U.S. Navy is shrinking but is still being assigned to littoral missions spread progressively more widely around the world. Antiship mines, safely delivered by U.S. submarines or standoff aircraft, could effectively shut down commercial and military shipping as a potentially effective coercive measure in a crisis short of direct combat. They could also be used protectively to prevent interference with U.S. naval force missions, and as an extension of the fleet for such tasks as bottling up an invasion force. Strategically employed, remotely controlled, smart minefields incorporating a distributed sensor system could be a cost-effective counter to the feared proliferation of quiet nonnuclear submarines.

International conventions signed by the United States forbid the laying of armed sea mines in international waters in peacetime unless they are continuously monitored and international shipping is warned of their location. Today, advanced sensor and networking technology, together with advanced ocean surveillance of shipping, could enable remote control of naval mines. This capability could set the stage for their legal use to forestall wider conflict or to set conditions favourable for U.S. naval force operations.

Operational Considerations for Mine Warfare

In reviewing future concepts and possible scenarios, the committee was impressed by the number and diversity of operational drivers basic to the conduct of effective mine warfare activities. The most pertinent operational considerations are the following:

- *Uncertain scenarios.* In planning for future contingencies, the U.S. Navy and the military in general must be prepared to adapt to a variety of scenarios, and to locales that are expected to be increasingly close to shore, in mineable waters, as the Navy continues to implement its "Forward...From the Sea" vision. These contingencies could cross the full spectrum of military operations, from military operations other than war, to small-scale contingencies, to major theatre wars.
- *Uncertain allied and coalition support.* A reduced U.S. military overseas infrastructure and varying access to foreign basing place a premium on robust afloat basing plus logistics and maintenance support in-theatre that is capable, timely, and available at the right locations.
- *Multimission conflicts.* Declining warship and aircraft squadron force levels combined with increased multimission demands in joint and coalition operations mean that multimission conflicts will occur, and various concepts of operation (CONOPS), including those associated with mine warfare, must realistically reflect expected asset availability.
- *Reduced time lines.* The time allotted to countering the mine threat has decreased. Fast-paced expeditionary and maneuver warfare reduces associated time lines allocated for achieving maritime battlespace superiority (including countering undersea threats such as mines).
- *Limited forces early in contingencies.* Some short-warning situations are inevitable, with the likely result that only a few forces will be in-theatre early (prior to the arrival of continental United States-based forces). These limited forces will have to deal with the potential threat from mines, as well as other threats.
- *Dispersed force operations.* In the future, surface warships and submarines may be dispersed throughout the theatre doing key task unit operations (strike, fire support, theatre air defense, and theatre ballistic missile defense) as opposed to operating primarily in close proximity to a battle group.

Warships so employed will have to provide much of their own self-protection against various threats, including mines.

- *Network-centric operations.* Future platforms and sensors involved in countermine operations would be nodes in an overall communications network.

A shared picture of operations and fused sensor data, including naval minefield information, would support interactive collaborative mission planning and enhance battlespace situation awareness.

- *Low tolerance for losses.* The objective of an adversary's area-denial strategy may be to produce unacceptable losses (not commensurate with stated U.S. military objectives) and thereby undermine U.S. military involvement and influence. It has been said that the loss of even a single U.S. warship (particularly if it involves a ship sinking and high loss of life) may for some lesser contingencies "inflict enough damage to make the political cost of involvement unacceptably high." Recent military losses in Lebanon (the 1983 Marine barracks destruction) and Somalia (the 1993 firefight in Mogadishu) are examples of such losses that were considered inconsistent with military objectives, resulting in eventual U.S. military disengagement and withdrawal.

FUTURE CAPABILITY—NEXT STEPS

History, the current and future threat projection, and other operational as well as considerations make clear that countermine warfare should concern the planners of future U.S. naval and joint forces at least to the same extent as air or submarine threats. Additionally, because of the great potential benefits to U.S. maritime operations that could result from U.S. employment of modern sea mines, such capabilities are worth preserving. Of particular importance are the intelligence, surveillance, and reconnaissance (ISR) aspects of mine warfare, since that is where mine warfare really starts, regardless of the specific purposes for which such information is ultimately used. It is the considered opinion of this committee that, in order to ensure the capabilities of the U.S. Navy into this new millennium, the priority and attention afforded to mine warfare must be increased dramatically and religiously sustained.

Most of the subsequent discussion in this report deals with problems the Navy must solve and programs the Navy must bring to fruition to ensure having an adequate mine warfare capability later in this decade. This focus on Navy programs is not meant to imply that the Marine Corps, the other military Services, the intelligence agencies, and the unified commands have negligible roles in mine war—they do not. As with most complex military operations, mine warfare operations are inherently joint. The unified commands actually operate the mine warfare forces in-theatre; the intelligence agencies provide vital ISR information; Marine Corps units must work closely with the Navy in any amphibious operations and interface with Army mine warfare (and other) operations ashore; Navy and Coast Guard units must work together closely in inshore mine warfare operations both overseas and, should the occasion arise, in U.S. waters; and the Air Force is trained and its bombers are configured to quickly deliver large quantities of naval mines.

Because the Navy's mine warfare programs are so potentially important, because developments in this warfare area have lagged behind those in other warfare areas, and because of the complexity inherent in establishing a new major area of naval warfare, the committee found it appropriate to offer a larger number of more detailed recommendations than is customary for reports of this kind. These recommendations provide the committee's best judgment on how current mine warfare programs can be strengthened to meet future naval force needs, how additional efforts should be developed to address future capability shortfalls, and how the naval forces can better leverage joint or national assets to meet their objectives.

MINE WARFARE AS A MAJOR NAVAL WARFARE AREA

The increasingly recognized importance of mines as a growing threat to the U.S. fleet and its freedom of maneuver, as well as to freedom of the seas generally, has fuelled the movement to place mine warfare in the mainstream of naval force planning and operations. The importance of the mine threat is reinforced by the strategic orientation of the naval forces—and U.S. joint forces generally—to expeditionary warfare along the littorals, where battle groups, amphibious forces, and the seaborne logistic support for all U.S. forces overseas will have to operate and where sea mines are most likely to be employed by hostile forces to try to impede U.S. access.

The United States has used sea mines as an instrument of diplomacy, to shape the naval battlespace, and to extend naval power into areas the fleet could not immediately guard on several occasions in recent decades. In the opinion of the committee, such U.S. use of sea mines should become more prevalent in the future as the potential for technologically advanced minefield surveillance and remote-control techniques could enable effective U.S. use of sea mines while adhering to international conventions in situations short of war.

All of these developments mean that mine warfare has risen to a level of significance that necessitates its designation as a major warfare area, similar in importance to air warfare, surface warfare, and submarine warfare. This requires that current approaches to planning, preparing, and organizing the naval forces be modified in several ways. Naval forces' exercises and the facilities for exercises and for developing new concepts of operation under mine warfare conditions must be enhanced. Personnel education, training, and career development require similar attention. Until naval personnel are fully qualified and knowledgeable in the mine warfare area, and are able to advance their careers from such an orientation, there will be little hope of raising mine warfare into the mainstream. And appropriate adjustments must be made in the budget for mine warfare to more fully meet the needs described in this report. It is important to note that the actions that need to be taken to elevate the importance of mine warfare would not lead to a significant growth of naval force structure, but rather to increased mine warfare capabilities within the force structure that is currently planned or one that emerges from current defense reviews.

Recommendation: The Secretary of the Navy, the Chief of Naval Operations, and the Commandant of the Marine Corps should take the steps needed to establish mine warfare as a major naval warfare area. Such an elevation in warfare status will require that the Department of the Navy (a) coordinate and improve the focus of its "mainstreaming" initiatives; (b) upgrade mine warfare-related readiness reporting, certification, training and education, and officer career planning; and (c) program, budget, and execute accordingly. Continual follow-up by these officials will be necessary to ensure implementation.

The major activities that need to be addressed if this recommendation is to be fully implemente. While each of these major activities is addressed separately, the committee believes that they are sufficiently interrelated that substantial progress will be needed in each area if the collective goal is to be achieved.

The Navy Fleet Engagement Strategy

In the fall of 1998 the Vice Chief of Naval Operations (VCNO) and the Assistant Secretary of the Navy for Research, Development, and Acquisition (ASN (RDA)) tasked responsible commands to develop plans of action and milestones (POA&M) to support the four Fleet Engagement Strategy pillars—doctrine and tactics, education and training, industry and technology, and public affairs— with these plans due in March 1999. The committee learned from briefings and reports commissioned by the Navy that as of December 1999, only about half of the plans had been developed and submitted to the Director, Expeditionary Warfare (N75), as designated in the task letters. To date, some additional progress has been made in each of these areas. Navy staff briefed this committee on shortfalls in the Fleet Engagement Strategy and a draft implementation plan intended to both address the shortfalls and define the schedule and the hierarchy of responsibility and accountability for "mainstreaming" mine warfare.

Mainstreaming mine warfare and adding organic MCM capabilities to the fleet is a significant and complex undertaking, critical to the ability of deployed carrier battle groups (CVBGs) and amphibious ready groups (ARGs) to attain and maintain sea battlespace dominance. Primary Navy emphasis is on phase five of countermine warfare, MCM, or countering mines after they have been put into the water. However, the roles intended for the dedicated and future organic MCM systems in the expected types of operations remain to be fully defined as experience is gained with organic MCM capabilities.

The proposed hierarchy relies on the existing Navy chain of command and places ultimate responsibility and accountability with the senior Navy leadership, specifically the VCNO. The ASN (RDA) would provide the linkage to the Secretariat and associated program executive offices. The Director, Expeditionary Warfare

(N75) would serve as the executive agent for the VCNO, addressing day-to-day issues and monitoring all facets related to mainstreaming mine warfare and facilitating the transition to organic MCM capabilities.

Three key architects would serve the VCNO, including the following:

- A capabilities architect (Commander in Chief, Atlantic Fleet (CINCLANTFLT) components to include the Commander, Second Fleet, supported by the other fleet CINCs and the fleet marine forces),
- A requirements architect (N75, supported by the other OPNAV codes and Headquarters, Marine Corps), and
- An acquisition architect (Deputy Assistant Secretary for Mine and Undersea Warfare, supported by other associated deputy assistant secretaries and program offices).

Although the year 2000 target dates have now all passed unmet, the Navy remains committed to mainstreaming mine warfare and to transitioning organic MCM capabilities to an initial CVBG by 2005. While some progress has been made toward tasks required to implement the Fleet Engagement Strategy, a comprehensive implementation plan has not yet been endorsed by the senior Navy leadership. To be successful, mainstreaming initiatives need to address issues ranging from command structure implications to training and education at both the schoolhouse and waterfront levels. Sustained high-level support is critical for the major cultural changes required for successful, fleet-wide mainstreaming of mine warfare.

Recommendation: The Chief of Naval Operations (CNO) and the senior Navy leadership should expeditiously establish an implementation plan that assigns responsibility and accountability to the appropriate officials to bring to fruition the mainstreaming of mine warfare, in particular the introduction of organic mine countermeasures capabilities. Such a plan should include the seven key elements— doctrine, organization, training, materiel, leadership and education, people, and facilities—detailed below.

Incorporating organic MCM capabilities into the fleet and mainstreaming mine warfare are integrally related. They succeed or fail together. Seven key elements are essential to this success or failure:

- *Doctrine.* Development of countermine warfare (CMW) CONOPS, tactics, and doctrine specifically defining the roles of organic and dedicated MCM relative to joint and naval missions.
- *Organization.* Development of an overall command structure that addresses the role of the mine warfare commander, CVBG and ARG staff billets, and a planned transition from current mine warfare coordinator to mine warfare commander.
- *Training.* Implementation of the needed schoolhouse (operations, intelligence, and Judge Advocate General (JAG)) and fleet training from the system level to the CVBG and ARG interdeployment training cycle (IDTC).
- *Materiel.* Implementation of the maintenance and logistics support plans needed for the transition of organic MCM systems to the fleet.
- *Leadership and education.* Establishment of an education program for developing naval leadership commitment to well-equipped and well-trained mine warfare forces, as well as to the key role of future organic MCM systems.
- *People.* Development of the necessary manning concepts for incorporating future organic MCM systems on multipurpose fleet units (surface combatants, submarines, aircraft), and establishment of attractive career paths for officers in the mine warfare community.
- *Facilities.* Development of various mine warfare-related support facilities to enhance tactical development, training and education, maintenance, logistics, and other facets of mine warfare.

Adequate CVBG and ARG Expertise

Independent of the transition to new organic MCM capabilities, deploying CVBGs and ARGs need to prepare for the likely mine threat by leveraging existing countermine warfare capabilities. For example, the mission areas required for CVBG and ARG certification prior to deployment already formally include the mine warfare mission area. Deploying force command structures currently include a mine warfare coordinator with the CVBG only, rather than a mine warfare commander for the CVBG or the ARG.

Effective execution of countermine warfare phases one through four—intelligence collection and surveillance, notification of imminent mining, interdiction, and post-interdiction intelligence evaluation and dissemination, involves not only the mine warfare commander, but also the other warfare commanders (i.e., those responsible for interdiction and for the execution of amphibious operations), the intelligence officer and intelligence support infrastructure, and the JAG staff to facilitate appropriate rules of engagement (ROE).

Currently, specific individual schoolhouse training and prior experience requirements do not include mine warfare, resulting in only limited mine warfare awareness and expertise embedded in CVBGs and ARGs. Each of these combat forces face potentially varied countermine warfare scenarios, particularly when operating apart, with the ARG typically in shallower, closer-to-shore waters than the CVBG units. Although current CVBGs and ARGs deploy with capabilities to plan and execute the first four phases of countermine warfare, the IDTC provides an existing process for expanding these capabilities as part of the mainstreaming initiatives.

The committee notes that the Commander, Second Fleet, has taken meaningful steps toward improving the mine warfare components and assessments in the routine predeployment joint task force exercises and the at-sea certification test for deploying CVBGs and ARGs. Evidence to date indicates that at least sporadic initiatives are under way to improve training. The command structure implications are addressed in the draft concept of operations (CONOPS), which has yet to be implemented, with the exception of Fleet Battle Experiment HOTEL. A more focused effort is required to raise the awareness and expertise of naval personnel fleetwide.

Predeployment Training, Fleet Exercises, and Readiness Reporting

Realistic scenarios for fleet training exercises are fundamental to instilling proper understanding of the entire mine warfare area. Proper training is as important for senior commanders and staffs as for individual ships or aircraft or personnel. Additionally, the importance of mine warfare to fleet operations means that mine warfare/MCM readiness must be a part of fleet readiness reporting, to the same extent as readiness to engage opposing missile, air, and submarine forces. Defense against mines should become a major element of the Navy's force protection initiative.

Historically, fleet exercises have tended to ignore the effects of mines on an operation: Time lines have been artificially shrunk to overcome the delays caused when mines are encountered, a unit encountering a mine has been "reconstituted" almost immediately, or the encount itself has been ignored completely. These procedures have tended to foster the idea, even if only subliminally, that mine damage is either imaginary or that it can be ignored as a real factor in operating the force.

To ensure development of mine warfare expertise in all participants in a fleet exercise, the likely consequences of an encounter with a mine have to be played out at least to the same degree that encounters with air or submarine attackers are accounted for. This will require a more versatile exercise mine system and procedures such as adjudication of the interaction by on-scene referees, removal of the unit from the exercise, rescue, medical evacuation of the "casualties," and salvage of the damaged ship. The argument that scarce training time will be diverted is perhaps specious, since the training imparted by an artificial response to a mine incident is suspect at best and can be considered to be counter-productive in the long run.

Similarly, readiness to conduct mine warfare must be reported as part of overall unit readiness, especially in view of the growing likelihood of mine encounters in littoral waters and in expeditionary operations. As the new organic MCM systems are introduced into the fleet, MCM readiness associated with those systems should become reportable in the ship's operational readiness training status (SORTS) report by each ship and aircraft squadron. Tactical aircraft squadrons and submarines that have mine delivery capabilities should routinely report their readiness to conduct such missions in SORTS. As the new mission capability assessment system (MCAS) is introduced, battle group commanders should begin reporting the collective readiness of their units to conduct mine warfare operations.

The mine warfare readiness and effectiveness measurement (MIREM) program (modeled after the SHAREM program for antisubmarine warfare (ASW)) has been under way for several years. The primary emphasis to date has been on evaluating the performance of dedicated MCM forces. The performance of existing organic MCM capabilities on current warships (surface combatants, submarines), such as their on-board high-frequency sonars and their signature control capabilities, have largely not been evaluated as part of MIREM exercises to date.

The committee concluded, based on examination of all these needs, that the mine warfare portions of fleet and subunit exercises and readiness reporting are not given the status of other warfare areas. Their relegation instead to secondary and unrealistic auxiliary positions fosters an inappropriate and inaccurate concept of the roles and importance of mine warfare in maritime operations among the officer corps from their most junior years.

Recommendation: The Department of the Navy should establish broad first-order force-protection requirements for naval units that will ensure adequate levels of countermine warfare capability, both active and passive.

Mine Warfare Battle Laboratory

The committee concluded that there is an urgent need for a mine warfare battle laboratory (1) as an essential adjunct to the ongoing effort to bring mine warfare into the mainstream of naval force planning and (2) to provide a facility for exploration of fleet mine warfare-related operational concepts and capabilities, to assess fleet mine warfare operational issues and doctrine, and, in war games and other exercises, to provide the means whereby mine warfare can be practiced realistically, accurately, and in real time by the war game or exercise participants.

Such a facility ideally must be a true extension of the fleet and should be sponsored, tasked, and controlled by a senior fleet operational entity. While the Navy's R&D centers and laboratories must naturally be involved with and supportive of the technical side of the battle laboratory, the primary sponsor and customer of the laboratory must be the operational side of the Navy. It is the consensus of the committee that the mine warfare battle laboratory should report to the numbered fleet commander(s) and should be located in, or be accessible to, a fleet concentration center such that it is visible, used, and useful to the fleet operators, directly or indirectly. A location in Ingleside, Texas, while not in geographic proximity to fleet centers, could be feasible, if funding and manpower resources are made available to clearly support robustly linking the laboratory with other fleet and R&D sites.

Also, to ensure adequate and appropriate attention to inshore countermine warfare, the Marine Corps would have to be a participant in battle laboratory activities, along with amphibious force commanders.

Recommendation: The CNO and the CMC together should establish a mine warfare battle laboratory under the auspices of the numbered fleet commander(s) and provide the resources necessary to ensure its effective utilization.

Individual Education, Training, and Career Development

For mainstreaming of mine warfare to be fully effective, officers must perceive expertise in mine warfare as career enhancing. To this end a desirable promotion path is needed for officers who have devoted career time to gaining expertise in mine and countermine warfare. At present such paths exists only to the 0–6 level, and only in the MH-53 airborne MCM and explosive ordnance disposal (EOD)/very shallow water (VSW) detachment communities. Such viable career paths also need to be established in the surface warfare and MH-60 helicopter communities. Selection of flag officers should increasingly value mine warfare knowledge and experience, which should become an explicit prerequisite for such key operational commands as Commander, Mine Warfare Command. Currently, such experience tends to be discounted, and there is a well-justified belief among many officers that assignment to a mine warfare post detracts from promotion prospects.

If attention to mine warfare is increased by making it a warfare area on a par with other warfare areas, this "second class" status for mine warfare officers is likely to disappear, but the issue needs continuing command attention at the highest levels of the Navy and the Navy Department until the change is securely in effect. The Navy has reportedly recently made a step in this direction by deciding to assign some of its most promising junior officers to command each of the 26 small mine-hunting and mines weeping ships. The extent to which the future assignments of these outstanding officers to additional tours in mine warfare billets would be considered appropriate has not been discussed with the committee.

Another facet of the Navy's mine warfare mainstreaming initiative also needs to be strengthened. There should be clear educational curriculum requirements for mine warfare disciplines, just as there are for naval surface, air, and undersea warfare, as well as much greater emphasis on mine warfare in officers' professional schools. Currently, for example, instruction in mine warfare history, technology, and operations constitutes a very minor part of the curriculum in the Naval Academy and the Naval War College, and it is given but 20 percent of the time that is given to antisubmarine warfare in surface warfare school. Aviation MCM training relies on on-the-job training. The need to incorporate mine warfare into the mainstream of naval force training and education is noted above, and the current state of inadequate attention to the necessary personnel planning and training for integration of the organic MCM systems.

Recommendation: The Secretary of the Navy, the CNO, and the CMC should ensure that the growing importance of mine warfare is emphasized in all appropriate Navy and Marine Corps formal education curricula and in officer career development practices. These curricula and career development criteria should place mine warfare expertise on a par with the emphasis given to air warfare, surface warfare, and submarine warfare.

Mine Warfare Budgets

The committee attempted a detailed examination of the budget devoted to mine warfare, in comparison with that devoted to other warfare areas. Assembling the budget for a warfare area is a notoriously difficult task, since it requires allocating the costs of large, multimission systems, such as Navy ships, into components devoted to each of the warfare areas. This, in turn, requires ascertaining the multiyear costs of several levels of subsystems and component equipment, and making judgments as to their specific applicability, by warfare area. Cost research to this level of detail did not prove possible within the resources available to the committee, even with the excellent support that the Navy furnished for the committee's deliberations.

However, the results of the committee's explorations in this area were sufficient to indicate that (1) the total Navy budget for sea mine warfare is small relative to that for air and missile defense, and (2) the budget for mines and mining, as part of that, is trivially small compared with that for strike warfare weapons (a few million dollars compared with several billion over the future year defense program (FYDP)), and may soon drop to zero. The budget that the Navy identifies with mine warfare, approximately $4.6 billion over the next 7 fiscal years, is devoted almost entirely to countermine warfare. Roughly one-third of the countermine warfare budget is for operations and maintenance (O&M) of the existing fleet of dedicated mine warfare forces, and another third is for ongoing development of the seven organic MCM systems.

As indicated in those chapters, there are many unfunded or underfunded needs in the mine warfare area. These deficiencies include, to reiterate but a few major examples:

- No funding to acquire a very shallow water and assault breaching system to support amphibious landings in this decade;
- Lack of funding to remedy important equipment shortfalls on the MCM and MHC classes of MCM ships;
- Inadequate funding for technologies (including advanced signal processing techniques) to find buried mines, and to support the objective of removing people and other mammals from the minefields—e.g., bottom-penetrating sonars, electric field sensors, and synthetic aperture sonars;
- Inadequate funding to maintain and verify the reduction of ship magnetic and acoustic signatures;
- Insufficient funds to populate the databases for the mine warfare environmental decision aids library (MEDAL), information that is essential for mine hunting and clearance in littoral waters and in ports important to U.S. and allied shipping;
- Lack of funding for necessary upgrades to the systems on the mine warfare command ship *Inchon* to replicate and extend such a capability to fully and effectively meet the needs of a two-ocean navy;
- Phasing out of the MH-53 helicopter needed for heavy-duty mines weeping because funds are not available, rather than for technical and operational reasons;
- Lack of funded preplanned product improvement programs for the organic MCM systems now being developed and soon to be entered into service;
- Disappearing funds for mines and mining capability;

- Inadequate funding to adequately exploit foreign mines as needed to design effective countermeasures; and
- Restriction of organic MCM to carrier battle group ships, leaving even new amphibious ships such as the LPD-17 with no active defences against mines.

Shortfalls such as these must be funded if the Navy is to meet all of its mining and countermine warfare responsibilities in the face of the shrinking Navy and the growing mine warfare threat. The committee's explorations suggest a serious imbalance in the allocation of funding among the various warfare areas. If mine warfare is to become a partner comparable in importance with air, surface ship, and submarine warfare in the naval forces' panoply of systems to enable expeditionary warfare, some redress of this imbalance is needed.

The committee did not have the budget analysis resources to make credible, detailed estimates of how much additional funding would be needed. However, it is estimated very roughly that the most important unfunded needs might be met by approximately doubling the budget remaining after the O&M funding for the dedicated forces and the organic system developments are accounted for over that period—in the neighborhood of an additional $1.5 billion over the next 5 years— about a 30 percent increase in annual spending on mine warfare. A detailed budget plan would show the extent to which part of this increase, or further funding beyond it, would be needed to meet the requirement for continuation or expansion of the mine countermeasures command ship concept (the mine control ship (MCS)-12, *Inchon* and/or its replacement(s)). Most such MCS funding would be needed later in, and beyond, the FYDP period.

The committee could not identify large amounts of mine warfare money that appeared to be allocated inappropriately or was being spent wastefully, so that shifting funds within the mine warfare complex of systems cannot solve the problem of serious shortfalls. It therefore appears to the committee that the Navy will have to allocate additional funds to mine warfare from other areas in the Navy budget by deferring some expenditures intended to meet threats that are less imminent.

9

Naval Port Security in the RIN

NAVAL PORT SECURITY OFFICES AND STAFF

In April 1943, an officer left for the United Kingdom to undergo training in security duties, and returned in October to take up office as Staff Security Officer at Naval Headquarters. At the same time, Naval Port Security Officers were appointed at Calcutta, Madras, Karachi, Chittagong, Bombay and Landing Craft Wing. Moreover, Naval Security-Intelligence Officers were appointed at other ports of India. Between October 1943 and January 1944, the R.I.N. obtained the services of Commander Campbell-Ross, R.N.V.R., to examine and suggest improvements in Port and Shipping Security. As a result, many new security measures were undertaken to introduce a larger degree of control. The Security Branch, like other branches in the services, suffered from an acute shortage of officers. On the recommendation of the Manpower Committee in 1944, intelligence and security duties at Karachi, Cochin, Madras and Chittagong were amalgamated. Thereafter, security arrangements at the ports showed progressive improvement. The number of security ratings originally allowed in April 1944 was cut down to 14, excluding the thirty with the Landing Craft Wing.

Inter-Services Security Education Department (I.S.E.D.)

In March 1944, Commander Campbell-Ross, R.N.V.R., and Commander Clairmonte, R.N.R., came to India to advise about the setting up of a Security Education Department in the R.I.N. Later, the Naval Security Education Department was amalgamated with the Inter-Services Security Education Department and formed part of the Inter-Services Security Directorate (I.S.S.D.). The education department consisted then of two wings the education wing and the production wing. Commander Clairmonte, R.N.R., was appointed officer-in-charge of the Inter-Services Security Education Department and Lieut. Commander Bruce Belfrage, R.N.V.R., as head of the Inter-Services Education Department (Education Wing). With the help of the Department of Information and Broadcasting, security education, drives were conducted at all ports and important centres with great success.

Inter-Services Security Co-ordination Section (I.S.C.S.)

With the formation of Inter-Services Security Directorate under the Director of Security, India Command, a close liaison was maintained with the security authorities of the other services through the Inter-Services Security Co-ordination section to which a representative of each Service was appointed.

Inter-Services Movements Security Control Directorate (I. Mov. S.C.)

Another addition to the Inter-Services Security Directorate was the Inter-Services Movement Control Directorate, which was responsible for all questions relating to security of sea, air, and land movements and merchant shipping and seamen, and formed a linkup with, and worked on the lines of security control in, the United Kingdom. The Director of Naval Intelligence Admiralty loaned a Lieutenant Commander as a Naval representative in this department.

Inter-Services Security Board (I.S.S.B.)

The Staff Security Officer, Naval Headquarters represented the Royal Indian Navy's interests on the Inter-Services Security Board. At the time of the separation of the East Indies Fleet and the British Pacific Fleet, the Royal Naval Intelligence Officer in Delhi was appointed as a representative of the Commander-in-Chief, East Indies Station. There was also a naval officer on the permanent secretariat of the Board.

General Headquarters Security Liaison Officers were made available to the Royal Indian Navy. These officers were asked from time to time to make tours of various H.M.I, ships and establishments to advise on security and morale amongst the personnel of the R.I.N. Their work proved very valuable.

Censorship

In order to improve censorship in the Services, the Naval Adviser on Censorship, Middle East (Captain W.K. Conlon, R.N.,) visited India in January 1944, and carried out a tour of ports to contact censor authorities, service and security representatives, and civilians connected with shipping, to advise them on common problems. His visit which terminated in March 1944, was most beneficial. He was loaned to the India Command, as Naval Adviser to the Director of Civil and Services Censorship (India) (D.C. & S.C.I.) His appointment proved most advantageous as censorship of naval mails was organised on a much sounder basis. WRINS censorship units were established at each of the ports and, in addition to being responsible for censorship of R.N. mails, they also undertook censorship of R.I.N. mails written in English.

MORALE IN THE R.I.N.

A section at N.H.Q.. was formed on 18 August 1945 to deal with questions affecting morale and to take over certain allied subjects from the Naval Law Branch. The head of the section was called the Staff Personnel Officer.

On 30 September 1946, though all censorship in the India Command ceased, particular attention was paid to morale reports received from ships and establishments and information received from other sources. These reports showed that operations in the Far East and the liberal grant of leave that was possible in many ships between July and December 1945 had a good effect on morale. Conditions of service, accommodation and messing were generally reported satisfactory. Physical fitness and medical attention were commented on very favourably from all sources. Ratings were greatly interested in their family affairs and the majority had confidence that the District Sailors', Soldiers' and Airmen's Boards were looking after the welfare of their dependents. Throughout the war, the morale of the service was indeed very high.

Welfare and Canteens

As regards welfare, there was, until early 1945, no co-ordination whatsoever, and the three Services were free to follow their own welfare activities. While taking all possible steps to ensure that adequate amenities and recreational facilities were made available to its personnel, the R.I.N. chose to concentrate its efforts mainly on family welfare. This was achieved by providing an adequate and efficient service for dealing with the multifarious problems which might adversely affect the rating's family during his service. Steps were also taken to build up a Royal Indian Navy Benevolent Association with sufficient resources to meet all possible claims upon it, whether from ratings themselves, or from their dependants. In other words, far more importance was attached by the R.I.N., in its efforts to stimulate and maintain morale, to mental confidence and contentment than to the satisfaction of physical needs and requirements, like food, amenities etc.

1939-1943

Prior to 1943 the R.I.N. had no welfare organisation. There was no money available for the provision of welfare. There was no proper system or established channel through the Naval Headquarters for dealing with civil authorities in the interest of navy personnel. Occasionally cases of very exceptional hardship were taken up by the Director of Personal Services at Naval Headquarters with the civil authorities, through the War Department. Attempts were also sometimes made by individual officers in the ships and establishments, by writing direct to the collectors, to assist in family cases, but in the absence of any proper system, or of any knowledge or official guidance as to how such matters ought to be handled, these odd attempts usually proved abortive and unsuccessful.

As regards amenities, sporadic local attempts were also made to obtain them from private organisations or through the good services of public-spirited civilians, and these attempts were sometimes successful. In general, however, very little progress was made in this direction, and when, for example, the first batches of officers and ratings were leaving India for the U.K. to man new construction ships, they were generally obliged-to leave without any amenity goods whatsoever, and even without any woollen comforts. These were, of course, invariably forthcoming from the welfare organisations in the United Kingdom, so that the service at that end was usually amply catered for—after its arrival there. Later, late in 1942 and 1943 drafts were, in fact, adequately supplied with woollen comforts and sheepskin jackets, collected under the kind auspices of Lady Fitsherbert from the Red Cross and other sources. As regards funds, the only funds available for giving monetary assistance to genuine cases of distress among R.I.N. personnel or their dependants was a small Benefit Fund. Its total resources did not at any time exceed an invested capital of 70,000, the income from which was used to dispense benevolence. The number of its beneficiaries was thus of necessity small, and the grants they received were paltry.

1943-45

Establishment of Welfare

In early 1943 provision was made for the establishment of a Welfare Organisation in Naval Headquarters. It was formed on 1 March, 1943, with the appointment of one Welfare Officer and one Welfare Accountant Officer, with the requisite office staff.

Two Welfare Touring Officers, one for the East Coast and the other for the West Coast, were shortly afterwards added. The organisation subsequently grew until, at its peak, it consisted of seven officers at naval ports (Bombay, Karachi, Chittagong, Calcutta, Vizagapatam, Madras and Cochin), an Officer-in-Charge of the R.I.N. Ratings' Rest Camp at Tindharia, an officer attached to the Fauji Dilkhush Sabha Entertainment Organisation in India, and a great many officers in ships and establishments, who were responsible for internal welfare duties. The main activities of R.I.N. Welfare from March 1943 until the end of the war may conveniently be summarised under three main heads: (a) individual and family welfare, (b) funds and amenities, and (c) the R.I.N. Benevolent Association.

INDIVIDUAL AND FAMILY WELFARE

Petitions

One of the first steps taken after the welfare organisation was set up was to issue an R.I.N. Order informing Commanding Officers that petitions of the ratings on matters relating to their or their immediate dependants, welfare should, in future, be forwarded to the Naval Headquarters. Within the first two months nearly 300 such petitions, many of them involving long and complicated negotiations with the civil authorities, were received. The two officers sanctioned for the organisation found themselves completely unable to cope with the volume of work. Within a very short time, it was necessary to obtain sanction for another officer, whose sole function was to set in motion the procedure for obtaining satisfaction or redress in family cases. Very soon he had an incredibly large number of files to deal with. Speedy results were not forthcoming, since the Service was still in the stage of feeling its way to find the most satisfactory mode of contacting the appropriate civil authorities, and settling family grievances.

The I.S.S.A.B.

Considerable use was also made of the existing army organisation, the Indian Soldiers' Board, whose title was changed, in April 1944, and was then called the Indian Sailors', Soldiers' and Airmen's Board. The Board maintained branches, called district boards, in all districts of British India, and was composed of prominent local individuals, i.e. Government officials, local welfare workers, vakils etc., with the Collector or Deputy Commissioner of the district always as the ex-officio chairman.

The Boards were grouped under a Provincial Board and the whole was controlled by a Headquarters Office, under the auspices of the War Department at New Delhi. In theory, their functioning was efficient, systematic, and rapid. Petitions were received by the Secretary; generally a paid official and whose office was often located in the Collector's office at the Headquarters town in the district. Where the petitions related, as 99% of them did, to remote villages in the district, they were passed on to the tehsildars concerned, who further passed them on to the local patwari, who in fact, generally did delegate his responsibility in the matter to a local welfare worker. The report reached the Service Headquarters along the same channels.

In practice, the system had grave defects, the most serious being an inevitable and, in some cases, quite inordinate delay in obtaining any answers at all. The passage of the petitions through the Board Office, the tehsildar, and the patwari to the village welfare worker, meant long delays. The experience of Naval Headquarters was that in many cases petitions remained outstanding from nine to nineteen months, without any effective action being taken. Often these petitions related to simple matters, such as permission to cut a tree or use thatching material. Another handicap was that at the level of the District Boards, very frequently its members and welfare workers, however willing and anxious to assist, lacked the necessary influence to do so. A number of cases occurred in which the Service was frankly informed that some local resident against whom a service man had formulated a complaint was "too influential a person" for the Board to deal with. Thirdly, there was the element of corruption and there were cases where the decisions of the District Boards had been influenced by coercion or greed.

But these should not lead to the impression that the Sailors', and Airmen's Boards were wholly ineffective. There were many Boards which did valuable service. It was found that, when the Collector saw a particularly deserving case or a glaring instance of inaction by the District Board, he took effective action to obtain redress.

Government Concessions

In addition, utmost care was taken to ensure that food concessions, educational concessions, tax remissions, etc. which were made available to serving personnel by the Central and Provincial Governments during the war, were brought to the notice of R.I.N. personnel through the medium of R.I.N. Fleet Orders, R.I.N. Temporary Memoranda, and printed and cyclostyled notices. Great care was taken to ensure that these notices actually reached the ratings for whom they were intended. Full publicity was also given, through the same media, to the considerable body of legislation which was introduced during the war with the object of protecting servicemen's interests on the legal side. Many ratings were benefited in this way and the interests of others were protected in legal matters under the provisions of the Indian Soldiers' (Litigation) Act, 1925, as read with the Indian Seamen (Litigation) Rules 1944.

Inside the Service

The individual welfare of officers and ratings was directly bound up with the various terms and conditions of their service and, in particular, with the rules governing, for example, pay, pensions, and clothing. Cases in which these rules appeared to require modification or were unduly harsh, were frequently taken up, from the welfare point of view, and in many cases modifications were obtained. Notable examples of this type of work were the initial steps taken to secure free treatment on full pay for personnel suffering from tuberculosis attributable to naval service; the extension of sick leave on full pay for an indefinite period (as opposed to the earlier six months limit), the modification of certain pension rules, the modification of the whole procedure for discharge, and the grant of very generous additional clothing, without payment, to boy trainees at H.M.I.S. *Bahadur* and H.M.I.S. *Dilawar*.

Welfare Tours

Early in 1945, family welfare was pursued in a new direction when the first welfare tour was undertaken in conjunction with a recruiting tour. An officer from the Welfare Section of Naval Headquarters, accompanied by a small party of selected ratings, was sent to Southern India to contact the families of ratings, to visit local officials and to discuss service welfare matters with them.

The welfare party visited Ratnagiri, Mangalore, Cannanore, Tellicherry, Calicut, British Cochin, Ernakulam, Alleppey and Trivandrum, and at all these places the meetings which were held were attended, amid great enthusiasm, by all local Officials. A number of vexatious cases which had been pending for long periods were settled on the spot, and the families of some 800 ratings were met, mainly by personal visits to their homes, in these towns and in the small villages in the immediate neighbourhood.

The tour was an unqualified success, subsequent morale reports received at the Naval Headquarters testified to the popularity of the idea amongst the ratings, and many appreciative letters were received from the families who had been visited and on whose behalf action had been taken locally. Another result of the first welfare tour was a noticeable speed-up in time taken by the local authorities to deal with representations from Naval Headquarters.

Priority Passages

One further aspect of individual welfare which deserves to be mentioned was the Priority Passage Scheme governing the passage to India of wives of R.I.N. personnel from countries outside India. This, from its inception in 1943, was handled by the Welfare Section and a large number of priority passages were obtained on behalf of both officers and ratings.

AMENITIES

Funds

The first and most important problem which faced the new welfare organisation was that of funds. In March 1943, the R.I.N. War Purposes Fund contained only Rs. 17,000. The A.C.E.S. (Amenities, Comforts, and Entertainments for the Service) Fund, provided by the Government of India, was also meagre, which, while useful for the provision of small amenities, was quite inadequate to provide for any large-scale welfare work. The officer-in-charge of welfare came to the conclusion that very little in the way of welfare would be attempted until the service was able to get hold of adequate funds. Appeals were, therefore, made to His Excellency the Viceroy, to all the Provincial Governors, and later to the public at large, and funds were soon forthcoming on a generous scale. As a result, it was possible during the succeeding years to carry through a very considerable programme of welfare work, at a cost of over 20 lakhs of rupees.

Supply of Small Amenities

A considerable portion of this sum was expended on the provision of small amenities such as gramophones, wireless sets, sports gear, woollen comforts, and in some cases refrigerators and soda-water machines. It was the "aim of Naval Headquarters that every ship, however small, should be supplied with at least one wireless set, one gramophone, and an adequate quantity of sports gear. Some difficulty was experienced in 1944 in obtaining sufficient wireless sets and gramophones to go round. This shortage, however, did not persist. Great difficulty, on the other hand, was experienced in the servicing and maintenance of wireless sets, which had to be carried out in spare time by Naval Stores Officer, Bombay, and his staff. One difficulty which was never solved was the provision of wireless sets for motor launches and landing craft. These craft were unable to run a mains wireless set and, although exhaustive enquiries were made, an adequate supply of battery wireless sets was never available anywhere in India. Similarly, the supply of gramophones fell far below requirements. At the time of the Munster Mission to India, the R.I.N. was successful in its bid for 500 mains and battery radios, a large number of gramophones, and also for refrigerators, all from the United Kingdom, but these amenities were not forthcoming until some six months after the end of the war, when, with the reduction in the size of Service, their arrival proved more of an embarassment than an asset.

Periodicals and Books

The welfare organisation also made itself responsible for the regular supply of reading material to the whole Service. After an initial period of difficulty with the postal services, and after the loss of many thousands of periodicals by theft in transit, an efficient distributing organisation for newspapers, magazines, and periodicals in English and in the Indian languages was built up at the Naval Headquarters, and nearly 35,000 papers were distributed each month, through service channels instead of the ordinary post. In addition, all shore establishments were provided with cash grants, to enable them to set up ratings' libraries, and books were supplied in periodical parcels to the ships afloat.

Clubs

In the early years of the war a frequent grievance was that the ratings going ashore at various ports in India had nowhere to spend their leisure hours. Welfare, therefore, undertook the setting up of a ratings' club at every port. The *Cornwallis* Fleet Club was built in Bombay, on a permanent scale, at a cost of nearly four lakhs of rupees. The club which was designed by an architect serving as a temporary officer in the R.I.N., was a handsome building with luxurious interior furnishings, containing two restaurants, a theatre, and a dormitory for 40 men. It was one of the finest Service clubs in India. At Chittagong, Calcutta, Vizagapatam and Cochin, temporary-style clubs were opened. No club was opened at Madras as there existed adequate club facilities for servicemen at that port. In Karachi various administrative limitations delayed the commencement of building operations, but, largely due to the generosity of His Excellency the Governor of Sind and of the Karachi Port Trust, a start was made in the middle of 1945 with the construction of a ratings' club, somewhat smaller than the Cornwallis Fleet Club, but on the same generous lines and designed for permanence.

Leave Facilities

Leave facilities for both officers and ratings received attention. The first step, as far as officers were concerned, was the publication of a small annual booklet containing full information about all the various hostels, clubs, etc., in all parts of India, which made special arrangements to cater for service officers on leave. In 1944, the R.I.N. opened its own Officers' Leave Hostel at Srinagar (Kashmir), and this functioned successfully throughout 1944 and 1945. The hostel was made available to junior officers of all Services. The R.I.N. was also responsible for initiating the proposal which eventually led to the grant of free road travel between Rawalpindi and Kashmir for all service personnel, both Indian and British.

A rest and convalescent camp for ratings was established at Tindharia (near Kurseong, on the Darjeeling-Himalayan Railway), but although the building was rented for over two years, administrative difficulties in obtaining Government sanction for ratings to proceed to the camp on duty, and not on leave, prevented the camp from coming into operation before the war was over.

Entertainments

Arrangements were made with the army welfare authorities to place Ensa and the Fauji Dilkhush Sabha entertainment organisation equally at the disposal of the R.I.N. Special parties were arranged to cater for the tastes of R.I.N. ratings, and these parties did invaluable work touring naval establishments and ports. In 1945, a naval officer was attached to the Fauji Dilkhush Sabha organisation in Calcutta, whose special duty it was to raise and to route Indian concert-parties for the R.I.N.

Ship Adoption

One of the most interesting features of the welfare programme was the Ship Adoption Scheme. The scheme was lunched by the Flag Officer Commanding, R.I.N., in 1943, when he appealed to Governors, Princes, and business community, and in a few cases, business firms, to adopt R.I.N. ships. The idea met with conspicuous success, and all the ships whose names had territorial connections were adopted immediately. It was somewhat more difficult to get the others adopted, but this was done eventually. Many ships benefited greatly from the scheme, receiving gifts both of amenities and of money from their adopters; but looked at from a national point of view, the main benefit derived from the scheme lay in the fact that good relations were fostered between the R.I.N. and the public, and that information about the navy was disseminated.

Delegations from many districts visited their adopted ships, and, where possible, these visits were returned by the ships' companies.

"Other Purposes"

The above paragraphs illustrate the main uses to which the R.I.N. War Purposes Fund and the Government A.C.E.S. Fund were put. Money from these funds were occasionally also diverted to "other purposes" not directly connected with welfare, but which provided for the Service certain benefits for which otherwise the Government could not sanction funds. Thus the War Purposes Fund gave a grant to the R.I.N. Hospital at Sewri for the purchase of a motor ambulance for the conveyance of officers' or ratings' wives from their residences in Bombay to the hospital; another grant was given from the War Purposes Fund to assist in financing the three so-called R.I.N. hostels, set up for the education of the sons of servicemen at Ratnagiri, Dapoli and Sangameshwar, and many grants were made as R.I.N. contributions, towards the financing of inter-service projects.

Dockyard Welfare

The R.I.N. War Purposes Fund financed the more important of the dockyard welfare schemes, namely, the provision of amenities in the dockyard hospital, clinic, children's creche, and so on, to the extent of over a lakh of rupees.

Sports Fund

Mention may be made of two other funds administered by Welfare—the R.I.N. Sports Fund and the R.I.N. Band Fund. The former was collected entirely from subscriptions paid by officers and ratings and was used for providing sports gear and for the maintenance of sports fields, tennis courts, etc.

Band Fund

The R.I.N. Band Fund was managed by Welfare Section from its commencement until the R.I.N. Band was actually formed. Subscriptions were collected from officers of the Service, and public appeals were also made. Within a short time a fairly large sum had been collected, to enable the Service to purchase instruments for a band of over 50 musicians. Government sanction was accorded in 1944 to the creation of Musician Branch and to the formation of the R.I.N. Band itself, and a Lieutenant was recruited into the Special Branch of the R.I.N.V.R. as Director of Music. In 1945, after the band instruments had been paid for, at a cost of about Rs. 40,000, the remainder of the fund, about 20,000/-, was handed over to the Flag Officer, Bombay, in whom administration of the band was then vested.

R.I.N. Maintenance Fund

In early 1945, the R.I.N.Maintenance Fund was established. The purpose of this fund was to collect an invested capital of at least 10 lakhs of rupees, the interest from which would be used in the postwar years to maintain those clubs, libraries, sports grounds, and other welfare institutions which the Service had been able to acquire for itself during the war. It then amounted to some seven lakhs of rupees.

THE R.I.N. BENEVOLENT ASSOCIATION

Purpose

Early in 1943 the R.I.N. Benefit Fund was reconstituted as "The R.I.N. Benevolent Association" and was registered under the Societies Act (1860). The aim of the Association, as stated in the Memorandum of Association, was the "relief of distress" among past and present officers and ratings of the Royal Indian Navy, Royal Indian Marine, Royal Indian Navy Reserve, Royal Indian Naval Volunteer Reserve and Royal Indian Fleet Reserve, and their dependants. A number of amendments to the Memorandum of Association and to the rules were subsequently made, the chief of these being the substitution of the words "hardship or distress" for "distress" and the inclusion of officers and auxiliaries of the WRINS and of nursing sisters of the R.I.N. Hospital, as potential beneficiaries.

Collection of Funds

In January 1944 the Welfare Section, having collected about 15 lakhs of rupees for amenity purposes, turned its attention to funds for the Benevolent Association, and an intensive drive was started. The target was set by Admiral Godfrey at 20 lakhs of rupees, a figure which, invested at 3%, would give the Association a permanent annual income of some Rs. 60,000 for benevolent purposes. The target figure was regarded as extremely high, but no efforts were spared to ensure that it should be attained. Appeals, signed by the Flag Officer Commanding, were made to almost every section of the people of India, and without exception they responded munificently.

In a space of 16 months, the total of 20 lakhs was reached and passed. The final subscription lists included the names of the Viceroy, all the Provincial Governors, many of the Indian Princes, Indian and British business firms, clubs, zamindars, cinema proprietors, churches, army units, and countless private individuals. A large subscription was also received from the King George's Fund for sailors in the United Kingdom.

The figures of actual collection show the rate at which money for the R.I.N. Benevolent Association was received. It will be seen that towards the end of 1944 over two lakhs per month was received regularly. The average for 1944 amounted to Rs. 4,000 collected every day of the year. The Flag Officer Commanding stated at a general meeting of the Benevolent Association that in his opinion no better manifestation of the high regard in which the people of India held their navy was required than the way in which they had supported its collection of funds for the Benevolent Association.

Expansion of Activities

As the funds of the Benevolent Association grew, so also did its activities expand. Perhaps equally important with the growth of its resources was the fashion in which between 1943 and 1945 the Association, a non-official body, carrying out its functions with private funds, was gradually woven into the administrative fabric of the Service, and became as much an integral part of the Naval Headquarters, and of the Service, as any of the administrative sections. Great care was taken to ensure that no deserving case went unassisted. A departure was made from the usual practice among charitable associations of taking no cognisance of hardship or distress unless the victim himself appealed for assistance. To this end, arrangements were made for the Medical Board papers of all ratings invalided from the service to pass first through the office of the Benevolent Association, and if it was possible for any assistance to be given to the ratings (especially further medical treatment at the Association's expense) then action was taken without waiting for an actual appeal from him. The Association speedily became known for the good work it was doing, ratings showed keen appreciation of it, and the number of its beneficiaries rose steadily from a few dozen to some 800. These include widows and families not eligible for service pensions, families whose service pensions were inadequate, those whose pensions were due but delayed, ex-ratings maintained in hospital for treatment for tuberculosis, leprosy, mental complaints, and so on.

R.I.N. CANTEENS

At the outbreak of war there was only one shore canteen in the Royal Indian Navy. It was accommodated in a small building inside the Dockyard at Bombay. In conformity with the usual practice of canteen administration in India, a contractor was responsible for the running of that canteen, stores being purchased by him from the Canteen Contractors' Syndicate. As the Royal Indian Navy expanded and acquired additional training establishments and operational bases, more shore canteens were opened on the contractor system, while ships purchased their requirements direct from the Canteen Contractors' Syndicate installations at the ports.

Towards the end of 1940 it was realised that the contractor system of canteen management, apart altogether from its normal and expected defects, was, as far as the R.I.N. was concerned, wholly unsatisfactory and unable to meet the particular requirements of the Service. Commanding Officers of most of H.M.I, ships and establishments had throughout displayed a desire to conduct their canteens on service lines. The opinion generally prevailed that the contractor system, though running on well-established and professionally efficient lines, was not satisfactory, in that it lent itself to abuses and tended to make divisional and other junior officers lose interest in the canteens aspect of their ratings' welfare. In addition, commanding officers found the Canteen Contractors' Syndicate frequently unable to meet urgent demands for canteen stores during the short periods that the ships were able to spend in the port. It was, therefore, decided that the Service should establish and manage its own ratings' canteens, as far as possible, and a beginning was made in this direction. By September 1942 there were nine ratings' canteens, and one families' canteen (or retail grocery shop) in Bombay all conducted on service lines with the assistance of civilian managers.

The New Policy

It was not until September 1943 that a Canteens Section was established at the Naval Headquarters, this being the first step towards the formation of an efficient canteens service within the navy. The section formed part of the Personnel Department and consisted of one reserve officer at the Naval Headquarters and one touring officer based on Bombay. The officer at the Naval Headquarters was specially selected on account of his experience in the retail trade in civilian life. The organisation was subsequently expanded by the addition of a staff officer at the Naval Headquarters, another touring Officer and two officers as Canteen Warehouse Managers in Bombay and Calcutta.

A long-term canteen policy for the Royal Indian Navy was then laid down. It consisted briefly of the building up a service-controlled wholesale and retail canteen administration. Canteen supplies were to be taken over in bulk from the Canteen Stores Department, and from that point their distribution, down to the final individual sale, was to be controlled by the Service, and all net profits derived from the sales were to accrue to the Service. In order to disrupt the existing supply procedure as little as possible, it was decided not to make an abrupt switch-over, but to transfer existing canteens gradually to the new system, and to ensure that all new canteens were opened in accordance with this principle.

To implement this policy, it was necessary that funds should be made available for the establishment of new canteens and for the improvement of those already existing. Accordingly, in November 1943, the Royal Indian Navy Canteens Improvement Fund was established by means of an advance of 3 lakhs of rupees from the R.I.N. War Purposes Fund. Cash grants from the improvement fund were made to ships and establishments, and the standard of existing canteens was greatly improved. In addition, between 1943 and March 1945, over 40 new service-run canteens were opened in H.M.I, ships and establishments, and by that date 95% of all ships and establishments were provided with canteen facilities.

The distribution of the bulk supplies purchased from the Canteen Stores Department required the establishment of R.I.N. Canteen Warehouses at the various ports. These warehouses, the equivalent of Canteen Bulk Issue Depots, were established in

Bombay, Calcutta, Karachi, Jamnagar, Vizagapatam and Madras. In December 1943, the Quarter Master General in India authorised R.I.N. Canteen Warehouses to purchase canteen stores at wholesale prices, thus enabling canteens in the R.I.N. to compete with contractors on equal terms and making possible the employment of a nucleus of civilian managers on attractive rates of pay.

By the middle of 1945, the canteen organisation had gone long past the experimental stage. Of the 95 canteens in the R.I.N., only three were then run by canteen contractors, and these were in the ports in which an approved contractor had been granted monopoly of all canteen supplies. The R.I.N. was thus in the position of being the only Service in the India Command (Indian or British) which ran its own wholesale and retail canteens organisation. This Was undoubtedly the greatest benefit to the Service, and the psychological benefit of an honestly administered canteen service was well worth the additional trouble involved, and far outweighed the monetary benefit accruing to the Service. Visitors to R.I.N. canteens had on a number of occasions commented upon the extremely high standard of cleanliness and comfort achieved in them. The successful establishment and operation of this service-run canteen organisation effectively dispelled the notion that contractors in India were indispensable. It proved that a service could run its canteens organisation successfully from a financial point of view. At the end of the war R.I.N. canteens were yielding a dividend (from profits) of Rs. 2,500 per month or 15% per annum. This money was paid into welfare funds, to be used for the benefit of the personnel of the service, and, in addition, over one lakh borrowed for the establishment of the Canteens Improvement Fund had been repaid.

MEDICAL CARE IN THE R.I.N.

Till 1942 members of the Indian Medical Department were seconded to the navy, but due to shortage of personnel and because of their own needs, the army was unable to second any more Warrant Officers of the Indian Medical Department. Instead, Emergency Commissioned Officers of the Indian Medical Service were selected from volunteers for secondment to the navy. This went on for about a year. At first, it appeared to be satisfactory, but later, the quality and number of volunteers for the navy began to fall. The Director General, Indian Medical Service, approached the Government and obtained sanction for direct recruitment to the Navy. This supplied the R.I.N. with medical officers who were keen to serve in the navy and gave a wider range of selection. Medical officers in the army were still seconded to serve in the navy, if they volunteered to do, and a few were taken in from time to time from that source. Emergency Commissioned Officers (E.C.Os.) of the I.M.S. began to be seconded to the R.I.N. from the latter half of 1942. In 1943, the army opened the Army Medical Training Centre (A.M.T.C.), at Poona and medical officers who joined the navy through the army had usually completed this course.

In 1944, a Medical Branch of the Royal Indian Naval Voluntary Reserve (R.I.N.V.R.) was formed consisting of officers of the I.M.S. (E.C.O.) and I.A.M.C. who had been seconded to the R.I.N. When direct recruitment of medical officers to the navy was opened, the new entrants were given a divisional officers' course of training at H.M.I.S. *Feroze*. Regular I.M.D. officers continued to serve in the navy as R.I.N. officers.

There were no other courses for medical officers in the navy. The Medical Directorate organised courses on various subjects for their medical officers; but these were not open to naval medical officers on account of the objections of the Finance Department. Later on, Finance agreed to permit one medical officer at a time to attend the army courses of instructions in malaria and in venereal diseases. There were altogether five medical officers who ultimately attended these courses. The courses in malaria were held in Malaria Institute, Delhi, and those for Venereal diseases at the General Hospital, Bangalore.

The system of appointing specialists in various branches of medicine and surgery did not exist in the Royal Indian Navy, nor was the system of graded specialists recognised. There were many medical officers of the status of specialists or at least of graded specialists in medicine, surgery, public health, ophthalmology and pathology, but they were denied this privilege. To obtain expert opinion and treatment, the R.I.N. appointed consultants from among the leading specialists in Bombay. They were given honorary naval ranks and were attached to the R.I.N. Hospital. They gave approximately three mornings a week of their valuable time to the R.I.N.

Sick Berth Attendants

Sick Berth Attendants were recruited directly for this branch. The educational standards required were matriculation or its equivalent. The response of volunteers to this branch was low and the entry was small. In 1943 the pay scale was favourably revised and the educational standard was lowered. There were also a few modifications in the physical standards. The result of modification in the standards and the rise of pay was that more men were available and the quota of Sick Berth Attendants was kept up. There was, of necessity, a sacrifice of quality for quantity, but the large number that trained for the navy was in consonance with the principle of rapid expansion which was essential for winning the war.

The demand for Sick Berth Attendants grew as war progressed. Many small ships of the R.I.N. carried Sick Berth Attendants who, apart from attending to minor ailments, were called to treat serious injuries received in action. This necessitated a proper training of the Sick Berth Attendants; hence a training establishment known as a S.B.A. Training Establishment, was opened in 1943 in Bombay. First it was housed in the gymnasium hall in Castle Barracks where instructions and demonstrations were given, and later it moved to the R.I.N. Hospital at Sewri. The programme of training was so arranged as to give them a good grounding in elementary anatomy, physiology, first aid and general sick nursing.

Medical Personnel and Equipment of Ships

Sloops of the R.I.N. carried one medical officer each. The ships had a complement of 210 to 250 officers and men and their duties entailed being at sea for a period extending up to three weeks in company with other ships, not carrying medical officers. Hence the medical officers had to be independent as far as they could in all matters including medical aid. The medical stores and equipment carried on board was of a comprehensive nature and included a large range of instruments and medicines to deal with most illnesses and emergencies on board.

The duties of the medical officers consisted of maintaining the ships company in health and countering threat to their well being. They arranged and organised for medical aid in emergencies and accidents either on board their own ships or in others in company. They also gave lectures and demonstrations in first aid and general principles of hygiene to the ship's company, to make them capable of rendering first aid when called upon to do so in an emergency. Lectures were also given on the prevention of venereal diseases.

For the assistance of medical officers on board there were two Sick Berth Attendants, one usually of the leading rate or even the petty officer rate (P.O.) and the other a S.B.A.I or S.B.A. II. They acted as nursing orderlies carrying out the treatment as ordered by the medical officer, and kept the sick bay clean. The Sick Bay Attendant had considerable influence over the rest of the ship's company who looked upon him with friendly respect. He was a great help in organising and helping in the running of lectures and demonstrations. During action, the S.B. As. were in charge of stretcher parties. They rendered first aid and transported the wounded to the sick bay for attention by the medical officer.

There was difficulty regarding stores of medical equipment in ships afloat. Immediately on the declaration of war the R.I.N. ships worked with, and under the orders of, the Royal Navy in various theatres, for example, Persian Gulf, Aden and the Red Sea. The Indian ships were, however, not fitted medically on the same scales as the R.N., the difference being considerable. The R.I.N. scales of medical stores and equipment were similar to the army and tended to be based more on the numbers of men to be looked after rather than on the idea of an independent unit or the nature of its duties. Parity with R.N., in medical equipment in the ship was necessary as the two navies were working in conjunction and there was reciprocity in the matter of medical aids and medical duties. To secure such a parity the Flag Officer Commanding, Royal Indian Navy, sanctioned making up of medical stores in R.I.N. ships up to the standard of Royal Navy by local purchase of articles and equipment required.

The Royal Indian Naval Hospital

Till 1943, the R.I.N. had no hospital of its own and, therefore, had to depend on the military or civil hospitals for the treatment of their cases. St. George's Hospital, Bombay, placed one of its wards at the complete disposal of the navy. Consequent on the expansion of the Service after the outbreak of war, the numbers of patients requiring hospitalisation rose. The military hospitals, because of their own needs, were hard put to provide for the navy also. It was first proposed to take over the St. George's Hospital,

Bombay, for naval use jointly with the R.N., but the negotiations were dropped as it meant depriving the civilian population of the hospital. The completed buildings of the Ramesh Premchand Sanatorium, Sewri, Bombay were placed at the disposal of the R.I.N. Though completed in 1940, the buildings were not equipped or furnished, perhaps due to the outbreak of war. Negotiations were taken up with the Bombay Corporation and the buildings were acquired for a 250-bed hospital for the R.I.N. It continued to be the only well-organised hospital for the Indian Navy in the country till it closed down in 1946 after the close of the war, when a R.I.N. wing of 120 beds was opened in the Combined Military Hospital (C.M.H.), Colaba, Bombay.

Campaigns

The Royal Indian Navy operated in almost all theatres of war extending from the North and South Atlantic in the west to the Java Sea and the Pacific Ocean in the east. Ships carried a medical officer and had a fairly roomy sick bay stocked with medical drugs and equipment.

1939-40

At the outbreak of war three sloops of the R.I.N. were attached to the R.N. and did duty in the Persian Gulf, Aden and the Mediterranean. Medical arrangements were in common with the R.N. who had Base Hospitals at various ports in the Persian Gulf and the Red Sea, to which all the R.f.N. sick were sent for hospitalisation and treatment.

1941-42

Ships of the R.I.N. took part in patrolling and escort duties in the Indian Ocean, the Red Sea and the Persian Gulf. They also took part in the recapture of Berbera and cleared mines from the harbour of Massawa, and were generally active up and down the coast of North Africa. Medical arrangements were similar to those in the Persian Gulf region. Two sloops of the R.I.N. took part in the Battle of the Java Seas. The *Sutlej* picked up a large number of survivors. The *Jumna* too was busy in anti-aircraft and anti-submarine patrols and suffered many casualties. All sick from these ships were landed ashore in Singapore. The *Jumna* and the *Sutlej* also took part in the landing of the Allied armies in Sicily.

The main work was convoy duties and bombarding shore batteries and affording fire cover to landing troops. Medical cover was provided in both the ships. Evacuation and hospitalisation was carried out by the R.N.

1943

H.M.I.S. *Narbada* and *Godamri* did escort duty in the Atlantic with the R.N. They depended on the latter for their medical supplies, transfer and hospitalisation ashore to naval hospitals. Ships in Red Sea, Persian Gulf and those in Burmese and Indian waters were chiefly engaged in patrol and convoy duties. They were based on ports where the local sick bay of hospital looked after the R.I.N. sick. A few of the ships of the R.I.N. were completely self-sufficient in point of medical cover.

1944-45

Navy played an important part in the Burma operations, the R.I.N. specially with its landing craft wing. In respect of the latter, medical arrangements were divided between R.I.N. and the Indian army consisting of Squadron Medical Officers for the Landing Craft Wing and Senior Medical Officer for the Headquarters Base. The Squadron Medical Officers were equipped with a minimum of essential stores and equipment to enable them to travel light. For evacuation of casualties and hospitalisation navy depended on the army. Medical arrangements on the whole worked well during the Burma operations.

Naval Surgeon awarded M.B.E.

Two difficult surgical operations performed at sea while a convoy was proceeding through enemy-infested waters in the Atlantic earned for Surgeon Lieutenant Chandra M. Dave, R.I.N.V.R., the M.B.E. (Military Division). In the words of the Commanding Officer of H.M.I.Sloop "his conduct and bearing, together with his surgical skill, have been of the highest order throughout these operations."

H.M.I. DOCKYARD BOMBAY

Visiting Bombay dockyard in 1775, a traveller named Parsons spoke highly of it. "Bombay boasts such a dry dock as perhaps. is not to be seen in any part of Europe, either for size or convenient situation". If Parsons had seen the dockyard during World War II, he would have been still more eloquent. Almost every campaign of the last 200 years from China and Abyssinia, between Egypt and the Cape of Good Hope, depended in some measure on Bombay for its fitting out and repairing of ships. Though the change from sail to steam greatly affected the fortunes of the dockyard, the world wars supplied a strong impetus to ship building and repairing. World War II, in particular, gave Bombay dockyard an importance never exceeded in the past. With Hong Kong and Singapore lost, it became almost the only naval dockyard in the northern hemisphere, east of the Suez, and Bombay workers repaired ships damaged in actions from the Mediterranean to the Coral Sea.

The outbreak of war in September 1939 found the dockyard lacking in both men and equipment for the immense tasks ahead, but it rose to the occasion. Though much hampered by having within its limits the depots, gunnery school, mechanical training and other establishments, the dockyard became a self-contained unit well-equipped with the machinery and gear, which were required for the handling of naval repairs. During the weeks before Hitler marched into Poland, the limited resources were working at full belt to make the ships of the Royal Indian Navy and its requisitioned vessels "in all respects ready for war". With men and machines working day and night, 17 vessels were handled concurrently in the first ten days of the war, with facilities designed for a much smaller number.

H.M.I. Dockyard was a civilian establishment in a service background and acted as a front-line organisation which performed the same functions of repair and maintenance towards warships as were carried out by those who looked after tanks, motor transport and aircraft in the army and the Air Force. With the dockyard rested the responsibility for ensuring that ships were properly prepared for war and were capable of remaining at sea and fighting under all conditions.

The dockyard was in many ways like a self-contained industrial town. Hemmed in on three sides by the built-up area of the city, and on the fourth by the harbour, the dockyard found it difficult to expand, but its productive area increased by 50 per cent. Five acres of nor-productive buildings were swept away to make room for stores and workshops. A hundred and seventy thousand square feet of new buildings sprang up, in every bit of available space. There were few trades one could not find there, from tailors to tinsmiths and optical experts to millwrights. Foundries and sawmills, engineering shops and gunsheds, stores and power plants crammed the whole dock area, which was policed by its own force of ex-service sepoys.

H.M.I. Dockyard was comparable to Chatham, during war, in the work it undertook. Under the direction of a Captain Superintendent of the R.I.N., it worked for six years at top pressure. The then Captain Superintendent was Captain R.R. Caws, R.I.N., who took over from Captain W.R. Shewring, R.I.N. One of the Departmental Chiefs had a cartoon on his desk showing a long queue, waiting at a door marked "Captains only. Refit coupons to be handed in here", while a figure on the bridge of one of the cluster of ships in the harbour had his telescope trained on an ominous banner. "Is your refit really necessary". The answer in the case of most dockyard "Customers" was not in doubt. Clients ranged from a destroyer with 70 feet of stern missing to a ship requiring a new stern. P & O Liners were converted into armed merchant cruisers, and nearly a score of passenger vessels were fitted out as troop transports and hospital ships. Many other ships were taken from their peace-time jobs to become local defence vessels. As the war progressed, the variety of tasks which had to be performed increased. A dozen ex-Norwegian whalers were converted and fitted out for mine-sweeping. Warships of the United States, Greek and Dutch Navies used the resources of the Bombay dockyard. In addition, the dockyard staff superintended the refitting of all naval vessels in the commercial docks.

The first big action damage repairs were carried out on the Cruiser H.M.S. *Capetown*, after being torpedoed off Massawa in April 1941. The destroyer H.M.S. *Kimberley*, which had her stern blown off by an enemy submarine in the Mediterranean in January 1942, was towed through the Suez Canal to the Bombay dockyard where a completely new stern was built into her and her nine ton main gear-wheel was trued up. The destroyer H.M.S. *Isis*, also damaged in the Mediterranean, reached Bombay under her own steam. After her damage had been patched up, she sailed for Singapore where, with refit 90% complete, she suffered fresh damage after a near miss from a Japanese plane. She was then towed to Surabaya where she received more attention from Japanese planes. In the end, she was towed back to Bombay, to be made fit for sea once more.

The dockyard's engineering department trebled its capacity after 1939. Housed in the century-old building erected as the "steam factory", it then possessed the most modern machinery, supplied since the war, partly from the United Kingdom, and partly as lease-lend material from America. Among the shining new machines, a veteran lathe, 98 years old, was still doing its job. Most spectacular wartime growth was that of the gun mounting organisation. In 1939 it consisted of one officer and one ordnance artificer. At the end of the war, it employed hundreds of men in workshops which were all wartime constructions. As supplier of guns to the Defensively Equipped Merchant Ships (D.E.M.S.), Bombay ranked as the third port in the Empire: in one year, it fitted over 500 guns of the size of oerlikons and above. For naval vessels, repairs were carried out on gun-mountings, Directors and optical instruments. The department coped with the requirements of almost any ship. The Naval Stores Officer, who supplied anything from a screwdriver to a motor-boat, had a job almost equal to that of big business. Forty-eight officers, 218 storehouse staff and 260 clerks were kept busy looking after the needs of ships which had 50,000 items to choose from (compared with a mere 10,000 at the start of the war). The Naval Stores Department in Bombay planned and manned stores in several other ports. A year's bill for goods to keep them all satisfied came to something like 400 lakhs of rupees.

Docks

The new "Torpedo" Dock which would take Bangors, Bathursts, Bassetts and up to "S" class submarines, eased the docking position in 1944. There were plans to install the electrical pumping machinery. Alterations were carried out to the floor of Bombay dock, so that the whole length of the dock was then on one level instead of three, enabling 2 sloops to be docked together instead of one, as formerly. Electrical high-duty dry dock pumps were installed in Duncan and Bombay Docks.

Cranage

A 15-ton crane was installed on West Wall, another between the two dry docks. A new 30-ton mobile crane was also commissioned. The new cranage system made for greater efficiency.

Compressed Air System

Air compressors for a ring main system throughout the whole yard to supply high pressure air to workshops and ships, were installed.

Signal Station

The ground floor or the signal station on the breakwater was demolished in order to permit wheeled traffic, i.e. small mobile cranes, compressors, generators, and trucks to pass on to the breakwater and, in effect, turn the breakwater into a series of refitting berths. Formerly, only very minor repairs were carried out at the breakwater.

Machine etc. Shops

The following shops equipped on a modern scale were created or adapted from previously existing shops, resulting in a greatly expanded output of work viz. platers, blacksmith, tinsmith, jointers, painters, welding, boiler, millwright, engine-fitters and foundry.

Torpedo Motor Workshop

It was found necessary to take over and expand a commercial garage and workshop, five miles from the dockyard, for the purpose of overhauling and maintaining the large fleet of Royal Indian Navy motor vehicles.

Labour Welfare

About the middle of 1943 comparisons were made between the dockyard and other large industrial establishments throughout India, in respect of wages, conditions of service and welfare arrangements. It was found that while the dockyard compared quite favourably in regard to wage increments, hours of work, leave, provident fund, bonus, medical treatment for employees etc., it compared badly in welfare arrangements, as, with the exception of Dockyard Canteen and grain shop, there were no welfare arrangements, and in addition workers' housing conditions were appalling. It was, therefore, proposed to the Government that a housing scheme, some 14 miles outside Bombay, incorporating all the usual amenities for workers' families, schools, hostel, shopping centre and recreation facilities, should be sanctioned; but owing to the shortage of building materials and the high rough estimate, Government was unable to accord its approval to it. The scheme was then revived in a modified form, alter being shorn of all amenities and the housing cut down to the barest minimum. Sanction in principle was then given. Recognising that while out of keeping with modern development, the plan would still provide better housing than had hitherto existed in the slums of Bombay, it was decided to proceed with the modified scheme. All these took a great deal of time, about 15 months, but in the meantime efforts were made to deal piecemeal with the welfare problem. A sum of Rs. 100,000 was placed at the disposal of the Flag Officer Commanding, Royal Indian Navy, by the Governor Bombay for providing (a) library (b) educational classes (c) workers' family dispensary (d) canteens (e) cinematograph apparatus and (f) recreational facilities embracing hockey, cricket, football and swimming to the dockyard workers. With the exception of (b) all these became flourishing activities and were acceptable to the workers.

Workers Family Dispensary

This was housed in a building in Hornby Road, Bombay, near Crawford Market, and was equipped on a modern scale. It was in charge of a well-qualified lady doctor assisted by a staff of six nurses who carried out a routine of house visiting ante-natal treatment, medical advice, and dealt with child welfare problems, as well as attending to out-patients and confinement cases at the dispensary itself. There were a large number of calls for advice and treatment from the dockyard workers. It might be added that the dispensary was quite a useful influence in checking absenteeism among the dockyard workers, who frequently used to leave work to escort ailing members of their families to their villages for treatment by local hakims. At the suggestion of the Dockyard Workers' Union, and with the approval of the Government of India, the Workers' Families Dispensary was renamed in 1945 the "Godfrey Clinic". This institution fully maintained its popularity with the workers. It would appear that a strong case existed for its retention as a permanent feature of the welfare organisation.

The Workmen's Institute

This provided indoor games, library, reading room and canteen. This was named the "Shewring Institute". This institution had a large membership, was financed by members'subscriptions and welfare funds.

Supervisory Staff

The withdrawal of technical supervisory staff attached to the dockyard on loan from the Admiralty during the later years of the war, had serious repercussions on output and efficiency. Twenty-five Indian technicians from the various departments were selected early in the year to be sent to the United Kingdom for training in naval dockyards, in order to replace the Admiralty staff withdrawn or time-expired. Negotiations for sending those men to England for training were pursued in 1946.

Sail Loft

Least war-like, but not least necessary in a corner of the yard, was the section where 300 tailors at their sewing machines were busy during the war period turning out uniforms for the R.I.N. Thousands of uniforms a year amounting to 75 per cent of the navy's needs, were made there. Thus in six years of concentrated efforts the historic naval dockyard in Bombay had made a distinguished contribution to victory worthily maintaining its 200-year old tradition.

10

Naval Diplomacy

Navies exist as part of a nation state's maritime policy, whose objective is to attempt to use the sea for one's own purposes while being in a position to prevent others from using it in ways which are to one's disadvantage. The functions of navies can be conceived as a trinity. The unity of the trinity is provided by the idea of the use of the sea. This is the underlying principle in the whole business of navies and foreign policy. The character of the trinity is then defined by the three characteristic modes of action by which navies carry out their purposes: namely *the military, the diplomatic and the* policing functions.

The Military Role should from the base of this triangle because the essence of all navies is their military character. It is navy's ability to threaten to use force-or to actually use force-which gives meaning to all its other modes of action. The diplomatic role of navies is concerned with the management of foreign policy short of the actual employment of force. Diplomatic application support state policy particularly in bargaining situations or in general international intercourse. The policing role is internally as much as extremely oriented. However, these functions are rarely concerned with the armed forces of other states. They are mainly concerned with extending sovereignty over the state's own maritime forces.

The diplomatic role, which concerns this study, has been an important one for the major navies, and involves a wide variety of operational tasks. The range of functions within this role encompasses, action with a degree of implicit or explicit coercion (negotiation from strength) to actions promising rewards (naval aid) to action seeking to oil the wheels of relationship by imposing an image (influence and prestige). Aims and subsidiary objectives of the diplomatic role that are relevant to us today are listed below:-

Negotiation from Strength

This enables the nation to do the following:-

(i) Reassure, strengthen, and change the behaviour-patterns of friendly States within the region, who may be challenged by external or internal threats.

(ii) Indicate to observers that a crisis is under control.

(iii) Support national policy through the threat of force from the sea.

(iv) Improve bargaining strength and the ability to affect the course of specific diplomatic negotiations.

Manipulation. This enables the following to be effected:-

(i) Gain or increase access to different countries.

(ii) Build-up foreign navies and create a proxy threat, while tying the 'target' nation to one's own policy.

(iii) Extend one's reach to distant waters, to manifest the right to be interested in happenings far away.

Prestige. This achieves the following:-

(i) Psychological reassurance to all Indian citizens, at home and abroad.

(ii) A favourable general image abroad, of India.

(iii) A powerful advertisement of India's industrial and technological prowess and the consequent creation of strong trade-incentive.

ASSETS OF WARSHIPS AS DIPLOMATIC INSTRUMENTS

Navy is the only service that can carry the image of sovereignty with it to other states. Its diplomatic potential, therefore, is significantly enhanced over that of Army or Air Force. It is also a self-contained unit of military power that can project itself into the heart of a target state. The ports visited are also usually the most important cities of target states.

Warships either singly, or in groups, can perform a range of tasks of social, humanitarian or political character, as well as of purely military character. The nonterritoriality of the medium on which warships operate and absence of resident population on the sea gives them advantages over the other branches of the armed forces. Warships are not only relatively mobile, they are also efficient carriers of their own firepower, troops, tanks, aircraft, landing craft and a variety of other military hardware. Warships, therefore, have many basic characteristics that make them highly suitable instruments of diplomacy.

Tenets of Naval Diplomacy

Naval diplomacy is carried out by means of five basic tenets. As mentioned earlier, the first two tenets, standing demonstration of power and specific operational deployment represent power politics. The rest, naval aid, operational visits and specific goodwill visits are naval influence politics. Political demonstrations of power are a time-honoured usage of major navies. A single warship carries out much naval diplomacy at the lowest level. It must be remembered that the ultimate targets of standing demonstrations of naval power are the brains of decision makers, and not their ships.

Specific operational deployments are invariably a special case of the standing demonstration. They refer to the use of one or more warships in a deliberate, determined and active sense in a crisis or low-level engagement. Naval aid includes a range of activities such as attachment of naval advisers, mine clearances, or salvage work in the aftermath of hostilities, disaster relief and requests for specific assistance from friendly countries.

Operational calls refer to port visits whose basic occasion is the satisfaction of the operational naval requirements of foreign warships operating in or transiting through a particular stretch of water. The basic requirements are rest for the crew and the replenishment of supplies. However, such visits can be used in attempts to make a favourable impression on the country concerned by the behaviour and turnout of the crew, the technological prowess of the country as embodied in the ship, general 'image' of the ship, and the entertainment and cultivation of selected locals. As in the case of operational calls, warships operating in or transiting through a particular area may carry out specific goodwill visits. However, the difference between the two is that whereas the former is an attempt to maximise the political effects of a necessary visit, the specific occasion of the latter is political. These visits are specific attempts to cultivate the host country, with the hope of accumulating diplomatic capital.

Joint Naval Exercises

Navy to navy relations tends to transcend geographical boundaries. This is because of the unique nature of demands, challenges, opportunities and romance of the seas. The navies of the world speak a language with distinctive word phrases, style of expression, develop a communality of minds, manners, customs and skills-actually it is sort of a common culture. This phenomenon provides coastal states that the oceans have made neighbours, a fertile soil to build friendship on. Joint naval exercises are, in addition to other forms of naval co-operation, therefore, an important instrument of State policy. Historically, it is clear that diplomacy exercised through naval power is not new. The chronological list of diplomacy employed by naval forces from 1919 to 1991 has been compiled by James Cable in his work 'Gunboat Diplomacy 1919-1991'. What is new is that naval diplomacy has become a significant preoccupation of academic thought and has therefore, been elevated to the lofty heights of naval missions. Due to the nature of naval diplomacy, all states have the advantage of being able to participate on an almost equal footing with every other state.

INDIA AND 'GUNBOAT DIPLOMACY'

'Gunboat diplomacy' as defined by James Cable "... is the use or threat of limited naval force, otherwise than as an act of war, in order to secure advantage, or to avert loss, either in the furtherance of an international dispute or else against foreign nationals within the territory or the jurisdiction of their own state." Coercive naval diplomacy or ' gunboat diplomacy' is often seen as a complement to diplomacy and an alternative to an actual conflict. Being a military form of diplomacy, it tends to produce effects more rapidly than other methods such as preferential trade agreement or financial assistance. 'Gunboat diplomacy' is traditionally a weapon employed by the strong against the weak.

The US with its strong navy and a committed political will has made the maximum use of 'gunboat diplomacy'. The US Navy has used 'gunboat diplomacy'to evacuate its nationals endangered in countries engaged in civil war, to carry out reprisal attacks and also to display national resolve. In Dec, 1982, the US deployed 14 ships off the Lebanese coast and carried out exercises to demonstrate US resolve to the Arab States and the Soviet Union. On the negative side, it is increasingly obvious that there is worldwide opposition to the use of coercive naval diplomacy. Carrying around the big maritime stick is no longer fashionable at least most certainly for the United States and other dominant regional powers. Also this form of diplomacy usually focuses on political and military objectives and has little or no impact on economic or cultural ones. It may also generate undue hostility and tension between assailant and victim (in part due to adverse public opinion) out of all proportion to the level of coercion, physical or otherwise, intended.

Applications of 'Gunboat Diplomacy' by India

'Gunboat diplomacy' here implies political demonstrations of power and specific operational deployment mentioned earlier. In the case of India this particular coercive form of naval diplomacy has not been applied much. This may be due to two reasons: one, that this would have further distanced us from our land and maritime neighbours and the second could be that the government has not comprehended the importance of this form of diplomacy.

There have been three instances of 'gunboat diplomacy' exercised by India:-

(a) The first instance was in Aug 1987 against Sri Lanka when two Indian frigates lay off Colombo ready to evacuate the Indian High Commission endangered by civil war. Actually this could also be construed as non-coercive diplomacy as they went on the invitation of President Jayawardhene.

(b) The second instance was in Nov 1988 when the Indian Navy foiled a coup de tat in Maldives, rescued hostages and sunk the ship carrying mercenaries.

(c) The third incident was the deployment of Indian Naval units during the Indo-Bangladesh negotiations in respect of the status of New Moore Island.

The only case of 'gunboat diplomacy' against India was in Dec 1971. A United States Task Force centred on the carrier Enterprise entered the Bay of Bengal, apparently to deter India from pushing to extreme her military victory over Pakistan. The move certainly attracted attention, but the influence it exercised is open to question. In the Indian context, the opportunities to engage in 'gunboat diplomacy' would be numerous in view of its superior military might compared to that of its maritime neighbours. However, New Delhi is out to disprove the theories of people accusing it of hegemonic designs. Towards this objective, the likelihood of India engaging in 'gunboat diplomacy' in future would be limited.

INDIA AND NON COERCIVE NAVAL DIPLOMACY

Over the years, India's perspective of naval diplomacy has included visits to foreign ports, the hosting of warships at Indian ports, foreign training, and joint operations against poachers/ pirates. These may be termed collectively under the head of non-coercive naval diplomacy.

The mere thirty warships of the Indian Navy at Independence were not the ideal tools for diplomacy but they still continued the practice of goodwill foreign port visits. This was very much a part of the traditions of both the Royal Navy and the Royal Indian Navy. For obvious reasons, the port visits of the Indian Navy were confined to the littoral states of the Indian Ocean. The most important of these, during the early days of independence was Prime Minister Jawaharlal Nehru's official visit to Indonesia. In June 1950, Nehru sailed abroad the Indian flagship "Delhi" to Jakarta, escorted by three Indian destroyers and frigates. Such goodwill visits, however, did not follow any strict pattern in terms of countries selected, the number of warships deployed, the duration of stay, or even the annual total number of visits. During 1965-70, for example, warships of the Indian Navy made visits to 34 countries. These varied from a low of single visit in 1965 to a high of 22 such visits to 19 countries in 1969. The majority of such visits during this period, however, took place to countries of the Indian Ocean littoral, along with a single visit to the United States.

Since the mid-1980s, the Indian Navy increased its visits to those countries in the Indian Ocean that expressed concern over the nature and extent of its expansion. For the past ten years, for example, the Indian Navy has visited ports in Indonesia and Malaysia virtually every year. This included the visit of two warships to Penang in 1990-91, to take part in the international fleet review that marked the fiftieth anniversary of Royal Malaysian Navy. During the period 1991-94 the Indian Navy visited 22 countries and approximately 25 ports. During the year 1997-98 naval ships visited Brunei, Bangla Desh, Mauritius, Seychelles, Tanzania, Mozambique, Kenya, Malaysia and Cambodia. Indian warships also visited ports in South Africa, China and Philippines in 1998-99.

Hosting Foreign Warship

Indian ports continue to host visits by foreign warships, including those from Australia, Indonesia, Malaysia, Russia, UK and the United States. Moreover, sensitive naval establishments, such as those on the Andaman and Nicobar Islands, and the submarine base at Visakhapatnam, have also been opened up to warships of a few foreign countries on a selective basis. Since 1991, naval ships from Australia, France, Indonesia, Malaysia, and Singapore, have visited Port Blair. Naval Ships of the Republic of Singapore visited Visakhapatnam for the first time in early 1996.

In view of its 'gunboat diplomacy' during 1971 Indo-Pakistan War, the entry of American ships to Indian Ports had been refused till the mid-1980's. During the 1990-91 Gulf War, however, US ships on their way to the war zone were allowed refuelling stops.

In November 1993, the first Chinese warship, a destroyer size training ship, visited Mumbai. Although the Chinese had visited the Indian Ocean in mid-1980s, no Indian port has been visited. In March 1995, the first visit of South African naval ship, a combat support vessel also took place at Mumbai. Specifically in the year 1997-98, naval ships of the US, UK, France, Malaysia, Italy, Germany, Thailand, Indonesia, Brazil, Turkey, Oman and Argentinean navies visited Indian ports. Later three fleet ships of South Korea visited India in 1998.

This feature of hosting foreign warships is prevalent throughout the world in this era of peace and co-operation. As an example, the PLA Navy ships including a Luhu Class destroyer Harbin, visited US naval bases at Pearl Harbour, Hawaii and San Diego, California in March 1997.

'Milan' Gathering of Ships. Since 1995 the IN has thrice hosted a multinational gathering of ships from five to seven countries at the Port Blair naval base of Andaman and Nicobar Islands in the Bay of Bengal. In Feb 1995 four warships from Indonesia, Thailand, Singapore and Sri Lanka along with India participated in 'Milan

95'. Two years later in Feb 1997, eleven warships from seven countries (Malaysia and Bangla Desh were the new nations which had joined the Milan) were involved in various activities, excluding joint naval exercises, for a five-day period. The third of this series of bi-annual gathering of ships, Milan 99 was held from 30 Mar-04 Apr 99. Malaysia did not participate in this Milan while the remaining five nations participated. These events were essentially social, cultural and sports get-togethers. This interaction provided a forum to foster friendship, strengthen cultural ties and promote confidence building amongst the naval fraternity of the region.

International Fleet Review. Indian Navy's first international fleet review was held, in Mumbai, in the second week of Feb 2001. Featuring over 70 ships, many of them foreign, which lined up at sea opposite the Gateway of India, it comprised an international parade at the Marine Drive involving naval marching contingents, military bands, several water-borne activities and a fly-past of over 60 aircraft. The fleet review, with the theme 'Brigades of Friendship', also hosted an international seminar on maritime diplomacy.

Disaster Relief

In addition to having been involved in disaster relief within the country, the Indian Navy has, no occasions, responded to requests from foreign governments to provide aid and disaster relief. One of the examples in 'Operation Madad', which was in response to the Maldivian request for relief supplies, when a massive tidal wave struck some of the islands in July 1991.

Naval Aid

The Indian Navy has been involved in specific diplomatic efforts in at lease four countries namely Sri Lanka, Mauritius, South Yemen and Maldives.

Piracy

The international law requires warships or other government vessels to repress piracy on the high seas. Anti piracy operations are another manner of exhibiting naval diplomacy in which both the Navy and the Coast Guard are engaged. The first case of piracy in Indian waters was reported on 16 Nov 99. An 8000 tonne Panamanian cargo vessel MV Alondra Rainbow was taken over by 15 pirates from Indonesia. This vessel was captured 270 miles off Goa in dramatic 12-hour joint operation by the Indian Navy and Coast Guard.

In another incident, on 24 Dec 99 the Indian Coast Guard captured a ship 'Gloria Kopp' off the Pondicherry coast and brought it to Chennai. The ship 'Kobe Queen –1, registered in Panama in 1976, which had left Istanbul on 09 Jul 99 after loading cargo, was 'hijacked' and its name changed to 'Gloria Kopp' before being diverted to west African waters instead of its destination of Reo Haina in Jamaica. On a global alert by the cargo insurance company, the Coast Guard intercepted the ship.

Miscellaneous

The other avenues of non-coercive naval diplomacy with regard to India pertain to the training of foreigners in India, hydrographic and technological assistance to foreign countries.

The Indian Navy trains personnel from foreign navies under the International Training and Economic Co-operation (ITEC) and Self Financing Scheme (SFS). During the year 1996-97, 119 officers and 136 sailors from foreign navies were trained in India. 48. The Indian Navy has modern hydrographic systems such as Multi-Beam Swath Echo Sounders, Automated Cartographic System and Photometry system for satellite image processing. For the first time, the Indian Navy undertook, and successfully completed, the survey of Oman's coastline in 1995. Hydrographic co-operation/ assistance with littoral countries is being actively pursued by the naval Hydrographic Department. Though not a direct means of naval diplomacy, technological assistance is an important activity and develops naval co-operation. India today has gained expertise to develop state of the art naval equipment and warships. The Indian Navy had developed the skill and infrastructure to maintain and operate these. These skills could be utilised in rendering technical assistance to neighbouring nations that need them.

Future Prospects

In the field of non-coercive naval diplomacy India has been quite active. There has been exchange of visits of both senior ranking naval officers and ships. The concept of 'Milan' gathering of ships is giant step to further naval co-operation with our eastern and far eastern neighbours. The Indian Navy has always been quick to respond to calls of aid from foreign countries. After the Pokharan – II explosions, naval diplomatic missions were almost negligible, especially in 1998. However, today things look brighter, ships from various nations are visiting India and Milan 99 was also conducted successfully. The road to further this form of diplomacy is clear for the Indian Navy. The International Fleet Review was a step in the right direction. However, there is scope for improvement in all the sub groups, especially foreign training, technical and hydrographic assistance.

INDIAN NAVY AND JOINT NAVAL EXERCISES

Joint naval exercises assume significance for the sake of expanding friendly relations and also enhancing national security. Common culture between navies, tend to transcend geographical boundaries. Conducted in international water, away from public gaze, sensitivity about sovereignty and other such things become non-issues.

In addition, joint naval exercises strengthen self reliance by testing it against international competition, enhances professional reputation and hence deterrent value for our navy and equally significantly provides valuable inputs for identifying areas for modernisation. Joint naval exercises could be low-keyed having the primary aim of fostering good relations. Participating units in these, are exercised in simple daytime manoeuvres, station keeping and basic seamanship drills at sea. The other types of exercises are those which expose navies to advanced tactics and techniques of other participating navies. Such exercises are much larger in scope and complexity and include operations on, under and above the sea. In the context of furthering naval diplomacy both types of naval exercises are important.

During the fifties and early fifties, our navy used to be a regular participant in the annual joint naval exercises of as much as four to six weeks duration in and off Trincomalee. These were held annually amongst the navies of India, Pakistan and Sri Lanka with the participation of the Royal Navy, and, at times, the Australian and New Zealand navies as well. Held in August, they came to be known by acronym JET (Joint Exercise, Trincomalee). In 1964, JET came to an abrupt end, in view of the increasingly antagonistic relations between India and Pakistan. Just over a year later. India was involved in a war with Pakistan. For over twelve years after the end of JET, the Indian Navy did not carry out any exercise with foreign navy. This was primarily because of the increased level of Cold War tensions, and the onset of superpower rivalry in the Indian Ocean. In these circumstances, India's non-aligned foreign policy did not allow any joint exercise to take place with the two major protagonists or their allies. However, there were two exceptions. One in 1977 during the brief period of Janata Party rule in the late 1970s. On this occasions India carried out a single joint multilateral naval exercise with Australia and New Zealand naval forces. Both the Indian and Australian naval forces were led by aircraft carriers. This was followed twelve years later in 1989 with a single joint bilateral naval exercise with warships of the Indonesian Navy off Surabaya.

Present Status of Joint Naval Exercises

In the seven year period, 1991-1998, 26 joint bilateral naval and coast guard exercises have been held with nineteen littoral as well as extra-regional navies of the Indian Ocean. The Indian Navy in the last four years has conducted joint naval exercises with many nations namely, Kenya, Iran, Kuwait, Oman, Saudi Arabia, Australia, Indonesia, Malaysia, Singapore, Philippines, France, Germany, South Korea, the UK and the USA.

However, the thrust of the joint naval exercises has been with the South East Asian states. Joint bilateral naval exercises have been conducted with all the four ASEAN states if the Indian Ocean rim. The Indian Navy has conducted the largest number of joint naval exercises with the Republic of Singapore, the seventh such exercise took place in 1998. The first joint naval exercise for the Indian Navy of this century was conducted with Singapore in end Feb 2000.

The scope of these exercises however, continues to remain limited, involving, at present, only one or two ships one each side. The Indian Navy in April 98 played host to a major exercise aimed at promoting co-ordination among the navies of friendly countries in conducting Search and Rescue operations in waters off the Indian sub-continent. Ships of navies of Bangla Desh, India, Indonesia, Singapore and Sri Lanka participated in the exercise known as Operation 'Madad'. In a bid to cultivate the Gulf countries India held joint naval exercises with Iran, Saudi Arabia and Kuwait, for the first time, in 1998.

Joint Exercises with the US Navy

The largest joint naval exercise conducted so far by the Indian Navy have been with the US Navy. Despite a virtual pandemonium in the Lok Sabha over the issue, the exercise was conducted smoothly as planned. The Indian Navy has carried out three joint bilateral naval exercises with US Navy, during 1992-97 (Malaba I-III). In the wake of India's nuclear tests of May 1998, all defence and naval co-operation with the US was stopped but these sanctions have now been lifted in the aftermath of the terrorist attacks on the World Trade Centre. The first exercise, with a major Western power after Pokhran-II, was carried out with the French Navy from Feb 28-29 2000. The French naval ships comprised their only operational aircraft carrier Foch, two other warships and one tanker.

Joint Exercises with Past Adversaries

There have been many instances in the recent past where nations involved in disputes and war have started exercising together as a first step towards developing friendly ties. Russia and Japan have traditionally regarded each other with suspicion. Half of Sakhalin Island, now Russia, was once controlled by Japan. And twice in the last century the two powers have gone to war i.e. during the Russo-Japanese War and World War II. More recently, relations between Japan and Russia have been strained by opposing claims over the southern Kuril Islands and by clashes between Japanese fishermen and the Russian Federal Border Service.

Russia and Japan set aside opposing territorial claims and disputes over fishing rights to join forces in the first naval exercises between the two Asian powers. The exercises took place in the Sea of Japan for three days in Sep 1998. Rear Admiral Nikolai Temerev, who led the Russian side, said the exercises showed the high level of readiness on the part of the 700 Japanese and 700 Russian participants. In addition to two antisubmarine ships from the Russian Pacific Fleet, two escort ships, a supply ship, five helicopters and two air crafts from Japan's Maritime Self Defence Forces participated in the exercises.

In another instance the UK and Argentine armed forces forgetting heir differences over the Falklands and the 1982 War conducted joint exercises from 3-6 Nov 1999 in the South Atlantic. It was the first time that forces from two countries exercised together outside UN auspices since the Falklands conflict 1982. The four day exercise involved ships and aircraft from the Navies and Air Forces of both countries establishing communications, then searching together for a fishing vessel reported sinking in waters to the south of the Falklands Islands.

The idea of having joint naval exercises with the Pakistan Navy seems too farfetched in the wake of the Kargil operations, the coup in Pakistan and the recent hijacking episode. It was prior to Kargil when building on the momentum of the bus diplomacy with Pakistan that the Indian Navy had proposed holding goodwill exchanges with Islambad.

The Chief of Naval Staff, Admiral Sushil Kumar in an informal chat with the media then had said, "If we can play cricket and our buses can come and go, why can't we have our ships sent to Pakistan and their ships coming here?"

However, things changed for the worse since then. Nevertheless, it would not be too farfetched to contemplate having joint naval exercises with Pakistan in the Arabian Sea and with China in the coming decades. With the passage of time this would seem more and more plausible, as it took 17 years after the war for the Royal Navy and the Argentinean Navy to exercise together.

Prospectus for Indian Navy

The conduct of Joint Naval Exercises (JNE), besides developing the Navy professionally, serves two basic purposes for India. These are listed below:-

(a) JNEs dispel concern over India's naval build up programme and expansion of power projection capabilities.

(b) JNEs also improve the nature of bilateral relations with nations. They are perceived to help instil as well as build upon, a military dimension to bilateral political relationship.

The Indian Navy has been engaged in joint exercises with a number of countries. There are, however, many navies that have not yet operated with the Indian Navy. The most significant of these is the Japanese Navy. Also, the thrust of the Indian Navy in the Western sector towards the Gulf of South Africa has been limited. These and other navies could be coaxed into conducting joint naval exercises to improve naval and subsequent political ties with these nations.

IMPENDMENTS IN INDIAN NAVAL DIPLOMACY AND THE WAY AHEAD

Is the Indian Navy doing all that it can in the diplomatic role? Where do we go from here?

Diplomacy in Naval Priority of Tasks

The Chief of Naval Staff Admiral Sushil Kumar, in his Navy Day 1999 message acknowledged that the Navy's contribution in enhancing naval diplomacy by way of joint exercises, port visits, foreign training and in joint operations against poachers/pirates has brought international acclaim to the Navy. This shows that the Indian Navy bestows high priority to diplomacy among its various missions. However, it is not known whether it has the backing of the Ministry of External affairs (MEA) or the Ministry of Defence (MoD). There is no doubt that the Navy has realises that the potential of naval diplomacy in immense and is attempting to do the most with resources available. The International Fleet Review conducted in Feb 2001, the first of its kind in India, amply demonstrated the naval will to promote diplomacy. The press that the event got in the international media proved beyond doubt that the India's image and that of the Indian Navy got a tremendous fillip due to the IFR. The next question is whether the resources available are adequate?

Force Level And Budgetary Constraints

The Naval budget has dwindled through the times. A balanced three-dimensional Navy should show our flag, carry the message of goodwill, reassurance and support to our friends, deter the adventure, the opportunist and deal firmly with our enemies. From being on the cover of Time magazine in 1989 it has gone almost to oblivion due to the drastic cuts as the Government has given impetus to the economy and liberlisation. The Navy continuously receives the least share of Defence expenditure among the three armed services. The dismal allocation can be realised by the fact that the Navy's budget for 1998-99 was only slightly higher than the pension for the services that year. In view of the increased costs of naval arms and equipment in the future, the Navy's share of the Defence budget is woefully short of the require amount.

The force levels of the Navy's principal combatants are rapidly decreasing. During the last five-year period (1995-2000) its principal combatants decreased by a fifth – from 40 to 32. Moreover, during the 2000-2015 period, they will decrease by as much as half – from 32 to 16 if no new acquisitions are planned after 2005. However, with the planned induction of some indigenous ships, procurement of Krivak III class ships and Ka-31 helicopters from Russia, the building plans of the Air Defence Ship and the likely procurement of the air craft carrier 'Gorshkov' the Navy again be a force to reckon with. Though naval diplomacy is not directly related to the force levels, it should be remembered that the diplomatic character of the navy comes from the military punch it is perceived to be capable of. A weak navy is not likely to succeed in any diplomatic activity and could offer the same role as a merchant ship might afford. The force level of the Indian Navy should be adequate to project an image of a modern, strong and well equipped navy.

Co-ordination between MOD, MEA and the Indian Navy

In all probability the impetus given to naval diplomatic activity in India has been the lone effort of the Navy. The MoD report 1997-98, as is the practice every year, relegated the report on co-operations with foreign countries to page 108, almost the end of the report. Moreover, the annual report of the MEA, does not acknowledge goodwill visits by Indian Naval Ships to foreign ports or the conduct of bilateral naval exercises. The official web site of the MEA has very concisely mentioned our international relations with various nations in their different web pages. Each web page is dedicated to one nation and explicitly mentions the visits of dignitaries exchanged between the two states. However, the port visits of naval ships and joint naval exercises conducted are conspicuous by their absence.

On the other hand, the Western nations are endeavoring to give fresh impetus to this important activity. The UK MoD in its Strategic Defence Review (SDR) has proposed the creation of a formal Defence Diplomacy Mission to make diplomacy a core Defence activity. This is aimed to give it greater priority and ensure that it is properly linked to the Government's broader policy objectives.

India too needs to have a Defence Diplomatic Mission established with a naval wing. In the interim a Naval Diplomacy Mission could be established which would comprise members from the MoD, MEA and the Indian Navy. The task of the mission should be initiated by the MEA. The diplomatic activities should not be incidental but be planned and well executed. Even seemingly trifle activities such as goodwill visits of our ships should be planned and thought over well and should not be adhoc. The PM of Singapore Mr Goh Chok Tok during his recent visit to the country mentioned that India was not putting enough effort in looking East. The establishment and promulgation of naval co-operations with our Eastern neighbours could be one of the first goals of the mission.

Areas of Naval Co-operation

Naval diplomacy, if reciprocated leads to naval co-operation. Naval co-operation whether bilateral or multilateral, comprises a wide variety of activities differing in scale, complexity and sensitivity. These range from traditional 'low level' activities such as personnel exchanges, ship's visits, attendance at fleet reviews, joint training (basic and specialised), hydrographic assistance, joint bilateral and multilateral exercises to high level activities such as information and intelligence exchanges,, warship design maintenance and construction, avoidance of incidents at sea (INSEA) agreements, joint operations in peacetime, co-ordinated patrols (anti piracy etc), co-operative maritime surveillance, enhanced inter-operability stressing jointness, joint doctrine development, mine counter measures, combined Sea Lines of Communications (SLOC) protection, and finally, the establishment of standing regional naval forces and joint operation in warfare. The importance of these activities depends upon the prevailing set of political relationship.

Shrinking defence budgets and growing commitments in the new world order will force navies into closer co-operation. Multinational naval integration is the way ahead. Co-operation agreements, outside NATO (North Atlantic Treaty Organisation) have been signed between the Belgian and the Royal Netherlands Navy, the French and Belgian Navy, the French and the Royal Navy as also between Latvia, Estonia and Lithuania in the Baltic. The atmosphere in the Indian Ocean Region (IOR) may not be conductive today to attempt establishment of standing regional naval forces on the lines of what NATO has done in the Atlantic, Adriatic and the Mediterranean seas. However, a collective security arrangement in the region, especially with US participation can be considered to cater to the security of all littoral states, including small and less developed countries. This would preclude 'gunboat diplomacy' and arbitrary exercise of power by any state. Meanwhile, a beginning can be made by the Indian Navy in the low level activities. With time the cooperation can be graduated to high-level activities like the joint protection of the Malacca Straits and other choke points of interest to us as also to our neighbours. This would require pointed and dedicated efforts from the MEA, MoD and the Navy.

The Way Ahead

Recommendations. In order to effectively utilise the Navy in support of Indian foreign policy the following recommendations are made:-

(a) It is imperative that the government (especially MEA) actually acknowledges the Navy's role in foreign policy. This would entail a formal recognition of its contribution, and the formulation of a comprehensive policy to actively involve the Navy in tasks of this nature. This would also necessitate a high level of co-ordination amongst MEA, MoD, Naval Headquarters and other related agencies, which is lacking at the present time. In effect, these changes would put an end to the often adhoc and arbitrary manner in which India naval diplomacy is being carried out and would also prevent opportunities for naval diplomacy from being missed.

(b) The activities of the Indian Navy in the diplomatic role need to be given wide publicity. In actual effect people need reminding of even the value of and reason for well-equipped and well-trained navies. Kindling current public interest in naval affairs is not easy. 'Out of sight, out of mind' has always been a public relations exercise for the navies the world over. Educating people on all aspects of the navy and role of naval diplomacy must be the responsibility of serving and retired officers, the government officials and the media. Dedicated efforts in this direction would have to be taken.

(c) Joint exercises have been conducted by the Indian Navy with many nations. However, there is scope of involving more navies like that of Japan, South Africa and the Gulf nations on a regular basis in these exercises, as has been done with our eastern neighbours.

(d) The Indian Navy being the largest in the region has a number of basic and specialised training academies and institutions throughout the country. A number of them regularly train personnel for selected foreign countries. However, considerable additional effort needs to be placed to further encourage the training of foreign naval personnel, may be even in specialised areas such as submarine warfare and in helicopter and Maritime Reconnaissance (MR) aircraft operations.

(e) The Indian Navy has been fortunate in gradually developing a state of the art hydrographic capability that is possibly the fourth largest in the world today. The Naval Hydrographic department (now termed as National Hydrographic Office) at Dehradun could organise and conduct training programs on a regular basis for naval officers of the Indian Ocean rim countries. The spare capacity of the service could be also be utlised to undertake surveys for other countries in the Arabic Sea and the Bay of Bengal. The conduct of Naval Hydrographic training and operation in a bilateral manner would enable the establishment of hydrographic department with navies of the Indian Ocean littorals which do not have them already, as well as enable the survey of large areas of the sea in a joint and co-ordinated manner.

(f) The three Defence shipyards in the country have developed a number of sophisticated warships. These include submarines, destroyers, frigates and corvettes along with patrol boats, minor coastal combatants and auxiliary ships which are presently in service with the Navy. The spare capacities in Indian defence shipyard could be utilised for the maintenance and repair, as well as the construction of ships for littoral as well as extra regional navies. This would earn goodwill and valuable foreign exchange for the country. The technical know-how acquired by the Navy in maintaining and operating these systems could also be used to provide technical assistance to these countries.

11

United States Naval Special Warfare Command and Group

The United States Naval Special Warfare Command (NAVSPECWARCOM, NAVSOC or NSWC) was commissioned on 16 April 1987, at Naval Amphibious Base Coronado in San Diego, California.

As the Naval component to the United States Special Operations Command, headquartered at MacDill AFB in Tampa, Florida, Naval Special Warfare Command provides vision, leadership, doctrinal guidance, resources and oversight to ensure component maritime special operations forces are ready to meet the operational requirements of combatant commanders.

BACKGROUND

Today's Naval Special Warfare operators can trace their origins to the Scouts and Raiders, Naval Combat Demolition Units, Office of Strategic Services Operational Swimmers, Underwater Demolition Teams, and Motor Torpedo Boat Squadrons of World War II. While none of those early organizations have survived to present, their pioneering efforts in unconventional warfare are mirrored in the missions and professionalism of the present Naval Special Warfare warriors.

To meet the need for a beach reconnaissance force, selected Army and Navy personnel assembled at Amphibious Training Base Little Creek, Virginia, on 15 August 1942 to begin Amphibious Scouts and Raiders (Joint) training. The Scouts and Raiders mission was to identify and reconnoiter the objective beach, maintain a position on the designated beach prior to a landing and guide the assault waves to the landing beach.

World War II

By the time the United States became involved in World War II, Adolf Hitler and his Axis forces had control over a large portion of Europe, Asia and North Africa. If the Allied forces were to stand a chance, there would have to be several full-scale landings. The US Navy decided that to do the job right required sending in their own.

They needed brave men to reconnoiter the landing beaches, take note of obstacles and defences and ultimately guide the landing forces in. Later, during the war, the Army Engineers passed down demolition jobs to the US Navy. They were to clear any obstacles and/or defences in the near shore area. Beginning a tradition that continues today, these brave men contributed immensely to the war effort.

Scouts & Raiders

The Navy Scouts and Raiders were created before the Underwater Demolition Teams (UDT) or Navy Combat Demolition Units (NCDU) (predecessors to the Navy SEALs). It was first formed in September 1942, nine months after the attack on Pearl Harbour, from the Observer Group, a joint Marine Corps-Army-Navy unit. The Observer Group was the first unit trained in amphibious reconnaissance. They trained in inflatable boat insertions from submarines around the Chesapeake Bay and at the Amphibious Training Base (ATB) Little Creek in Virginia and in Fort Pierce, Florida. They were training for an intense clandestine mission in North Africa.

However, the Observer Group was disbanded, with the Marine Corps counterpart forming the Amphib Recon Company; the Army/Navy unit formed the Scouts and Raiders and continued its deployment to North Africa as planned, where they earned eight Navy Crosses. This was just the first of many war-time missions for the versatile Scouts and Raiders.

First Group

The first group included Phil H. Bucklew, the "Father of Naval Special Warfare," after whom the Naval Special Warfare Center building is named. Commissioned in October 1942, this group saw combat in November 1942 during Operation Torch, the first allied landings in Europe, on the North African coast. Scouts and

Raiders also supported landings in Sicily, Salerno, Anzio, Normandy, and southern France.

Second Group

A second group of Scouts and Raiders, code-named Special Service Unit #1, was established on 7 July 1943, as a joint and combined operations force. The first mission, in September 1943, was at Finschafen on New Guinea. Later operations were at Gasmata, Arawe, Cape Gloucester, and the East and South coast of New Britain, all without any loss of personnel. Conflicts arose over operational matters, and all non-Navy personnel were reassigned. The unit, renamed 7th Amphibious Scouts, received a new mission, to go ashore with the assault boats, buoy channels, erect markers for the incoming craft, handle casualties, take offshore soundings, blow up beach obstacles and maintain voice communications linking the troops ashore, incoming boats and nearby ships. The 7th Amphibious Scouts conducted operations in the Pacific for the duration of the conflict, participating in more than 40 landings.

Third Group

The third Scout and Raiders organization operated in China. Scouts and Raiders were deployed to fight with the Sino-American Cooperation Organization, or SACO. To help bolster the work of SACO, Admiral Ernest J. King ordered that 120 officers and 900 men be trained for "Amphibious Roger" at the Scout and Ranger school at Fort Pierce, Florida. They formed the core of what was envisioned as a "guerrilla amphibious organization of Americans and Chinese operating from coastal waters, lakes and rivers employing small steamboats and sampans." While most Amphibious Roger forces remained at Camp Knox in Calcutta, three of the groups saw active service. They conducted a survey of the upper Yangtze River in the spring of 1945 and, disguised as coolies, conducted a detailed three-month survey of the Chinese coast from Shanghai to Kitchioh Wan, near Hong Kong

NAVAL COMBAT DEMOLITION UNITS

In September 1942, 17 Navy salvage personnel arrived at ATB Little Creek, Virginia for a one-week concentrated course on demolitions, explosive cable cutting and commando raiding techniques. On 10 November 1942, this first combat demolition unit succeeded in cutting a cable and net barrier across the Wadi Sebou River during Operation Torch in North Africa. Their actions enabled the USS *Dallas* (DD-199) to traverse the river and insert Army Rangers, who proceeded to capture the Port Lyautey aerodrome.

Plans for a massive cross-channel invasion of Europe had begun and intelligence indicated that the Germans were placing extensive underwater obstacles on the beaches at Normandy. On 7 May 1943, Lieutenant Commander Draper L. Kauffman, "The Father of Naval Combat Demolition," was directed to set up a school and train people to eliminate obstacles on an enemy-held beach prior to an invasion. On 6 June 1943, LCDR Kaufmann established Naval Combat Demolition Unit training at Fort Pierce. By April 1944, a total of 34 NCDUs were deployed to England in preparation for Operation OVERLORD, the amphibious landing at Normandy.

On 6 June 1944, in the face of great adversity, the NCDUs at Omaha Beach managed to blow eight complete gaps and two partial gaps in the German defences. The NCDUs suffered 31 killed and 60 wounded, a casualty rate of 52%. Meanwhile, the NCDUs at Utah Beach met less intense enemy fire. They cleared 700 yards (640 m) of beach in two hours, another 900 yards (820 m) by the afternoon. Casualties at Utah Beach were significantly lighter with six killed and eleven wounded. During Operation OVERLORD, not a single demolitioneer was lost to improper handling of explosives.

In August 1944, NCDUs from Utah Beach participated in the landings in southern France, the last amphibious operation in the European Theatre of Operations. NCDUs also operated in the Pacific theatre. NCDU 2, under LTjg Frank Kaine, after whom the Naval Special Warfare Command building is named, and NCDU 3 under LTjg Lloyd Anderson, formed the nucleus of six NCDUs that served with the Seventh Amphibious Force tasked with clearing boat channels after the landings from Biak to Borneo.

OSS Operational Swimmers

Some of the earliest World War II predecessors of the SEALs were the Operational Swimmers of the Office of Strategic Services, or OSS. Many current SEAL missions were first assigned to them.

OSS specialized in special operations, dropping operatives behind enemy lines to engage in organized guerrilla warfare as well as to gather information on such things as enemy resources and troop movements.

British Combined Operations veteran LCDR Wooley, of the Royal Navy, was placed in charge of the OSS Maritime Unit in June 1943. Their training started in November 1943 at Camp Pendleton, California, moved to Santa Catalina Island, California in January 1944, and finally moved to the warmer waters of The Bahamas in March 1944. Within the U.S. military, they pioneered flexible swimfins and diving masks, closed-circuit diving equipment (under the direction of Dr. Chris Lambertsen), the use of Swimmer Delivery Vehicles (a type of submersible), and combat swimming and limpet mine attacks. In May 1944, General Donovan, the head of the OSS, divided the unit into groups. He loaned Group 1, under Lieutenant Choate, to Admiral Nimitz, as a way to introduce the OSS into the Pacific theatre. They became part of UDT-10 in July 1944. Five OSS men participated in the very first UDT submarine operation with the USS *Burrfish* (SS-312) in the Caroline Islands in August 1944.

UNDERWATER DEMOLITION TEAMS

On 23 November 1943, the U.S. Marine landing on Tarawa Atoll emphasized the need for hydrographic reconnaissance and underwater demolition of obstacles prior to any amphibious landing. After Tarawa, 30 officers and 150 enlisted men were moved to the Waimânalo Amphibious Training Base to form the nucleus of a demolition training program. This group became Underwater Demolition Teams (UDT) ONE and TWO.

The UDTs saw their first combat on 31 January 1944, during Operation Flintlock in the Marshall Islands. FLINTLOCK became the real catalyst for the UDT training program in the Pacific Theatre. In February 1944, the Naval Combat Demolition Training and Experimental Base was established at Kîhei, Maui, next to the Amphibious Base at Kamaole. Eventually, 34 UDT teams were established. Wearing swim suits, fins, and dive masks on combat operations, these "Naked Warriors" saw action across the Pacific in every major amphibious landing including: Eniwetok, Saipan, Guam, Tinian, Angaur, Ulithi, Peleliu, Leyte, Lingayen Gulf, Zambales, Iwo Jima, Okinawa, Labuan, Brunei Bay, and on 4 July

1945 at Balikpapan on Borneo, which was the last UDT demolition operation of the war.

The rapid demobilization at the conclusion of the war reduced the number of active duty UDTs to two on each coast with a complement of seven officers and 45 enlisted men each. The Korean War began on 25 June 1950, when the North Korean army invaded South Korea.

Beginning with a detachment of 11 personnel from UDT 3, UDT participation expanded to three teams with a combined strength of 300 men. As part of the Special Operations Group, or SOG, UDTs successfully conducted demolition raids on railroad tunnels and bridges along the Korean coast. On 15 September 1950, UDTs supported Operation Chromite, the amphibious landing at Incheon. UDT 1 and 3 provided personnel who went in ahead of the landing craft, scouting mud flats, marking low points in the channel, clearing fouled propellers, and searching for mines. Four UDT personnel acted as wave-guides for the Marine landing.

In October 1950, UDTs supported mine-clearing operations in Wonsan Harbour where frogmen would locate and mark mines for minesweepers. On 12 October 1950, two U.S. minesweepers hit mines and sank. UDTs rescued 25 sailors. The next day, William Giannotti conducted the first U.S. combat operation using an "aqualung" when he dove on the USS *Pledge* (AM-277). For the remainder of the war, UDTs conducted beach and river reconnaissance, infiltrated guerrillas behind the lines from sea, continued mine sweeping operations, and participated in Operation Fishnet, which severely damaged the North Korean's fishing capability.

NAVY SEALS & SWCC

Although Naval Special Warfare personnel comprise less than one percent of U.S. Navy personnel, they offer big dividends on a small investment. SEAL and SWCC units' proven ability to operate across the spectrum of conflict and in operations other than war in a controlled manner, and their ability to provide real time intelligence and eyes on target, offer decision makers immediate and virtually unlimited options in the face of rapidly changing crises around the world.

SEALs

SEALs are Special Operations Command's force-of-choice to conduct small-unit maritime military operations which originate from, and return to a river, ocean, swamp, delta or coastline. This littoral capability is considered more important now than ever, as half the world's infrastructure and population is located within one mile (1.6 km) of an ocean or river. Responding to President John F. Kennedy's desire for the Services to develop an Unconventional Warfare (UW) capability, the US Navy established SEAL Team ONE and SEAL Team TWO in January 1962. Formed entirely with personnel from Underwater Demolition Teams, the SEALs' mission was to conduct counter guerrilla warfare and clandestine operations in maritime and riverine environments.

Navy SEALs have distinguished themselves as an individually reliable, collectively disciplined and highly skilled maritime force. Because of the dangers inherent in NSW, prospective SEALs go through what is considered by many military experts to be the toughest training in the world. The intense physical and mental conditioning it takes to become a SEAL begins at Basic Underwater Demolition/SEAL (BUD/S) training. SEAL candidates begin BUD/S training at the Naval Special Warfare Center, NAB Coronado, California. This six-month course of instruction focuses on physical conditioning, small boat handling, diving physics, basic diving techniques, land warfare, weapons, demolitions, communications, and reconnaissance.

First Phase trains, develops, and assesses SEAL candidates in physical conditioning, water competency, teamwork, and mental tenacity. Second (Diving) Phase trains, develops, and qualifies SEAL candidates as competent basic combat swimmers. During this period, physical training continues and becomes even more intensive. Emphasis is placed on long distance underwater dives with the goal of training students to become basic combat divers, using swimming and diving techniques as a means of transportation from their launch point to their combat objective. This is a skill that separates SEALs from all other Special Operations forces. Third Phase trains, develops, and qualifies SEAL candidates in basic weapons, demolition, and small unit tactics. Third Phase concentrates on teaching land navigation, small-unit tactics, patrolling techniques, abseiling, marksmanship, and military explosives. The final three and a half weeks of Third Phase are spent at NALF San Clemente Island, where students apply all the techniques they have acquired during training.

SDVTs

SEAL Delivery Vehicle Teams' historical roots began during WWII with the earliest human torpedos to see use: Maiale, used by Italy's Decima Flottiglia MAS, and Chariots, used by British commando frogmen. Naval Special Warfare entered the wet submersible field in the 1960s when the Coastal Systems Center in Panama City, FL developed the Mark 7, a free-flooding SDV of the type used today, and the first SDV to be used in the fleet. The Mark 8 and 9 followed in the late 1970s. Today's Mark 8 Mod 1 provides NSW with an unprecedented capability that combines the attributes of clandestine underwater mobility and the combat swimmer. The Advanced SEAL Delivery System (ASDS) program that would have provided NSW a new (dry) submersible for long range infiltration missions was abandoned in 2009.

SWCC

The exclusive mission of Special Warfare Combatant-craft Crewmen operators is to expertly drive and provide small-caliber gunfire support on specialized high-tech, high-speed, and low-profile Surface Combatant Craft to secretly infiltrate and exfiltrate Navy SEALs on Special Operations missions worldwide. These missions include direct action on land, sea, coastline or rivers (such as strikes, captures, and ship take downs by Visit, Board, Search, and Seizure), special reconnaissance, Coastal Patrol and Interdiction of suspect ships and surface craft, counter-terrorism operations, riverine warfare, deception operations, search and rescue operations, and foreign internal defense missions. Although SEALs and SWCC undergo different training programs, both are focused on special operations in maritime environments. The SWCC program includes extensive training on craft and weapons tactics, techniques, and procedures. Like SEALs, SWCC must show physical fitness, possess strong motivation, be combat focused, and maintain responsiveness in high stress situations.

The SWCC designation is a relatively new Naval Special Warfare career path that is independent of the regular line Navy. Today's Special Boat Teams have their origins in the PT boats of WWII and the "Brown Water" naval force that was created in 1965 at the onset of the Vietnam War. Patrol Coastal and Patrol Torpedo ships are the ancestors of today's Cyclone class patrol ships and Mark V Special Operations Craft.

STRUCTURE

Global War on Terror

NSW is committed to combating the global terrorist threats. In addition to being experts in special reconnaissance and direct action missions, the skill sets needed to combat terrorism; NSW is postured to fight a dispersed enemy on their turf. NSW forces can operate from forward-deployed Navy ships, submarines and aviation mobility platforms as well as overseas bases and its own overseas units.

War in Afghanistan

In response to the attacks on America Sept. 11, 2001, Naval Special Warfare forces put operators on the ground in Afghanistan in October. The first military flag officer to set foot in Afghanistan was a Navy SEAL in charge of all special operations for Central Command. Additionally, a Navy SEAL captain commanded Combined Joint Special Operations Task Force (CJSOTF) South. Commonly referred to as Task Force K-BAR, the task force included Navy, Army, Air Force and Coalition Special Operations forces. During Operation Enduring Freedom, NSW forces carried out more than 75 special reconnaissance and direct action missions, destroying more than 500,000 pounds of explosives and weapons; positively identifying enemy personnel and conducting Leadership Interdiction Operations in the search for terrorists trying to escape by sea-going vessels. Operation Red Wing, a counter insurgent mission in Kunar Province, Afghanistan, involved four Navy SEALs and took place on 28 June 2005. The SEALs were on a mission to try to find a key Taliban leader. However, goat herders stumbled upon their hiding place and alerted local Taliban fighters, and they were subsequently surrounded by Taliban forces. The four SEALs requested back up after the 150+ Taliban had surrounded them. In the attempt to rescue the four SEALs on the ground a chinook helicopter containing members of SEAL delivery team one and several Army "Nightstalker" commandos was shot down. This is the biggest single loss of life for Naval Special Warfare forces since World War II. A firefight ensued, killing three SEALs. The fourth,

Marcus Luttrell, was protected by local villagers and later rescued by the US military.

SEAL Lieutenant Michael P. Murphy was posthumously awarded the Medal of Honor for actions in Afghanistan's Kunar Province. SEAL Senior Chief Petty Officer Dan Healy was awarded the Bronze Star with Combat "V" for Valor, Purple Heart, and Afghanistan Campaign Medal, posthumously.

Iraq War

Naval Special Warfare has played a significant role in Operation Iraqi Freedom, employing the largest number of SEALs and SWCC in its history. NSW forces were instrumental in numerous special reconnaissance and direct action missions including the securing of the southern oil infrastructures of the Al Faw peninsula and the off-shore gas and oil terminals; the clearing of the Khawr Abd Allah and Khawr Az Zubayr waterways that enabled humanitarian aid to be delivered to the vital port city of Umm Qasr; reconnaissance of the Shatt al-Arab waterway; capture of high value targets, raids on suspected chemical, biological and radiological sites; and the first POW rescue since WWII. Additionally, NSW is also fighting the war on terrorism in other global hot spots including the Philippines and the Horn of Africa. SEAL Petty Officer Second Class Michael A. Monsoor was posthumously awarded the Medal of Honor for actions in Ramadi, Iraq.

NAVAL SPECIAL WARFARE DEVELOPMENT GROUP

The Naval Special Warfare Development Group, (formerly known as MOB 6, SEAL Team SIX, and MARESFAC) based in Dam Neck, Virginia, is responsible for U.S. counterterrorist operations in the maritime environment. The Naval Special Warfare Development Group has as a primary function intelligence, counter-intelligence, investigative, and national security work, and the provisions, the United States Code cannot be applied to this organization in a manner consistent with national security requirements and considerations.

It's origin can be traced to the aftermath of the failed 1980 attempted to rescue American hostages at the Iranian Embassy (Operation Eagle Claw). Prior to this, the SEALs had already begun CT training, including all 12 platoons in SEAL Team One on the West Coast. On the East Coast, however, elements of the SEAL Team Two had taken the issue one step father. They formed a dedicated two-platoon group known as isMOB SixlB (short for Mobility Six) in anticipation of a maritime scenario requiring a CT response and had begun training (including the development of advanced tactics such as isfast ropingld) to that end. Yet, as was the case with the US Army's initial CT unit-Blue Light-and Delta Force, only one group was needed and could be recognized as official. With the formal creation of SEAL Team Six (a name selected primarily to confuse Soviet intelligence as to the number of SEAL Teams in operation) in October 1980, MOB Six was demobilized. A large number of members, however, including the former MOB Six commander, were asked to join the fledgling group. With prior experience from these operators, aggressive leadership, and an accelerated training program, SEAL Team Six was declared mission-ready just six months later.

Training for Six was conducted throughout the United States and abroad, both on military and civilian facilities. Exchange programs and joint trainings were expanded with the more experienced international teams such as Germany's GSG-9, Great Britain's Special Boat Squadrons (SBS), and France's combat divers. In all cases, emphasis was placed on realism in training, in accordance with the Train as you Fight, Fight as you Trainln philosophy popular amongst most of the world's leading special operations and CT units. Six participated in a number of operations, both overt and covert, throughout the 1980's before being revamped and renamed. The reasons for this transformation are vague, however the primary factor cited has been the need for the unit to evolved out of a poor reputation of the group within the Navy.

A great deal of controversy was generated due to charges of misappropriation of funds and equipment by team members, as well as the conviction of unit founder Cdr. Richard Marcinko on charges of conspiracy, conflict of interest, making false claims against the government, and bribery. He was sentenced to nearly two years in a Federal penitentiary in addition to being forced to pay a $10,000 fine. Despite this turn of events, Marcinko is still revered in some SEAL circles as an almost mythical figure. This status was attained, in no small part, to a best selling-book series which centers around fictional maritime special operations and counterterrorism.

The US government has described the Naval Special Warfare Development Group as having been established to oversee development of NSW tactics, equipment, and techniques. This, of course, is only partly true. The unit is under the direct command of NAVSPECWARGRU, however it is also a component of Joint Special Operations Command (JSOC-Pope AFB, North Carolina), along with other CT units such as Delta Force and the 160th Special Operations Aviation Regiment (SOAR). It is believed that DEVGRU maintains its own helicopter support unit (2 Sqns. with 18 HH-60H for SEAL transport and support), but trains frequently with the 160th SOAR, especially in support of ship assaults, which frequently make use of the small MH-6 "Little Bird", operated exclusively by the 160th.

Organization and manpower of the Group is a classified, and can only be guessed at. It is estimated that NSWDG now numbers approximately 200 operators, broken down by teams, much like the British SAS and Delta Force.

Most recently, it has been reported that there are currently four such teams within the group, assault units Red, Blue, Gold, and a special boat unit, Gray.

The missions of these units are, again, a cause for speculation, however it is logical that they are specialized amongst themselves, perhaps along the lines of the SAS – Mountain, Mobility, Boat, and HALO troops (within a single Squadron). It is also possible that these units may have focus on specific target types instead, such as shipping, oil rigs, and structures, (although this scenario seems less likely due to the obvious need for all members of the Group to be current and proficient should a large scale operation arise).

There is also an administrative and testing section, which numbers approximately 300 personnel. These individuals are responsible for the actual testing and development of new NAVSPECWAR equipment, including weapons. It has been reported that DEVGRU is one of only a handful of US units authorized to conduct pre-emptive actions against terrorists and terrorist facilities (NOTE: Red Cell once shared this charter, although it was never put into practice before the unit was disbanded). DEVGRU operators reportedly fire an average of 2,500 to 3,000 rounds per week in training.

Operations

1983-SEAL Team Six members were also responsible for the rescue and evacuation of Governor Sir Paul Scoon from Grenada during Operation Urgent Fury. Four SEALs were lost to drowning during helicopter insertion offshore. Other aspect of the operation included the securing of a radio transmitter which resulted in heavy contact with Grenadian forces.

1985-Six deployed to the site of the Achille Lauro hijacking in anticipation of a possible assault on the vessel.

1989-The unit took part in Operation Just Cause as part of Task Force White, which included SEAL Team Two. Their primary task, along with Delta Force, was the location and securing of Panamanian strongman Manuel Noriega.

1990-They again operated in Panama as part of a secret operation code-named "Pokeweed" which had as its goal the apprehension of Colombian drug lord Pablo Escobar. The mission was unsuccessful due to poor pre-assault intelligence. By some accounts, Six was deployed from the US aircraft carrier USS Forrestal offshore, although other sources dispute this claim [the ship's summary history discloses no operations in Panamanian waters during 1990].

1991-SEAL Team Six reportedly recovered Haitian President Jean Bertrand Aristide under cover of darkness following the coup which deposed him.

1991-Six was also part of contingency planning for the shooting down Saddam Hussein's personal helicopter with Stinger missiles, although this operation never got beyond the planning stage.

1996-The unit reportedly deployed to Atlanta, Georgia as part of a large US counterterrorist contingency plan for the 1996 Summer Olympics. (NOTE: The Federal Bureau of Investigation's Hostage Rescue Team [HRT] is responsible for domestic CT and was the primary response unit).

UNITED STATES NAVY SPECIAL WARFARE DEVELOPMENT GROUP

SEAL Team SIX is the U.S. Navy's main counterterrorist unit, whose operatives are drawn from the current SEAL ranks. The unit was created as part of the Joint Special Operations Command in 1980. The origin of SIX can be traced to the aftermath of the failed 1980 attempt to rescue American hostages at the Iranian Embassy (Operation Eagle Claw). Prior to this, the existing SEAL teams had already begun counterterrorism training, including all 12 platoons in SEAL Team One on the West Coast. On the East Coast, however, elements of the SEAL Team Two had taken the issue one step farther. They formed a dedicated two-platoon group known as "MOB Six" *(Mobility Six)* in anticipation of a maritime scenario requiring a CT response and had begun training to that end.

Six was formally created in October 1980, and an accelerated training program made the unit mission-ready just six months later. At the time, only two SEAL Teams were in existence; popular knowledge backed up by actual SEAL claims say that the name was chosen to confuse Soviet intelligence as to the number of SEAL Teams in operation. It became officially operational in 1981.

In 1987, the unit was given the official title of 'Naval Special Warfare Development Group' (NAVSPECWARDEVGRU, or simply DEVGRU). Reasons for the name change are varied, ranging from operational security, the team's reputation, all the way down to charges leveled at Six founder and now-public figure Richard Marcinko. Whatever the truth behind these, the name "SEAL Team Six" is no longer in use, although most military servicemen and many civilians still recognize them as "SEAL Team Six."

DEVGRU's mission is to provide intelligence and counter-terrorism services for the Dept of the Navy and the overall U.S. Special Operations Command, in addition to providing management for the development and testing of technologies under consideration for use by Naval Special Warfare forces such as SEALs. Both DEVGRU and Delta Force train together from time to time as well as deploy together when the need arises. The unit is currently based out of Dam Neck, Virginia and administrative control is under Naval Special Warfare Command.

DEVGRU is said to be composed of six different teams. Red for Assault with an Indian as mascot, Gold as the Premier Assault Team, Blue for Assault, Gray for Transportation, Black for Recon and/or Surveillance, and, finally, Green for New personnel who are in training. Each team has "Cells", such as an Evasion and Recovery Cell (the new name for E&E is now E&R), a Force

Protection Cell (military version of VIP Protection detail), a Sniper Cell, etc..

At any one time all members of the team will be in one of three categories on the base:

1. SPECTRA (pronounced "spec-tray" and standing for Special Training where the team goes to HALO, shooting schools, etc.)
2. Standby (this team is on-standby-via beeper-within a certain distance from base and ready to deploy at a moment's notice)
3. Deployment (this team is overseas, for instance conducting foreign training with a host nation, acting as security at an embassy, performing missions as needed, etc.).

An executive order by President Clinton added DEVGRU to those units excepted from the contents of Title 5, Section 7103 of the US Code.

History

The origins of ST6 can be traced to the aftermath of Operation Eagle Claw, the failed 1980 attempt to rescue American hostages at the U.S. Embassy in Iran. During the Iran Hostage Crisis in 1979, Richard Marcinko was one of two Navy representatives for a Joint Chiefs of Staff task force known as the TAT (Terrorist Action Team). The purpose of the TAT was to develop a plan to free the American hostages held in Iran which culminated in Operation Eagle Claw. In the wake of the operation's disaster at Desert One, the Navy saw the need for a full-time dedicated Counter-Terrorist Team and tasked Marcinko with its design and development.

Marcinko was the first commanding officer of this new unit which he named SEAL Team Six (at the time, the US Navy had only two SEAL teams. Marcinko purportedly named the unit Team Six in order to confuse the Soviet intelligence as to the number of SEAL Teams in operation). It became officially operational in 1981. The men in the unit were handpicked by Marcinko himself from across the US Navy's Special Operations personnel. SEAL Team Six would be known as the US Navy's premier counter-terrorist unit. It has also been compared to the US Army's Delta Force. Marcinko held the command of SEAL Team Six for three years from 1980–1983 instead of what was typically a two-year command in the Navy at the time. SEAL Team Six was formally created in October 1980, and an intense, progressive work-up training program made the unit mission-ready six months later. Prior to this, the existing SEAL teams had already begun counter-terrorism training, including 12 platoons in SEAL Team One on the West Coast. On the East Coast, however, elements of the SEAL Team Two had taken the issue one step further. They formed a dedicated two platoon group known as "MOB Six" *(Mobility Six)* in anticipation of a maritime scenario requiring a counter-terrorism response and had begun training to that end. In 1987, a new unit was formed, given the official title of 'Naval Special Warfare Development Group' (NAVSPECWARDEVGRU, or DEVGRU) after SEAL Team Six was dissolved. Reasons for the disbanding are varied. But the name "SEAL Team Six" is often used in reference to DEVGRU because of their similarities as a maritime counter-terrorism unit.

Recruitment, selection, and training

In the early stages of creating SEAL Team Six, Marcinko had been given only six months to get ST6 up and running. This meant that there was a timing issue and Marcinko had little time to create a proper selection course, similar to that of Delta Force, and as a result hand-picked the first plankowners of the unit himself after assessing their Navy records and personally interviewing each man. It has been said that Marcinko regretted not having enough time to set up a proper selection process/course. All applicants came from the UDTs and east and west coast SEAL teams.

Marcinko's criteria for recruiting applicants was combat experience due to the fact that he would know they could perform under fire; language skills were vital, as the unit would have a worldwide mandate to be able to communicate with the local population if needed; union skills, in order to be able to blend in as civilians during an operation; and finally SEAL skills. Each member of SEAL Team Six was selected in part because of the different specialty skills each man brought with him to the unit. The training schedule was intense. The claim had been made by one former Team member that in one year SEAL Team 6 fired more rounds of ammunition than the entire US Marine Corps. The emphasis was on shooting skills, range firing, CQB, and stress shooting in a variety of conditions.

As with most aspects of the unit being highly classified, information regarding the process of recruitment and selection for the NSWDG is also scarce, but what is speculated and is known is that the selection and training for the unit hasn't changed dramatically since its creation. All applicants come from the "regular" SEAL teams and the Navy's Explosive Ordnance Disposal units, unless applying for support positions (in which there have been open advertisements on the web for support personnel). It can be inferred from the quality of their pool of applicants that those considered are in peak physical condition, maintain an excellent reputation as an operator within the Naval Special Warfare community, and have done operational deployments with a SEAL Team where an operator will have picked up invaluable experience. As a result, the candidate will usually be in his 30s. As ST6 was recruiting the best and brightest SEALs/UDTs from the regular teams, this created animosity between the unit and the "regular" teams that their best SEALs were being poached for the unit.

Those who pass the stringent recruitment and selection process, will be selected to attend a six to seven month Operators Training Course. Candidates will join the units training wing known as "Green Team." The training course attrition rate is extremely high; at least half the class will fail the course. During one selection course, out of the original 20 candidates, only 12 completed the course. All candidates are watched closely by DevGru instructors and evaluated on whether they are suitable to join the individual squadrons. Like all Special Operations Forces units that have an extremely intensive and high-risk training schedule, serious injuries or death among operators can result. SEAL Team Six/DevGRU have lost several operators during training, including parachute accidents and CQB training accidents, but this is necessary in order to make training realistic. It is presumed that the unit's assessment process for potential new recruits will be completely different from what a SEAL operator has come across in his career and will test the candidate's mental capacity rather than his physical condition, as he will have already completed Basic Underwater Demolitions/SEAL training.

Candidates will be put through a variety of advanced training courses, that can include courses led by civilian instructors. These can include Free-climbing, Advanced Unarmed Combat techniques, defensive and offensive driving, Advanced Diving, and Survival,

Evasion, Resistance and Escape. All candidates must perform at the top level during selection and the unit instructors evaluate the candidate during the training process. Any candidate not performing to the highest level will be returned to his previous unit. Once they have been selected they will be assigned to one of the Tactical Development and Evaluation Squadrons.

Organization and structure

The organization and structure of NSWDG is highly classified, and can only be speculated on. It is estimated that NSWDG currently numbers approximately 200 operators, broken down by color-coded squadrons. Most recently, it has been reported that there are currently four such squadrons within the group, assault units Red, Blue, Gold, Black and a special boat unit, Gray. Red for Assault with an Indian as mascot, Gold as the Premier Assault Team, Blue for Assault, Gray for Transportation, Black for Recon and/or Surveillance, and, finally, Green for New personnel who are in training.

Each team has "Cells", such as an Evasion and Recovery Cell (the new name for E&E is now E&R), a Force Protection Cell (military version of VIP Protection detail), a Sniper Cell, etc. SEAL Team Six/NSWDG became separated from the normal US Navy organization and structure; civilian dress was adopted and rarely did operators wear their traditional naval dress uniforms and anything else associated with the military was removed such as saluting and rank hierarchy. Both officers and enlisted members will address each other by their nickname or first name. The typical military clean-cut look was scrapped and operators could grow their hair long; beards and mustaches could also be maintained.

Commanding Officers

- Commander Richard Marcinko – Nov 1980 to July 1983
- Captain Robert A. Gormly – 1983 to 1986
- Captain Thomas E. Murphy – 1986 to 1987
- Captain Richard T.P. Woolard – 1987 to 1990
- Captain Ronald E. Yeaw – 1990 to 1992
- Captain Thomas G. Moser – 1992 to 1994
- Admiral Eric T. Olson – 1994 to 1997

- Vice Admiral Albert M. Calland III – June 1997 to June 1999
- Vice Admiral Joseph D. Kernan – 1999 to 2002
- Rear Admiral Edward G. Winters, III – 2002 to 2004
- Captain Eric Prescott
- Rear Admiral Brian L. Losey
- Rear Admiral Scott P. Moore.

Roles and responsibilities

When SEAL Team Six was first created it would be devoted exclusively to counter-terrorism with a worldwide maritime responsibility. Its objectives would include targets such as ships, oil-rigs, naval bases or other civilian or military bases that were accessible from the sea or inland waterways. SEAL Team Six would also be tasked in covertly infiltrating a hot spot somewhere in the world to carry out reconnaissance or security assessments on US military bases and US Embassies. Although the unit was created as a maritime counter-terrorism unit, it has become a multi-functional Special Operations unit with multiple roles. After SEAL Team Six was disbanded and renamed, the official mission of the NSWDG is to test, evaluate and develop technology and maritime, ground and airborne tactics applicable to Naval Special Warfare forces such as Navy SEALs. DEVGRU is one of only a handful of U.S. special mission units authorized to use pre-emptive actions against terrorists and their facilities. DEVGRU and the Army's Delta Force train together and deploy together on counter-terrorist missions usually as part of a joint special operations task force (JSOTF). The CIA's highly secretive Special Activities Division (SAD) and more specifically its elite Special Operations Group (SOG) recruits operators from SEAL Team Six. Joint Navy SEALs and CIA operations go back to the famed MACV-SOG group during the Vietnam War. This cooperation still exists today and is seen in the wars in Iraq and Afghanistan.

Operational deployments

The majority of the operations assigned to the NSWDG are classified and may never be known to the public. However, there are some operations in which the unit has been involved where certain details have been made public.

Operation Urgent Fury

On October 13, 1983, the Grenadian Army, controlled by former Deputy Prime Minister Bernard Coard, overthrew the government of Grenada in a bloody coup d'état, creating a Communist regime. The severity of the violence, coupled with Coard's hard-line Marxism, caused deep concern among neighboring Caribbean nations, as well as in Washington, D.C. Adding to the US's concern was the presence of nearly 1,000 American medical students in Grenada. The new leader of the Grenadian government, Maurice Bishop, aligned Grenada with Cubans, Soviets, and communist organizations. The Reagan administration reviled the leftist government for being too closely allied to Cuba and the Soviet Union. On October 25, Reagan decided to act and United States invaded the small island of Grenada.

SEAL Team Six's Assault Group Three was to conduct a static line drop with boats a few miles away from the Grenadian coast. One of two C-130 cargo planes transporting the SEALs to their drop point veered far off course. A rain squall accompanied by high winds broke out just before the SEALs conducted the drop. Four out of the eight SEALs that made the drop drowned and were never seen again. After the disastrous insertion, Assault Group Three was told to stand-by and began preparing for the next mission. The next mission was to go to the governor's mansion and secure Governor-General Paul Scoon, protect him and his family and move them out of the combat area. A second mission was to capture and secure Grenada's only radio station so that it couldn't be used by the local military to incite the population or coordinate military actions. There was almost no intelligence for either of these operations.

Governor-General's Mansion

To reach the governor-general's mansion, the SEALs were flown in on Blackhawk helicopters that morning, and fast-roped to the ground while under fire. As they approached from the back of the mansion, the team found Scoon hiding. The SEALs then continued to clear the rest of the house and began to set up a perimeter to ensure security. Soon the mansion started to take fire from men armed with AK-47s and RPGs. As the incoming fire started to increase, Governor-General Scoon and his family were moved to a safer location in the house. After the incoming fire had decreased, three men wearing Cuban uniforms approached the mansion, all of them carrying AK-47s. The SEALs shouted for the three men to stop where they were. When the three men heard the yells, they raised their weapons. The SEALs opened fire on the Cubans and killed them almost instantly.

Soon afterward, two BTR-60PBs rolled up to the mansion's gates. One of the BTRs at the mansion's front gate opened fire. Just as the SEALs were about to fire a LAW anti-tank rocket, the BTR backed off and left with the other BTR. When the SEALs had inserted on to the compound, they left behind their long-range SATCOM radio on a helicopter. The only communications the team had were through MX-360 radios. The team used the radios to communicate with a SEAL command post on the island to call in air strikes. As the radios started to die, communications with the SEAL command post became weak. Once all the radios had finally died and the SEALs urgently needed air support, the SEALs used a regular house phone to call JSOC. JSOC was able to get a AC-130 Spectre gunship to hold station over the SEALs' position to provide air support.

When morning came, a group of Force Recon Marines arrived to extract the SEALs, Governor-General Scoon, and his family to a helicopter extraction point. As the team left the compound, they noticed splattered blood and discarded weapons all around. The helicopter finally arrived and extracted everyone to safety.

Radio Station

Assault Group Three and another squad from SEAL Team Six flew to the radio station on a Blackhawk helicopter. The helicopter took small-arms fire on the insertion. Once the team unloaded it overran the radio station compound. The SEALs were told to hold the station until Governor Scoon and a broadcast team could be brought in. After the team took control of the compound, it was not able to make radio contact with the SEAL command post. The SEALs set up a perimeter while they continued to try to make radio contact. As this was happening, a BTR-60 rolled up to the compound and 20 Grenadian soldiers disguised as station workers piled out. The soldiers carried weapons even in disguise. The SEALs ordered the soldiers to drop the weapons. The soldiers opened fire but were shot down almost instantly. Afterwards the SEALs continued laboring to make radio contact when another

BTR and three trucks were spotted coming towards the station. The trucks carried a dozen soldiers each. The SEALs quickly conducted a defensive maneuver as the soldiers flanked the building. The BTR covered the front entrance with its 14.5 mm KPV heavy machine gun. The incoming fire on the SEALs position was becoming devastatingly heavy and the SEALs were running out of ammunition. The SEAL team knew that their only option was to change their original plan of holding the radio station and instead destroy the radio transmitter, and head to the water following their pre-planned escape route out behind the station across a broad meadow that led to a path that cut between cliffs and a beach. The meadow was terribly exposed to Grenadian fire. The team leapfrogged across the exposed ground and took heavy fire. The team finally reached the end of the field, cut through a chain-link fence and ran into dense brush. The SEALs quickly followed the path to the beach. One SEAL had been wounded in the arm. The Grenadians were still in pursuit, so the SEALs waded into the water and began swimming parallel to the shore until they found cliff ledges to conceal themselves. The SEALs remained hidden until long after the Grenadians had given up the search. Once the SEALs were convinced that the Grenadians had given up, the team jumped back into the water and swam out to sea. The SEALs were in the water close to six hours before a rescue plane spotted them and vectored a Navy ship to pick them up.

Operation Restore Hope

During Operation Restore Hope and Operation Gothic Serpent in Somalia, DEVGRU was a part of Task Force Ranger. TF Ranger was made up of operators from Delta Force, the 75th Ranger Regiment, the 160th SOAR, the 24th Special Tactics Squadron, and unknown number of SEALs from DEVGRU. Eric T. Olson, John Gay, Howard Wasdin, Homer Nearpass, and Richard Kaiser were the five SEALs that fought in the Battle of the Black Sea during the last mission of Operation Gothic Serpent to capture the warlord Mohamed Farrah Aidid.

Bibliography

Alden, John Doughty: *The Fleet Submarine in the U.S. Navy: A Design & Construction History,* Naval Institute Press, 1979.

Bagnasco, Erminio: *Submarines of World War Two,* Naval Institute Press, London, 1977.

Baldeo Sahai: *Indian Navy - A Perspective : From the Earliest Period to Modern Times,* Publications Division, Ministry of Information and Broadcasting, 2006, xiv, 280 p, ISBN : 81-230-1354-X, Price : Rs. 300.00 Details

Blair, Clay: *Silent Victory: The U.S. Submarine War Against Japan,* New York: J.P. Lippincott Company, 1975.

Campbell, John: *Naval Weapons of World War Two.* Annapolis: Naval Institute Press, 1985.

Compton-Hall, Richard: *Submarine Warfare: Monsters & Midgets.* Blandford Press, 1985.

Duncan, Francis: *Rickover and the Nuclear Navy: The Discipline of Technology.* Naval Institute Press, 1990.

Edward J. Marolda : *The U.S. Navy in the Vietnam War: An Illustrated History,* Washington: Brassey's, 2002.

Everitt, Don & Holmes, Harry: *K Boats: Steam-Powered Submarines in World War I.* Naval Institute Press, 1999.

Galantin, Ignatius: *Submarine Admiral: From Battlewagons to Ballistic Missiles.* University of Illinois Press, 1995.

Hezlet, Arthur: *Electronics and Sea Power.* New York: Stein and Day, 1975.

Hiranandani, G.M. : *Transition to Eminence : The Indian Navy 1976-1990,* Lancer Pub, Delhi, 2005.

James, Lawrence: *Raj: The Making and Unmaking of British India Naval Warfare,* New York: St. Martin's Press, 1997.

Julian S. Corbett: *Some Principles of Maritime Strategy,* Annapolis, MD: Naval Institute Press, 1988.

Keegan, John: *The Price of Admiralty: The Evolution of Naval Warfare,* Penguin Group, 1988.

Kumar, R. : *Role of I.N.A. and Indian Navy,* Commonwealth Pub, Delhi, 2008.

Liu, F.F.: *A Naval Warfare History of Modern China: 1924-1949,* Princeton University Press, 1956.

Padfield, Peter: *War Beneath the Sea: Submarine Conflict During World War II.* John Wiley & Sons, 1998.

Paul C. Scotti: *Coast Guard Action in Vietnam: Stories of those who Served,* Central Point, Oregon: Hellgate, 2000.

Perry, Milton F.: *Infernal Machines: The Story of Confederate Submarine and Mine Warfare.* Louisiana State University Press, 1985.

Poluhowich, John J.: *Argonaut: The Submarine Legacy of Simon Lake.* Texas A&M University Press, 1999.

Salve, M.V. Salve: *Nuclear Powered Submarine : A Retrospect and Fundamentals,* Sumit Enterprises, Delhi, 2010.

Schafer, Louis: *Confederate Underwater Warfare: An Illustrated History.* McFarland & Co., 1996.

Schratz, Paul R.: *Submarine Commander: A Story of World War II and Korea.* University Press of Kentucky, 1988.

Index

N

O

P

R

S

T

W

□□□